Coloured Revolutions and Authoritarian Reactions

Between 2000 and 2005, colour revolutions swept away authoritarian and semi-authoritarian regimes in Serbia, Georgia, Kyrgyzstan and Ukraine. Yet, after these initial successes, attempts to replicate the strategies failed to produce regime change elsewhere in the region. The book argues that students of democratization and democracy promotion should study not only the successful colour revolutions, but also the colour revolution prevention strategies adopted by authoritarian elites. Based on a series of qualitative, country-focused studies the book explores the whole spectrum of anti-democratization policies, adopted by autocratic rulers and demonstrates that authoritarian regimes studied democracy promotion techniques, used in various colour revolutions, and focused their prevention strategies on combatting these techniques.

The book proposes a new typology of authoritarian reactions to the challenge of democratization and argues that the specific mix of policies and rhetoric, adopted by each authoritarian regime, depended on the perceived intensity of threat to regime survival and the regime's perceived strength vis-à-vis the democratic opposition.

This book was published as a special issue of *Democratization*.

Evgeny Finkel is Assistant Professor of Political Science, George Washington University, USA. His articles have been published in *Comparative Politics, Democratization, East European Politics and Societies, Global Society, Genocide Studies and Prevention,* and several other journals.

Yitzhak M. Brudny is the Jay and Leonie Darwin Chair in Russian Studies, The Hebrew University of Jerusalem, Israel. He is the author of Reinventing *Russia: Russian Nationalism and the Soviet State, 1953–1991* (Harvard University Press, 1998), and the principal editor of *Restructuring Post-Communist Russia* (Cambridge University Press, 2004). His articles on Russia and the former Soviet Union have appeared in numerous journals and edited volumes.

Coloured Revolutions and Authoritarian Reactions

Edited by
Evgeny Finkel and Yitzhak M. Brudny

Routledge
Taylor & Francis Group

LONDON AND NEW YORK

First published 2013
by Routledge
2 Park Square, Milton Park, Abingdon, Oxfordshire OX14 4RN

Simultaneously published in the USA and Canada
by Routledge
711 Third Avenue, New York, NY 10017

First issued in paperback 2015

Routledge is an imprint of the Taylor & Francis Group, an informa business

British Library Cataloguing in Publication Data
A catalogue record for this book is available from the British Library

ISBN 13: 978-1-138-94521-0 (pbk)
ISBN 13: 978-0-415-63957-6 (hbk)

Typeset in Times New Roman
by Taylor & Francis Books

Publisher's Note
The publisher would like to make readers aware that the chapters in this book may be referred to as articles as they are identical to the articles published in the special issue. The publisher accepts responsibility for any inconsistencies that may have arisen in the course of preparing this volume for print.

Contents

Citation Information

The chapters in this book were originally published in *Democratization*, volume 19, issue 1 (February 2012). When citing this material, please use the original page numbering for each article, as follows:

Chapter 1
No more colour! Authoritarian regimes and colour revolutions in Eurasia
Evgeny Finkel and Yitzhak M. Brudny
Democratization, volume 19, issue 1 (February 2012) pp. 1-14

Chapter 2
Russia and the colour revolutions
Evgeny Finkel and Yitzhak M. Brudny
Democratization, volume 19, issue 1 (February 2012) pp. 15-36

Chapter 3
Questioning democracy promotion: Belarus' response to the 'colour revolutions'
Elena Korosteleva
Democratization, volume 19, issue 1 (February 2012) pp. 37-59

Chapter 4
Oil in the family: managing presidential succession in Azerbaijan
Scott Radnitz
Democratization, volume 19, issue 1 (February 2012) pp. 60-77

Chapter 5
Coloured by revolution: the political economy of autocratic stability in Uzbekistan
Jennifer Murtazashvili
Democratization, volume 19, issue 1 (February 2012) pp. 78-97

Chapter 6
Tajikistan: authoritarian reaction in a postwar state

Lawrence P. Markowitz
Democratization, volume 19, issue 1 (February 2012) pp. 98-119

Chapter 7
Democracy promotion, authoritarian resiliency, and political unrest in Iran
Güneş Murat Tezcür
Democratization, volume 19, issue 1 (February 2012) pp. 120-140

No more colour! Authoritarian regimes and colour revolutions in Eurasia

Evgeny Finkel[a,b] and Yitzhak M. Brudny[c]

[a]Department of Political Science, University of Wisconsin-Madison, Madison, USA;
[b]Program on Order, Conflict, and Violence, Yale University, New Haven, USA;
[c]Department of Political Science & Department of History, The Hebrew University of Jerusalem, Israel

Between 2000 and 2005, colour revolutions swept away authoritarian and semi-authoritarian regimes in Serbia, Georgia, Kyrgyzstan and Ukraine. Yet, after these initial successes, attempts to replicate strategies failed to produce regime change elsewhere in the region. This introductory article argues that students of democratization and democracy promotion should study not only the successful colour revolutions, but also the colour revolution prevention strategies adopted by authoritarian elites. The article proposes a new typology of authoritarian reactions to the challenge of democratization and presents the main findings of the special issue, devoted to the analysis of authoritarian reactions to colour revolution in the post-communist region and in Iran.

From 2000 to 2005, a series of popular protests, which later became known as 'colour revolutions', swept away authoritarian and semi-authoritarian regimes in Serbia, Georgia, Kyrgyzstan and Ukraine. The common trigger of these revolutions was an attempt by the authoritarian leaders to falsify election results in their favour. These revolutions established a repertoire of non-violent, sometimes successful, regime change strategies. In other Eurasian states, however, attempts to replicate key strategies, so successful in the earlier colour revolutions, such as peaceful protests, public demands for democratization, the use of election monitoring and post-election mass protests to contest fraudulent elections, failed. Moreover, in Eurasian countries where no serious attempt to launch a colour revolution was made, governments nonetheless chose to avoid the possibility of regime change by adopting policies often publicly described as 'anti-colour insurance'. The elites of Russia, Belarus, Azerbaijan, Iran and several Central Asian authoritarian states sought to alleviate the threat of a colour revolution by focusing on several key political and intellectual strategies, namely attacks on independent civil society and political opposition, limits on electoral competition and efforts to ideologically delegitimize colour revolution ideas and techniques as subversive and alien to their country's culture and traditions. In this special issue we argue that understanding authoritarian strategies of democracy prevention is therefore no less important than understanding strategies of democracy promotion.

The goal of this special issue is to provide the conceptual framework through which these authoritarian strategies can be compared and analysed in depth by focusing on six major country cases in which these strategies were systematically applied. We construct this conceptual framework around one key question, namely, why, despite the different institutional designs, economic structures and resources available to their leaders, did the authoritarian states of Eurasia adopt a largely similar repertoire of democracy prevention strategies?

Based on the analysis of post-Soviet and Iranian anti-colour revolution policies, we argue that authoritarian regimes studied democracy promotion techniques, used in various colour revolutions, and focused their prevention strategies on combatting these techniques. Thus, the 'modular'[1] nature and the form of colour revolution determined the repertoire of democracy prevention policies adopted and eventually helped to stall the spread of this wave of regime change. While we do observe some variation in choices of strategies within this repertoire, we argue that the specific mix of policies and rhetoric, adopted by each authoritarian regime, depended on the perceived intensity of threat to regime survival and the regime's perceived strength vis-à-vis the democratic opposition.

This introductory article makes several theoretical and policy contributions. First, while previous studies[2] focused on the pro-democracy opposition learning and imitative capabilities as instrumental in driving regime change, this special issue emphasizes the important, but understudied, topic of authoritarian learning as a factor in democracy prevention. Second, we contribute to the literature on democratization and authoritarianism by expanding the analysis of democracy prevention policies to ideational, ideological and rhetorical realms. Autocrats, we show, not only *employ* repressive strategies to ensure their survival, they also try to *convince* their citizens that authoritarianism is a superior alternative to electoral democracy. This special issue also demonstrates that there is no linear relationship between regime violence and regime capabilities – both an extremely weak (Tajikistan) and a fairly strong (Belarus) autocratic government fended off a colour revolution challenge without using large-scale repression. Finally, this special issue contributes to democracy promotion literature by showing that in order to be successful, pro-democracy activists have to take into account authoritarian states' learning capabilities and be constantly innovative in their strategy choices.

In the following pages we will provide a review of the existing literature on colour revolution in Eurasia, and demonstrate how the theoretical frameworks, developed by previous studies of colour revolutions, inform our analysis of autocrats' anti-colour policies. Next, by focusing on the case studies presented in this special issue, we will show the repertoire of authoritarian reactions to colour revolutions. This repertoire represents in essence the 'mirror image' of the repertoire of the colour revolution activists. Finally, we will highlight the reasons for the variation in democracy prevention policies across the region.

Colour revolutions: summary and review of a scholarly debate

Over the last years, colour revolutions have received a substantial amount of scholarly attention. Some optimistically and sometimes euphorically viewed these cases of regime change as genuine democratic breakthroughs that were going to have substantial, positive and permanent effects.[3] Other accounts were more cautious and sceptical[4] and some were overtly pessimistic about the real impact of colour revolutions on the quality of democracy in the affected countries.[5] In addition to evaluating the impact of these cases of attempted regime change, leading scholars, such as Mark Beissinger, Valerie Bunce, Sharon Wolchik, Henry Hale, David Lane, Michael McFaul, Joshua Tucker, Lucan Way, Stephen White, and numerous others, participated in lively debates on the causes and origins of colour revolutions.[6]

However, despite the significant scholarly interest in colour revolutions, the actions of broadly similar authoritarian governments that were not overthrown have not been fully explored. Methodologically, this makes many works on colour revolutions subject to the critique of case selection based upon a dependent variable because they do not address those cases in which, paraphrasing Arthur Conan Doyle, the colour revolution did not bark. Important steps in the right direction have been made by Bunce and Wolchik, Hess, and Kalandadze and Orenstein, who include in their analysis not only the cases of successful regime change, but also the cases of successful repression of pro-democracy, protest movements.[7] Authoritarian resistance to democracy has also been addressed in the *Democratization* special issue on democracy promotion before and after colour revolution,[8] and several chapters in a recent book, edited by Valerie Bunce, Michael McFaul and Kathryn Stoner-Weiss.[9] Yet a comprehensive and detailed analysis of Eurasian autocrats' reactions to colour revolutions (and democratization more generally) is still lacking.[10] The main motivation behind this special issue is to contribute to addressing this gap in the literature on democratization and authoritarian reactions to it.

Stoner-Weiss argues that there is a certain difficulty in studying countries in which a colour revolution or pro-democracy mass protests has failed to take off. The reason for this difficulty (and a possible explanation for this lack of scholarly attention) is that 'it is always harder to explain a nonevent, something that never happened, than to find factors that explain something that actually did take place'.[11] Yet while in many Eurasian states the colour revolution was, indeed, a 'non-event' incumbents' policies, designed to prevent the colour revolution, were not. 'The spread of the impetus for political change does not necessarily produce actual change, especially not the faithful imitation of the original model', notes Weyland. 'Governments often do not passively fall to the spread of contention but design an active response' by cracking down on the challengers or partially giving in to their demands without giving up power.[12] Therefore, authoritarian governments' policies, we argue, require studying and analysing. Furthermore, scholars of colour revolutions and democratization more broadly have to recognize, as Silitsky noted, that 'democrats and revolutionaries are not the only ones who can learn from the past and apply new knowledge to fulfill their political goals. Indeed, their antagonists appear to have mastered the science and craft of democratic transitions in order to stop the contagion at their borders'.[13] The analysis of colour revolutions will be incomplete without sufficient attention to the topic of the prevention of such revolutions.

Why then are some authoritarian leaders more successful at fending off the threat of a colour revolution than others? A structure-centred perspective is put forward by Lucan Way, who argues that the survival of incumbent autocrats is certain when one of the following conditions exists – (1) highly institutionalized party rule backed by a non-material source of cohesion such as revolutionary tradition or highly salient ideology; (2) an extensive, well-funded, and cohesive coercive apparatus; or (3) state discretionary control over the economy.[14] However, by emphasizing structural factors, this explanation neglects (or deems irrelevant) the actual incumbents' anti-colour policies, which often did not focus on strengthening the ruling party, the coercive apparatus or the rulers' grip over the economy. In Russia and Belarus, as the contributions to this special issue show, the authorities devoted substantial efforts to ideological issues, such as presenting the anti-national and predatory nature of the pro-democracy organizations and ideology. In the case of Tajikistan, notes Markowitz, the very weakness and fragmentation of the ruling elite actually contributed to regime stability. Furthermore, parties with revolutionary traditions rarely exist in the post-communist region, and the only party that does enjoy a revolutionary legacy, the Communist Party, is generally excluded from the government.[15] Therefore, a much more detailed, fine-grained perspective is needed to explain not only *why* but also *how* authoritarian rulers coped with threats to their rule.

Contrary to Way's structuralist approach, Vitali Silitsky concentrates on autocrats' actions and policies, aimed at preventing a colour revolution in their domain. These policies, described by Silitsky as 'pre-emptive authoritarianism', take several forms: (1) tactical pre-emption, that is, attacks on the opposition, the civil society, and their infrastructures; (2) institutional pre-emption, which focuses on changing the fundamental rules of the political game to the incumbents' advantage; and (3) cultural pre-emption – the manipulation of public consciousness and collective memory to spread stereotypes and myths about the opposition, the West, and democracy in general.[16] While in general we demonstrate the validity of Silitsky's argument, our goal is to study a wider set of questions: to what extent were these 'pre-emptive authoritarianism' policies triggered by colour revolutions, rather than by a general desire to consolidate political power; what are the forms and content of pre-emption policies beyond Silitsky's case study of Belarus; and why did particular governments focus on specific pre-emption policies?

In addition to the scant literature that explicitly deals with states in which the colour revolution failed to achieve regime change or simply did not materialize, we also suggest using the existing literature on successful colour revolutions as a basic theoretical framework to understand anti-colour authoritarian policies. The scholarship on the causes and origins of colour revolutions can be divided into several groups.

Some authors present a long list of factors that led to the overturn of authoritarian regimes in Serbia, Georgia, Kyrgyzstan and Ukraine. Thus, McFaul lists seven factors – a semi-autocratic regime, an unpopular incumbent, a united opposition, an ability publicly to expose electoral fraud, independent media, the opposition's ability to mobilize people to take to the streets, and divisions among the regime's coercive forces – as important factors in explaining the success of the revolutions.[17] A largely similar, but even longer, nine-point list is presented by Kuzio, who argues that the success of the colour revolution is determined by the existence of such factors as: a competitive (that is, semi-) authoritarian state facilitating space for the democratic opposition; 'return to Europe' civic nationalism that assists in mobilizing civil society; a preceding political crisis that weakened the regime's legitimacy; a pro-democratic capital city; unpopular ruling elites; a charismatic candidate; a united opposition; mobilized youth; and regionalism and foreign intervention (Russia or the European Union).[18]

Other works can be classified as macro, meso, and micro perspectives on the colour revolutions. The macro-level approach focuses on the structural factors that affect the success or the lack of a colour revolution. The most visible example of the macro perspective is an article by Lucan Way published in the *Journal of Democracy*, which argues that structural factors, namely the strength of a country's ties to the West, and the strength (or more precisely, the weakness) of the incumbent party and state are the 'real causes' of the colour revolutions.[19] Meso-perspectives emphasize the importance of sub-national level actors, such as dissatisfied business people who were willing and able to provide financial, logistical and media support to the opposition[20] or youth movements that spearheaded the generational protests of the post-communist generation against the older cohort of power holders.[21] The successful defeat of authoritarian rulers also depends heavily on the extent to which the opposition and their allies were able to use novel and sophisticated electoral strategies, as argued by Bunce and Wolchik.[22] A micro-level (and the most overlooked) perspective in the field of colour revolutions focuses on decisions of individuals, psychological factors and motivations for participation in mass protests that led to colour revolutions. Thus, it is the realization that an electoral fraud has been committed by the authorities that makes citizens take to the streets and participate in anti-government protests.[23]

The special issue contribution to the colour revolutions debate

In this special issue we propose a typology of authoritarian governments' reactions to colour revolutions. This typology is based both on Silitsky's framework of tactical, institutional and cultural pre-emption, as well as key arguments of the scholarship on colour revolutions. Faced with the threat of regime change, author-itarian incumbents can and do rely on at least one of five major strategies – *iso-lation, marginalization, distribution, repression, persuasion*.[24] The authoritarian government can attempt to isolate itself from unwanted external influences by refusing to register foreign non-governmental organizations (NGOs), by withhold-ing visas from election observers, or by shutting down and censoring media outlets. It can marginalize or almost completely eliminate the opposition by tinker-ing with electoral legislation, limiting opposition leaders' access to mass media, and by presenting the opposition in a highly negative light, such as being greedy, corrupt and unpatriotic pawns of foreign powers. It can reward loyalists or buy off important or potentially threatening groups. It can also punish by with-holding benefits, rents or income from subversive elites and businesspeople, force challengers into exile, or have them imprisoned or disappear. Finally, the govern-ment can try to convince the population that the opposition's democratic ideals are alien to the country's history, tradition and identity, funded by foreign security ser-vices, or driven by US and Western geopolitical and economic interests.

We show that each of these strategies can be applied at the macro, micro and meso levels. Thus, isolation can be pursued by severing the country's ties with the West (macro level), by limiting the ability of foreign NGOs to operate in the country (meso level) or by denying visas to individual journalists or election observers (micro level). Similarly, repression can be directed against society as a whole, specific groups, such as opposition parties, individual democracy acti-vists, or people who dare to take to the streets to protest electoral fraud.

In this special issue we identify the actual construct of these anti-colour pol-icies by focusing on five post-Soviet authoritarian states – Azerbaijan, Belarus, Russia, Tajikistan and Uzbekistan. These countries were chosen because they rep-resent different geographic regions (Europe, Caucasus, Central Asia), and vary in terms of size, natural resources, regime type, levels of social development, invol-vement in internal and external violent conflicts, and regime strength and stability more generally. Furthermore, each of these states borders at least one country that witnessed a successful colour revolution, thus exacerbating the authorities' sense of threat. In addition, we focus on Iran, which is located outside the region in which the colour revolutions took place and does not share a border with any of the 'revolutionary' states, yet nonetheless provides an illuminating case for a com-parison drawn from outside the post-communist orbit. By presenting a series of qualitative, country-focused studies we aim to explore the whole spectrum of potential anti-democratization policies, ranging from preventing elite splits at the top (the case of Azerbaijan), to establishing supervision bodies at the commu-nity level (Uzbekistan); from brutally and violently cracking down on protesters (Iran), to using very limited physical force (Belarus); from staging mass rallies (Russia), to fearing any type of mass mobilization (Tajikistan). Our main findings, however, are that the strategies adopted by the governments of these diverse states follow a similar logic of isolation, marginalization, distribution, repression and persuasion and that the specific policies are shaped by regimes' perceived intensity of a threat to regime survival and the regime's perceived strength vis-à-vis the democratic opposition.

Another major finding of our collaborative effort is that colour revolutions, although limited to a handful of states, had a significant political impact on authoritarian and semi-authoritarian countries across Europe and Asia. Based on numerous interviews with local elites, scholars, opposition activists, as well as an analysis of official publications and statements and on-site observations, the contributors to this special issue demonstrate that colour revolutions created an acute feeling of threat among authoritarian elites, which led them to adopt policies designed to prevent the possibility of a colour revolution in their respective countries. Furthermore, the case studies show that rather than igniting a fourth wave of democratization, as numerous activists, scholars and politicians had hoped, the fear of colour revolutions made (at least temporarily) the existing authoritarian and semi-authoritarian regimes even more politically closed, repressive, and arguably less prone to democratize and reform than they had been before the colour revolutions took place. The articles in this special issue show that restrictions on NGOs, an almost complete elimination of independent electoral monitoring, and an anti-liberal state ideology in Russia; a barrage of vehemently anti-Western propaganda and threats of long imprisonment to participants of anti-government protests in Belarus; and the retrenchment of democratic reforms in Tajikistan were driven by the fear of further colour revolutions in the region. Furthermore, while the danger of new colour revolutions in Eurasia seems to have passed, the institutions and policies designed to assist authoritarian rulers in thwarting the danger of potential regime overthrow are by and large still firmly in place.

Continuing the old debate between structure and agency, this special issue provides a wide range of perspectives on authoritarian reactions and policies. The focus on power holders' persuasion and ideology construction efforts (Belarus, Russia) or palace politics (Azerbaijan) is supplemented with structural explanations (Tajikistan) or attempts to find a middle ground between the two. Obviously it is beyond the scope of this special issue to resolve the structure versus agency debate, but based on our findings we do suggest that in the study of authoritarian reactions to the threat of democratization, the focus on agency, especially that of the top leaders, is well founded. After all, even structural factors, viewed by Way as crucial to autocrats' survival – highly institutionalized party rule, an extensive and cohesive coercive apparatus, and the state's control over the economy – are outcomes of political actors' actions and decisions.

We also find that although coercion and repression do play a role in authoritarian resistance attempts, no government relies on naked coercion alone. States differ in their attempts to create and promote the ideological foundations of the existing regime. At the same time, all states under review adopt policies aimed at ideologically legitimizing the government, either as promoting a unique version of democracy (Russia), or as being economically effective (Belarus), or simply as an antidote to widespread disorder (Tajikistan).

The economy is another important sphere of governments' preventive activities and we argue for a more detailed examination of economic issues, the extent of corruption and the density of clientelistic networks – topics which are often overlooked in the literature on colour revolutions. Economic growth by itself, as the Ukrainian case has clearly demonstrated, is insufficient to prevent a colour revolution. Targeted distribution of social and monetary benefits, on the other hand, proves to be a much more effective strategy of authoritarian governmental survival. Social security benefits for senior citizens in Belarus, pensions to families of martyrs and veterans in Iran, and internships in Gazprom for *Nashi* members in Russia fulfill the same function of creating a substantially large group of citizens dependent on the regime for their livelihood and wellbeing, and therefore willing to take actions in support of the government when the government is challenged by the pro-democratic opposition.

Russia, Belarus, Azerbaijan, Uzbekistan, Tajikistan and Iran: summary of the main findings

The picture of authoritarian reaction to colour revolutions that emerges from the contributions that comprise this special issue is of a complex and multifaceted set of policies which are unique for each country but drawn from the same repertoire of potential actions. Each regime adopts a particular blend of democracy prevention policies, concentrating on the issues that are perceived as the most threatening for the ruling elites. Table 1 summarizes different aspects of each country's anti-colour revolution strategies and their intensity.

Russia, note Finkel and Brudny, did not experience revolutionary attempts despite sharing a border with two 'coloured' states – Ukraine and Georgia.[25] This lack of a colour upheaval is even more puzzling given the fact that in the early and mid-2000s the country still enjoyed at least some media freedom, political pluralism, and independent civil society groups and youth organizations, determined to replicate various colour revolution techniques – factors that the literature on colour revolutions regards as important for their occurrence. The Orange Revolution in Ukraine created an acute sense of threat among the Russian elites and the Russia contribution discusses efforts that have been undertaken by the Kremlin to prevent a coloured upheaval in the country. Russian anti-colour revolution policies

Table 1. The focus of authoritarian reactions to colour revolutions.

	Isolation	Marginalization	Distribution	Repression	Persuasion
Russia	Low	Medium	Low	Low	High
Belarus	High	Medium	High	Medium	Medium
Iran	High	Low	Medium	High	Medium
Tajikistan	Low	Low	Low	Low	Low
Uzbekistan	Medium	Medium	High	Medium	Medium
Azerbaijan	Low	Medium	Low	Medium	Low

took various forms, such as the creation of state-sponsored institutions claiming to represent civil society, electoral legislation reforms and a weakening and marginalization of the opposition parties. The main focus, however, was on studying key democracy promotion techniques, and faithfully replicating them *against* a potential colour revolution. The pro-Putin youth movement *Nashi* and attempts to create an official state ideology are the most prominent examples of these authoritarian learning, imitation and replication techniques, generally understudied both by the scholars of authoritarianism and of democratization.

Unlike Russia, Belarus did experience a colour revolution attempt. Yet, despite a faithful replication of strategies that proved to be so successful in neighbouring Ukraine,[26] colour revolution failed to materialize in Belarus. Furthermore, Lukashenka's regime, arguably 'the last dictatorship in Europe'[27] needed no use of excessive violence to fend off the challenge. The explanation, argues Korosteleva, lies in the simple and often overlooked fact that non-democratic regimes can and often do enjoy genuine popular support and legitimacy.[28] The case of Belarus, argues the article, teaches us that colour revolution tactics can be applied in virtually any state; their success, however, often depends on factors that are beyond the control of Western democracy promoters and local pro-democratic opposition activists. Capitalizing on the Soviet past, Lukashenka, as the Belarus case study shows, succeeded in persuading the local population of the efficiency and supremacy of his non-democratic regime.

Substantial persuasive efforts, argues Tezcür, were also undertaken by the Iranian government.[29] Alarmed by the US invasion of Afghanistan and Iraq, and threatened by George W. Bush's democracy promotion discourse, Teheran's authorities, the article argues, clearly viewed the colour revolutions as a blueprint to follow in attempts to overthrow the Islamic regime. While hostility to the American philanthropist and financial backer of many pro-democracy NGOs, George Soros, was widespread throughout authoritarian states of Eurasia, nowhere was it more pronounced than in Iran, where Soros was dubbed the 'American-Zionist capitalist', plotting to overthrow the regime.[30] The case of Iran also clearly shows that authoritarian rulers' persuasion and framing strategies do not automatically ensure success. The Green (yet another colour) Movement in Iran was able to stage violent pro-democratic mass protests against the large-scale falsification of the 2009 presidential election results. The Iranian case can also provide a useful comparative case, outside the post-Soviet region, for further analysis and evaluation of various Orange, Rose or Tulip movements. In particular, it allows us to test arguments that the colour revolutions were essentially the revolt of the post-Soviet generation, or that the success of the colour revolutions was affected by the post-1991 privatization reforms.[31]

In some cases, however, deliberate persuasion efforts were hardly needed. As Markowitz points out, in Tajikistan any attempt at mass mobilization is viewed with suspicion, as it reminds citizens of the mass mobilization that led to a bloody and devastating civil war in the early and mid-1990s.[32] Another legacy of the civil war that determined the nature of Tajikistan's government's reaction to the colour revolution was the strength (or more precisely, the lack thereof) of the state and its institutions. Weakened by internal divisions, the state could pursue only mild or moderate anti-democratization policies. Viewed in a broader comparative perspective, the case of Tajikistan suggests an interesting link between state strength and authoritarian backlash and survival policies. Compared to the mild and moderate reaction of other states discussed in this special issue, such as Kazakhstan and Belarus, it might be argued that strong *and* weak autocrats are more likely to pursue moderate backlash policies, whereas countries with medium state capacity (such as Russia) are more likely to forcefully react to any democratization threat. Hopefully, further research will determine the link between state strength and anti-democratization policies.

State strength and weakness, while intuitively compelling concepts, are not easily defined. Moreover, in authoritarian states, which often do not possess or are not willing to share essential information about their economy, bureaucratic apparatus, or government capacity, the situation is even more complicated. Jennifer Murtazashvili's article on Uzbekistan – one of the most closed and authoritarian states in the world – tries to unpack the puzzle of state strength by focusing on the state's economic performance, capacity for repression and the co-optation of local institutions.[33] Uzbekistan, notes Murtazashvili, contains all the ingredients observers had long argued would lead to not only to regime change but civil war: suppression of the market economy and political and religious repression. Yet, the autocratic regime in Uzbekistan has remained remarkably stable in the face of revolutions in neighbouring countries. The secret of Uzbekistan's authoritarian stability, argues the article, is not simply in the government's ability and willingness to repress its opponents, but to combine this repression with wide distribution of material benefits and co-optation of local and traditional institutions. The analysis of Uzbekistan also suggests a need to move beyond the urban bias that characterizes current research on colour revolutions. Colour revolutions were undoubtedly an urban phenomenon and capital cities were the main arenas of clashes between the government and the opposition. At the same time, rural and small town populations also play a role in determining the success or failure of colour revolutions, and these groups should also be included in the analysis.

Co-opting local and traditional institutions, however, might be a successful strategy for colour revolution prevention, but this is not the only way to achieve this goal. In Azerbaijan, notes Radnitz, the main focus of Aliev family survival and consolidation activities was on preventing splits among the ruling elites.[34] Authoritarian regimes, he argues, can survive long after they lose popular support and, therefore, the immediate threat to the power holders was not from 'people in rural areas who lacked clean water and suffered from high unemployment', but from members of the elite who 'drive around Baku in shiny Mercedes Benzes and invest in multi-million-dollar condominiums overlooking the Caspian Sea'. The former, from the Aliev's point of view, are much less threatening than the latter. A divided elite has been widely recognized as a necessary component of successful colour revolutions,[35] and David Lane goes even further, viewing these events as 'revolutionary coup d'états',[36] thus highlighting the impact of elite conflict. What has not been studied, however, is how authoritarian governments, threatened by colour revolutions, prevent splits and impose unity among the elites. Radnitz's article provides important insights from Azerbaijani 'palace politics' and hopefully this line of research will be pursued by further studies.

In sum, in this special issue we aim to contribute to the literature on colour revolutions, democratization and authoritarianism, by expanding the analysis of colour revolutions to cases that did not experience regime change and by demonstrating which factors contributed to authoritarian regime survival in Eurasia. We propose a new typology of autocrats' reactions to the threat of democratization and look at how different non-democratic states coped with the challenge of democratization. We also highlight the desirability of expanding analysis of authoritarian rulers' survival strategies beyond the institutional, legislative and economic realms and to invest more effort in studying authoritarian regimes' persuasion strategies and attempts to create new ideological foundations of their rule. Finally, this special issue attempts to demonstrate the importance of authoritarian learning and the capacity of autocratic regimes to study democracy promotion techniques and to focus their democracy prevention efforts precisely on the policies and topics on which democracy promoters concentrate, sometimes replicating democracy promotion techniques *against* the pro-democratic opposition.

Against the background of the current wave (late 2011) of mass mobilization in Tunisia, Egypt, Libya, Syria and other Arab states, understanding the mechanisms of authoritarian rulers' reactions to democratization challenges is an imperative for scholars of democracy and authoritarianism. We hope that the articles presented in this special issue will not only enrich our understanding of colour revolutions and authoritarian reactions to them, but will also pave the way to further research that will cover not only post-Soviet Eurasia, but also other regions.

Acknowledgements

This special issue is an outcome of collaborative efforts of numerous people in the United States, United Kingdom, and Israel. We wish to express our gratitude to the authors, numerous anonymous reviewers, the journal editors and the participants of the 2010 American Political Science Association and 2009 American Association for the Advancement of Slavic Studies panels, in which several papers of this special issue were first presented. We also thank Mitchell Orenstein for his comments on the earlier draft of the contribution and those who assisted in proofreading and editing.

Notes

1. Beissinger, 'Structure and Example in Modular Political Phenomena'.
2. Ibid.; Beissinger, *Nationalist Mobilization and the Collapse of the Soviet State.*
3. See, for example, Åslund, *How Ukraine Became a Market Economy and Democracy*; Karatnycky, 'Ukraine's Orange Revolution'.
4. Hale, 'Democracy or Autocracy on the March? The Colored Revolutions as Normal Dynamics of Patronal Presidentialism'.

5. Kalandadze and Orenstein, 'Electoral Protests and Democratization'.
6. Beissinger, 'Structure and Example in Modular Political Phenomena'; Beissinger, 'An Interrelated Wave'; Bunce and Wolchik, 'Defeating Dictators'; Bunce and Wolchik, 'Democratising Elections in the Postcommunist World'; Bunce and Wolchik, 'Favorable Conditions and Electoral Revolutions'; Bunce and Wolchik, 'Getting Real About "Real Causes"'; Hale, 'Democracy or Autocracy on the March?'; Lane, '"Coloured Revolution" as a Political Phenomenon'; McFaul, 'Transitions from Postcommunism'; Tucker, 'Enough!'; Way, 'The Real Causes of the Color Revolutions'; White, 'Is There a Pattern?'.
7. Bunce and Wolchik, 'Defeating Dictators'; Hess, 'Protests, Parties, and Presidential Succession Competing Theories of Color Revolutions in Armenia and Kyrgyzstan'; Kalandadze and Orenstein, 'Electoral Protests and Democratization: Beyond the Color Revolutions'.
8. *Democratization* 16 (2009).
9. Bunce, McFaul, and Stoner-Weiss, *Democracy and Authoritarianism in the Postcommunist World*.
10. But see Ambrosio, *Authoritarian Backlash*; Wilson, 'Coloured Revolutions: The View from Moscow and Beijing'.
11. Stoner-Weiss, 'Comparing Oranges and Apples: The Internal and External Dimensions of Russia's Turn Away from Democracy', 255.
12. Weyland, 'The Diffusion of Regime Contention in European Democratization, 1830–1940', 1156–7.
13. Silitsky, 'Contagion Deterred: Preemptive Authoritarianism in the Former Soviet Union (the Case of Belarus)', 275.
14. Way, 'Resistance to Contagion: Sources of Authoritarian Stability in the Former Soviet Union', 230.
15. A notable exception to this rule is Moldova.
16. Silitsky, 'Contagion Deterred: Preemptive Authoritarianism in the Former Soviet Union (the Case of Belarus)', 276.
17. McFaul, 'Transitions from Postcommunism'.
18. Kuzio, 'Democratic Breakthroughs and Revolutions in Five Postcommunist Countries'.
19. Way, 'The Real Causes of the Color Revolutions'.
20. Radnitz, 'The Color of Money: Privatization, Economic Dispersion, and the Post-Soviet 'Revolutions'.
21. Nikolayenko, 'The Revolt of the Post-Soviet Generation: Youth Movements in Serbia, Georgia, and Ukraine'.
22. Bunce and Wolchik, 'Defeating Dictators'.
23. Tucker, 'Enough!'
24. For an additional, and in some aspects similar typology, see Ambrosio, *Authoritarian Backlash: Russian Resistance to Democratization in the Former Soviet Union*.
25. Finkel and Brudny, 'Russia and the Colour Revolutions'.
26. Silitsky, 'Contagion Deterred: Preemptive Authoritarianism in the Former Soviet Union (the Case of Belarus)'.
27. Marples, 'Europe's Last Dictatorship'.
28. Korosteleva, 'Questioning Democracy Promotion'.
29. Tezcür, 'Democracy Promotion, Authoritarian Resiliency, and Political Unrest in Iran'.
30. 'Take This Conspiracy Seriously!' The editorial describes Soros as 'the Zionist American capitalist who has strong ties with the Zionist lobby, and some even call him the "unofficial American agent" in the Third World countries. He is the sponsor and executor of "velvet revolution" or coloured revolution projects'.

31. Nikolayenko, 'The Revolt of the Post-Soviet Generation'; Radnitz, 'The Color of Money'.
32. Markowitz, 'Tajikistan: Authoritarian Reaction in a Postwar State'.
33. Murtazashvili, 'Coloured by Revolution'.
34. Radnitz, 'Oil in the Family: Managing Succession in Azerbaijan'.
35. See, for instance, McFaul, 'Transitions from Postcommunism'.
36. Lane, '"Coloured Revolution" as a Political Phenomenon'.

Notes on contributors

Evgeny Finkel is PhD Candidate, Department of Political Science, University of Wisconsin-Madison, and a Research Fellow, Program on Order, Conflict, and Violence, Yale University, USA. His articles have been published and are forthcoming in *Comparative Politics*, *East European Politics and Societies* (with Y. Brudny), *Global Society* and several other journals.

Yitzhak M. Brudny is the Jay and Leonie Darwin Chair in Russian Studies, The Hebrew University of Jerusalem, Israel. He is the author of *Reinventing Russia: Russian Nationalism and the Soviet State, 1953–1991* (Harvard University Press, 1998), and the principal editor of *Restructuring Post-Communist Russia* (Cambridge University Press, 2004). His articles on Russia and the former Soviet Union have appeared in numerous journals and edited volumes.

Bibliography

Ambrosio, Thomas. *Authoritarian Backlash: Russian Resistance to Democratization in the Former Soviet Union*. Burlington: Ashgate, 2009.

Åslund, Anders. *How Ukraine Became a Market Economy and Democracy*. Washington, DC: Peterson Institute for International Economics, 2009.

Beissinger, Mark. 'An Interrelated Wave'. *Journal of Democracy* 20, no. 1 (2009): 74–7.

Beissinger, Mark. *Nationalist Mobilization and the Collapse of the Soviet State*. New York: Cambridge University Press, 2002.

Beissinger, Mark. 'Structure and Example in Modular Political Phenomena: The Diffusion of Bulldozer/Rose/Orange/Tulip Revolutions'. *Perspectives on Politics* 5, no. 2 (2007): 259–76.

Bunce, Valerie, Michael McFaul, and Kathryn Stoner-Weiss, eds. *Democracy and Authoritarianism in the Postcommunist World*. New York: Cambridge University Press, 2010.

Bunce, Valerie, and Sharon Wolchik. 'Defeating Dictators: Electoral Change and Stability in Competitive Authoritarian Regimes'. *World Politics* 62, no. 1 (2010): 43–86.

Bunce, Valerie, and Sharon Wolchik. 'Democratising Elections in the Postcommunist World: Definitions, Dynamics and Diffusion'. *St. Antony's International Review* 2, no. 2 (2007): 64–89.

Bunce, Valerie, and Sharon Wolchik. 'Favorable Conditions and Electoral Revolutions'. *Journal of Democracy* 17, no. 4 (2006): 5–18.

Bunce, Valerie, and Sharon Wolchik. 'Getting Real About "Real Causes"'. *Journal of Democracy* 20, no. 1 (2009): 69–73.

Finkel, Evgeny, and Yitzhak M. Brudny, 'Russia and the Colour Revolutions'. *Democratization* 19, no. 1 (2012): 15–36.

Hale, Henry. 'Democracy or Autocracy on the March? The Colored Revolutions as Normal Dynamics of Patronal Presidentialism'. *Communist and Post-Communist Studies* 39, no. 3 (2006): 305–29.

Hess, Steve. 'Protests, Parties, and Presidential Succession Competing Theories of Color Revolutions in Armenia and Kyrgyzstan'. *Problems of Post-Communism* 57, no. 1 (2010): 28–39.

Kalandadze, Katya, and Mitchell Orenstein. 'Electoral Protests and Democratization: Beyond the Color Revolutions'. *Comparative Political Studies* 42, no. 11 (2009): 1403–25.

Karatnycky, Adrian. 'Ukraine's Orange Revolution'. *Foreign Affairs* 84, no. 2 (2005): 35–52.

Korosteleva, Elena. Questioning Democracy Promotion: Belarus' Response to the 'Colour Revolutions'. *Democratization* 19, no. 1 (2012): 37–59.

Kuzio, Taras. 'Democratic Breakthroughs and Revolutions in Five Postcommunist Countries: Comparative Perspectives on the Fourth Wave'. *Demokratizatsiya* 16, no. 1 (2008): 97–109.

Lane, David. '"Coloured Revolution" as a Political Phenomenon'. *Journal of Communist Studies and Transition Politics* 25, nos. 2–3 (2009): 113–35.

Markowitz, Lawrence P. 'Tajikistan: Authoritarian Reaction in a Postwar State'. *Democratization* 19, no. 1 (2012): 98–119.

Marples, David. 'Europe's Last Dictatorship: The Roots and Perspectives of Authoritarianism in "White Russia"'. *Europe-Asia Studies* 57, no. 6 (2005): 895–908.

McFaul, Michael. 'Transitions from Postcommunism'. *Journal of Democracy* 16, no. 3 (2005): 5–19.

Murtazashvili, Jennifer. 'Coloured by Revolution: The Political Economy of Autocratic Stability in Uzbekistan'. *Democratization* 19, no. 1 (2012): 78–97.

Nikolayenko, Olena. 'The Revolt of the Post-Soviet Generation: Youth Movements in Serbia, Georgia, and Ukraine'. *Comparative Politics* 39, no. 2 (2007): 169–88.

Radnitz, Scott. 'The Color of Money: Privatization, Economic Dispersion, and the Post-Soviet 'Revolutions'. *Comparative Politics* 42, no. 2 (2010): 127–46.

Radnitz, Scott. 'Oil in the Family: Managing Presidential Succession in Azerbaijan'. *Democratization* 19, no. 1 (2012): 60–77.

Silitsky, Vitalii. 'Contagion Deterred: Preemptive Authoritarianism in the Former Soviet Union (the Case of Belarus)'. In *Democracy and Authoritarianism in the Postcommunist World*, ed. Valerie Bunce, Michael McFaul, and Kathryn Stoner-Weiss, 274–99. New York: Cambridge University Press, 2010.

Stoner-Weiss, Kathryn. 'Comparing Oranges and Apples: The Internal and External Dimensions of Russia's Turn away from Democracy'. In *Democracy and Authoritarianism in the Postcommunist World*, ed. Valerie Bunce, Michael McFaul, and Kathryn Stoner-Weiss, 253–73. New York: Cambridge University Press, 2010.

'Take This Conspiracy Seriously!'. *Jomhuri-ye Eslami*, June 11, 2007.

Tezcür, Güneş Murat. 'Democracy Promotion, Authoritarian Resiliency, and Political Unrest in Iran'. *Democratization* 19, no. 1 (2012): 120–40.

Tucker, Joshua. 'Enough! Electoral Fraud, Collective Action Problems, and Post-Communist Colored Revolutions'. *Perspectives on Politics* 5, no. 3 (2007): 537–53.

Way, Lucan. 'The Real Causes of the Color Revolutions'. *Journal of Democracy* 19, no. 3 (2008): 55–69.

Way, Lucan. 'Resistance to Contagion: Sources of Authoritarian Stability in the Former Soviet Union'. In *Democracy and Authoritarianism in the Postcommunist World*, ed. Valerie Bunce, Michael McFaul, and Kathryn Stoner-Weiss, 229–52. New York: Cambridge University Press, 2010.

Weyland, Kurt. 'The Diffusion of Regime Contention in European Democratization, 1830–1940'. *Comparative Political Studies* 43, nos. 8–9 (2010): 1148–76.

White, Stephen. 'Is There a Pattern?'. *Journal of Communist Studies and Transition Politics* 25, nos. 2–3 (2009): 396–412.

Wilson, Jeanne. 'Coloured Revolutions: The View from Moscow and Beijing'. *Journal of Communist Studies and Transition Politics* 25, nos. 2–3 (2009): 369–95.

Russia and the colour revolutions

Evgeny Finkel[a,b] and Yitzhak M. Brudny[c]

[a]Department of Political Science, University of Wisconsin-Madison, Madison, USA;
[b]Program on Order, Conflict, and Violence, Yale University, New Haven, USA; [c]Department
of Political Science & Department of History, The Hebrew University of Jerusalem, Israel

The colour revolutions, and especially the Orange Revolution in Ukraine, are widely perceived as major international setbacks to Putin's Russia. The Ukrainian events alarmed Russian elites, who feared the possibility of a local colour revolution during the 2007–2008 electoral cycle. To thwart the perceived colour revolution threat, Russian authorities adopted strategies that combined a political, administrative and intellectual assault on the opposition and Western ideas of democracy promotion. An integral part of this assault was, first, an attempt to create a mass youth movement, Nashi, as a counterweight to the various youth movements that were the driving forces behind the colour revolutions in Serbia, Georgia and Ukraine. Second, it was an attempt to delegitimize the idea of liberal democracy itself, labelling it subversive and alien to the Russian national character. We argue that Russian reactions to the 'colour revolution threat' provide important insights into what an authoritarian regime, such as that in Russia, perceives as the most threatening aspects of democratizing activities by domestic and international actors.

Introduction

Colour revolutions, especially the Orange Revolution in Ukraine, caught the authoritarian regime of Vladimir Putin by surprise. During the 2004 Ukrainian presidential elections campaign, numerous Kremlin-affiliated political consultants worked for Victor Yanukovich, the defeated candidate who tried to rig the elections, while Yanukovich's candidacy was publically endorsed by Putin.[1] Since 2005, substantial efforts have been devoted to preventing the Ukrainian scenario in Russia.

The goal of this article is to study how Russian authorities reacted to the threat of colour revolution and democratization more broadly. The first key argument of this article is that the Russian authoritarian regime successfully copied democracy promotion strategies in order to prevent a democratic outcome. In short, democracy promotion tools became, in the hands of the Russian government, democracy prevention strategies. In this article we will show that Russia, like other authoritarian regimes in the region, adopted a range of policies aimed at preventing non-violent democratic regime change. The Kremlin, as we will demonstrate in this article, confronted the threat of colour revolution by putting restrictions on civil society and independent media, tinkering with electoral legislation and limiting independent electoral monitoring capabilities. Our second main argument is that while studies of colour revolutions and the attempts to counter them tend to focus on institutional and economic factors,[2] the analysis should be expanded to the regime's attempts to build popular support and legitimacy. In this article we focus on such components of democracy prevention as the Russian authorities' attempt to create a pro-government mass youth movement and its heavy investment in the development and articulation of a new official ideology.

Several scholars have proposed exhaustive theoretical frameworks to explain why colour revolutions occurred. For example, McFaul lists seven factors – a semi-autocratic regime, an unpopular incumbent, a united opposition, an ability to publicize electoral fraud, independent media, the opposition's ability to mobilize people to take to the streets, and the divisions among the regime's coercive forces.[3] Kuzio suggests another framework with nine, mainly similar, factors, including: a competitive- (that is, semi-) authoritarian state facilitating space for the democratic opposition; 'return to Europe' civic nationalism that assists in mobilizing civil society; a preceding political crisis that weakened the regime's legitimacy; a pro-democratic capital city; unpopular ruling elites; a charismatic candidate; a united opposition; mobilized youth; and regionalism and foreign intervention (Russia or the European Union).[4]

In the following pages we show how the Russian government's policies, aimed at countering the colour revolution threat, focused on precisely the fields crucial for colour revolution success. Restrictions on non-governmental organizations (NGOs) and new electoral legislation were designed to weaken the opposition and to move Russia's previously semi-authoritarian regime towards full-blown authoritarianism. The limitations on electoral monitoring eliminated the opposition's ability to publicize electoral fraud, and the independence of the media was further limited. Yet some factors, such as the popularity of the incumbent, mobilized youth, active attempts to counteract real and perceived Western meddling in Russian politics, and the existence of a pro-Western ideology could not be addressed by purely institutional measures and new legislation. Therefore, the creation of a pro-government mass youth movement and the promotion of anti-colour ideology became important components of the Kremlin's anti-colour strategies.

Restricting civil society[5]

The role played by various NGOs – especially the pro-democracy youth movements such as *Otpor* in Serbia, *Kmara* in Georgia, and *Pora* in Ukraine – made scholars and politicians alike realize the importance of independent civil society as one of the key promoters of colour revolutions.[6] One of the first steps taken by Putin after the Orange Revolution was significantly to reduce the role and the independence of NGOs in Russia. In May 2004, even before the Orange Revolution in Ukraine, President Putin argued that receiving grants from influential foreign foundations had become the priority task for many NGOs.[7] However, only after the Orange Revolution was a controversial draft law, designed to significantly constrain NGOs' independence, discussed and adopted by the Duma – the lower house of the Russian Parliament. Although the draconian original draft law was somewhat softened after a campaign led by human rights organizations in Russia and abroad, the restrictions on the NGOs remained substantial.[8]

In parallel to attacks on NGOs, Russia's authorities also engaged in a systematic effort to create new political institutions purported to represent a variety of societal interests. The culmination point of these policies was the establishment in 2005 of the Civic Chamber (*Obshchestvennaya Palata*), an official state body, designed to act as mediator between the citizens, NGOs and the authorities.[9] The Civic Chamber's 126 members were elected in three stages. At the first stage, the president appointed 42 members, who elected an additional 42 members, representing civic groups and organizations, willing to take part in the work of the Chamber. Together, these 84 members elected the last 42, representing regional and inter-regional NGOs. Therefore the election process almost completely ensured that only people approved by the authorities became members of the Chamber and that this institution would not challenge those who held power. The Chamber, nonetheless, had no real powers or any other ability to affect the decision-making process or to lobby citizens' interests vis-à-vis the authorities.

Electoral legislation reforms

In addition to cracking down on the independent NGOs, the authorities also sought to weaken the opposition and to prevent it from posing any real threat to the regime. Although the opposition in Russia was weak and fragmented to begin with, in 2005–2006 the pro-government United Russia party, which controlled the parliament, introduced new laws aimed to weaken it even more. The legislation raised the electoral threshold from 5% to 7% and eliminated the single member district component of Russia's electoral system.[10] These legislative changes effectively deprived members of the pro-democratic opposition of any real chance to get elected. The new registration rules also forbade the creation of electoral alliances. Further limits on the registration of parties and new requirements on party membership and regional representation ensured that only one opposition party, the hard line anti-Western Communist Party (KPRF), would be represented in the legislature.[11] This situation, notes Ryabov, created enormous advantages for United Russia, which was (and still is) closely intertwined with the state apparatus and enjoyed virtually unrestricted access to financial and administrative resources.[12]

The government had also tightened its grip over the major media outlets. Opposition media do exist in Russia, but the majority of Russian citizens rely on the main government-owned (or controlled) television channels for information on politics.[13] The government had also practically eliminated any independent electoral monitoring, both domestic and international. In the 2007 parliamentary elections, the Organization for Security and Co-operation in Europe (OSCE) refused to send an elections monitoring mission to Russia, 'indicating that the Russian government had imposed restrictions that would make it impossible to verify the veracity of the election'.[14] The same scenario took place during the 2008 presidential elections. Domestically, Russia has only one independent election-monitoring NGO, which operates in fewer than half of the country's regions and enjoys a very limited ability even to monitor, much less influence the quality of the Russian electoral process and to 'drive home the point that voting results were falsified'.[15]

Yet, none of these measures and policies were unique to Russia. Other authoritarian states throughout Eurasia were also actively engaged in cracking down on independent civil society, attempting to control the media, and tinkering with electoral legislation. What makes Russia different from other authoritarian states is the incumbents' investments in creating a new ideology, which ruled out the possibility of colour revolution, including establishment of a mass youth movement that replicated colour revolution techniques *against* a colour revolution. The next sections will discuss each of these policies.

The Nashi youth movement

Despite the existence in Russia of numerous youth political groups either as wings of existing parties or as independent organizations, studies show that members of the younger generation are usually not interested in political activities of any kind.[16] However, the colour revolutions in Serbia, Georgia, Kyrgyzstan and Ukraine, and the role played by young people in these events,[17] alarmed the Kremlin. Although attempts to create pro-government and pro-Putin youth movements had been made even before the Orange Revolution, the events in Ukraine gave a new urgency to these efforts.

It is unclear whether the Kremlin's worries were justified – a survey, conducted by Mendelson and Gerber indicated that only 3% of Russians under the age of 30 favoured some type of Orange Revolution in Russia, while more than 70% of the respondents said that they definitely did not want an Orange Revolution to take place in their country. Furthermore, the Ukrainian events were largely seen by young Russians as a plot, orchestrated by foreign intelligence agencies.[18] Still, from the authorities' point of view, the stakes were too high to tolerate the risk of the youth drifting toward revolution. The emergence in Russia of several youth movements aimed at promoting a colour revolution, such as the Russian *Pora* (a youth movement with the same name was the driving force behind the Orange Revolution in Ukraine) made the possibility of protests, led by the pro-democratic youth, even more threatening.[19] Therefore, a pro-government *mass* youth movement was needed, the government decided, to combat the colour revolution activists and to ensure the loyalty of young people to the regime. However, the existing pro-Putin youth movements, first and foremost the 'Marching Together' (*Idushchie Vmeste*), were too small, unreliable and ineffective to prevent Ukrainian-style mass protest from appearing in Moscow. By creating 'Nashi' (2005) the regime chief ideologue and Deputy Chief of Presidential Administration Vladislav Surkov and the Kremlin's most prominent political consultant Gleb Pavlovsky envisioned a new type of disciplined, well-trained mass youth movement, which could defeat the Orange activists by using their own weapons during the 2007–2008 elections cycle.

Marching Together

The first plans to create a pro-Putin youth movement emerged immediately after Putin became the president of Russia. Already in 2000, Vasily Yakemenko, a former presidential administration official, had created an organization named Marching Together (with Putin of course).[20] To attract new members, Marching Together provided its activists with such benefits as heavily subsidized movie tickets, free internet several hours a week, a swimming pool for movement members and almost cost-free participation at the summer camp on Lake Seliger (later to become the hallmark of Nashi activities).[21] The existence of numerous perks facilitated an increase in membership, although the loyalty and motivations of the new members were questionable. Because of its relatively small membership base and weak ideological commitment, Marching Together was perceived by Surkov and Pavlovsky as unable to counterbalance the highly motivated groups that led the colour revolutions in Serbia, Georgia and Ukraine. Recognizing the need to create a new type of pro-Putin youth movement, Surkov and Yakemenko created Nashi.[22]

Nashi – creation, ideology and antifascism

Nashi, officially named 'The Youth Democratic Antifascist Movement Nashi' was established on 15 April 2005. The movement was headed by a council of five federal commissars, although the undisputable leader of Nashi at that time was Vasily Yakemenko. Russia, according to Yakemenko, is threatened both by external and internal enemies. External forces strive to dominate Eurasia, while internal enemies seek either to return to the oligarchic capitalism of the early 1990s, or to establish in Russia a fascist regime. As stated by Nashi's leader, Russia's opposition was in its essence 'the unnatural alliance of liberals, fascists, sympathizers of the West and ultranationalists, international foundations and international terror, united by one and only thing – the hatred for Putin'.[23] Interestingly, the same phrase was later printed virtually verbatim in the Kremlin's United Russia party electoral leaflet.[24] The official goal of Nashi was to confront and defeat this alliance in order to preserve Russia's sovereignty and territorial integrity, to modernize the state and to foster the development of an active civil society.[25]

The founding congress also adopted the movement symbol – a white and red banner with diagonal (St Andrew) cross, reminiscent of the tsarist era Russian navy banner. The red colour symbolizes the heroic (presumably Soviet) past, while white represents the bright future. The Nashi Manifesto, approved by the movement's Constituting Assembly, presented world history as a competition between nations, claiming that the current generation of young Russians has a unique chance to lead their country towards global leadership.[26] Otherwise, the Manifesto argues, Russia will be destined to subordination and exploitation by external forces. Young Russians have to defend their country's sovereignty in a way their grandparents did 60 years ago during World War II. The Manifesto urges the modernization of the state in accordance with Putin's plans, but claims that such modernization cannot be achieved by the generation of 'defeatists', who lost the Soviet Union, allowed the crisis of the 1990s and ruled Russia during Yeltsin's years.

Nashi's ideology emphasized that the main goal of the movement is to protect the regime from the domestic and external Orange threat.[27] This outlook inevitably required constant readiness to recognize and confront the enemy and implied a certain degree of anti-Western feelings. As Mendelson and Gerber demonstrate, Nashi members[28] are more anti-American than other young people in Russia.[29] However, Nashi was not interested in global politics per se and paid attention only to those international controversies which were seen as threatening the current Russian regime.

In March 2007 Nashi held a rally in downtown Moscow attended by more than 15,000 activists, gathered to celebrate the seventh anniversary of the Putin presidency. Along with a display of youth support for Putin and his policies, the action was also directed against the West and its perceived hostile intentions towards Russia. Movement activists distributed a flyer, designed as a survey, which explained who was the main enemy of Russia. One of the rhetorical questions asked what the West was trying to achieve in Russia, and the answers proposed that the goal of the US and its allies was 'to establish external rule over Russia'. Moreover, the leaflet depicted the US as a 'voracious predator', eager to take advantage of an 'Orange' coup initiated by the opposition leaders and militarily to intervene in Russia under the pretext of dispatching North Atlantic Treaty Organization (NATO) peacekeeping forces to guard the nuclear facilities and gas and oil pipelines.[30] Similar and even more vehemently anti-Western leaflets were produced by Nashi in December 2007. Devoted to the Duma elections, the leaflets presented what Nashi claimed to be the 'cases of Western intervention in the post-communist electoral processes' (Serbia, Georgia and Ukraine) and described the US's aggressive attitude towards Russia. Although initially Nashi officials took responsibility for creating and distributing the leaflets, they later denied the movement's connection to the flyer.[31] Thus, this section demonstrates how Nashi's ideology and actions served to protect the regime from the colour revolution threat and to counterbalance several key components of successful colour revolutions elsewhere, namely the existence of a strong pro-Western civic nationalism and the ability of Western actors to intervene in Russia's affairs. The movement's loyalty to Putin, the attacks on his critics and labelling them 'fascists' also served to promote regime legitimacy and to mobilize the movement's members in support of the leader.

Orange techniques against the Orange threat

As previously mentioned, the nightmare of the Russian political elite was a colour-style mass protest in Moscow. Crowds of protesters, against which Nashi was established to fight, had to be confronted by even bigger crowds of government supporters. According to Nashi estimates, several months after the establishment of the movement it could count on the support of several thousand members and almost 100,000 sympathizers.[32] The first occasion to demonstrate Nashi's ability to organize mass action came in May 2005 during the celebrations of the 60th anniversary of victory over Nazi Germany. The 'Our Victory' march brought to the streets of Moscow more than 60,000 Nashi supporters from 30 regions – an unprecedented number of rally participants in post-1991 Russia. This action was a clear mark of Nashi's organizational strength, although some participants from provincial towns admitted that they participated in the march only because they were promised 'a free tour to Moscow', financed by the movement.[33] Later that year Nashi organized a summer camp for several thousand members on Lake Seliger in Tver' region, after which President Putin held a meeting with the most active commissars. Seliger camps became a tradition, with the number of participants growing each year. During their stay at Seliger, the activists receive intensive ideological and physical training, which should make them ready to act decisively against any possible revolutionary threat. The discipline at Seliger is strict: alcohol, filthy language or missing classes are not allowed. In summer 2007, hundreds of participants were expelled from the camp for violating these rules. It also should be noted that the rank and status of those officials who visit the camp rises every year. While the 2005 camp attracted mostly Kremlin political consultants, parliamentarians and regional leaders, in 2008 both main candidates to succeed Putin, Sergei Ivanov and Dmitry Medvedev visited Seliger and met with the activists.[34]

Obviously, mass actions and happenings, such as the 'Our Victory' march and Seliger camps require considerable amounts of money, estimated in the tens of millions of dollars. Although movement rank and file do not receive financial rewards for their activities, Nashi nonetheless has to sustain a network of regional offices and finance its numerous activities. The exact level of movement expenditure is kept secret. According to data provided by *Kommersant*, one of Russia's most respected daily newspapers, the activities of each regional Nashi office cost between US$20,000–30,000 a month, while for the 2007 Seliger camp alone the movement had to pay more than 20 million US dollars.[35] According to Russia's business newspaper *Vedomosti*, Nashi and organizations affiliated with the movement received from the state budget more than US$15 million in the form of grants and state contracts.[36] Yet it seems that the bulk of financial support for movement activities comes from private sources, mostly big companies and corporations.[37] It appears that sponsors just cannot refuse to support a movement affiliated with the Kremlin and Putin personally. As Yakemenko bluntly put it: 'the refusal to finance a Nashi project means lack of patriotism'.[38]

A distinctive feature of colour revolutions, and especially the Orange Revolution in Ukraine, was the colourful, 'carnival-like'[39] atmosphere of mass protests which featured numerous artistic performances, rock and folk concerts and even public weddings of protest participants. Imitating these carnival-style techniques was an innovation brought by Nashi to Russian politics. Actions such as sending tens of thousands of activists dressed as Santa Claus to distribute New Year presents to veterans, or masquerade-like marches of movement members dressed in World War II-era Red Army uniform, not only attracted significant media attention, but also clearly distinguished Nashi from other youth movements and created a positive image of an innovative, fun and colourful organization. Strikingly resembling the Orange Revolution 'Maidan weddings',[40] the 2007 Seliger camp witnessed a simultaneous wedding of more than 20 couples of movement activists. On the Day of National Unity (4 November) 2005, Nashi promised that each of the movement's members would carry out at least one noble deed, such as assisting veterans and pensioners, feeding homeless people or presenting flowers to people on the streets.[41]

An additional important feature of the colour revolutions was the use of new media, especially the internet, to organize and mobilize pro-democratic activists for mass protests.[42] Hence, it is hardly surprising that Nashi devotes significant attention to the new media, especially the internet. The movement has a well-developed, colourful and almost constantly updated website (www.nashi.su). Interestingly enough, and quite symbolically, the movement chose not to use the standard Russian domain country code '.ru', and opted for the relatively rare country code '.su', which stands for the Soviet Union. The movement also has a number of affiliated thematic websites, devoted to specific areas of Nashi activities. Additional 'colour' tactics that had to be countered by Nashi were the use of exit polls and election observers to discredit official results and trigger mass protests.[43] The 'Our Elections' programme, initiated by Nashi in 2005, was the movement's response to this exit polls threat. The goal of the programme was to train 3500 movement observers to take part in the 2007–2008 elections. The pilot programme was put into practice during the 2005 Moscow City Duma elections. Three parties – United Russia, Free Russia and the Just Russia Party – included Nashi members in their observers' quota – 100 in the United Russia list and 500 for each of the two other parties. Moreover, movement observers also received special training from the Central Elections Committee chairman.[44]

Nashi: incentives for counter-revolution

The creation of Nashi and the heavy involvement in its activities of Putin's chief ideologue and Deputy Chief of Presidential Administration Vladislav Surkov and the Kremlin's leading political consultant Gleb Pavlovsky, inevitably created tensions between Nashi and the ruling party, United Russia. Initially, when Nashi was created, several high ranking United Russia officials called the movement 'storm troopers' and ruled out the possibility of cooperation with Yakemenko. Furthermore, United Russia has its own youth wing, the 'Young Guard of United Russia'.[45] Relations between the two bodies proved to be rather strained. On numerous occasions the Young Guard and Nashi had no other choice but to cooperate, despite the constant feud over influence and privileged access to the Kremlin. Nashi, as the bigger and significantly more visible organization always had a significant advantage over the Young Guard which is associated with a political party and not with Putin personally. A good indicator of the two movements' relative strength was the list of United Russia candidates for the 2008 Duma elections. As a result of the elections two prominent Nashi activists entered the Duma, while none of the Young Guard leaders could secure inclusion into the party list.

The association with Putin, his power and prestige, is also meant to serve as an additional incentive to attract the politically apathetic Russian youth and to draw them into pro-regime political actions. Membership in the movement was presented as a good investment not only in the country's but also in one's personal and professional future. According to the movement's ideology, Nashi activists were trained to view themselves, and were often treated by the authorities, as the next generation of the Russian elite.[46] Despite their anti-bureaucratic rhetoric, Nashi activists nonetheless aspired to become members of the country's governing class. Not surprisingly, the movement has often been compared to *Komsomol* – the youth wing of the Soviet-era Communist Party and the breeding ground for the future leading cadres. Nashi members, particularly university students from economics, management and business administration departments, often do internships in various governmental and semi-governmental bodies such as federal ministries, the presidential administration, regional governments and the state natural gas monopoly, Gazprom. Movement activists were also entitled to take courses at the Higher School of Management, a prestigious training ground for senior government bureaucracy.[47] Moreover, recognizing the need to study from the West its management and scientific techniques and skills, Nashi initiated a project allowing a number of movement activists to pursue academic education in countries such as the United Kingdom, United States and Ireland.[48]

A central place in Nashi's pantheon was reserved for Putin. According to the movement's ideology, and unlike 'Marching Together', Nashi supported and admired Putin not only because he was president, but because of his policies and actions. For example, in October 2007 Nashi held a mass rally, attended by more than 10,000 activists, which was devoted to Putin's birthday. Posters prepared by Nashi members expressed their admiration for Putin and thanked the president for: stability, peace in Chechnya, Stabilization Fund, Winter Olympic Games, and urged him to stay with the movement forever. The newly established school-age wing of Nashi, the *Mishki* (Little Bears) also called on the president, whom they see as 'mega-super brown bear', to lead their organization.[49]

Although Nashi support for Putin often took forms that were reminiscent of the Stalin personality cult, it could be also seen as an instrumental attempt to strengthen the movement rank and file's loyalty to the president, and to ensure that the 'unpopular incumbent' predicament would not be repeated in Russia. Furthermore, as the studies in this special issue demonstrate, even a relatively small but loyal, organized and well-equipped praetorian guard was often sufficient to substantially reduce the threat to the regime. While Nashi was clearly not a military force or a riot police, it did create an in-house 'security service', called the Voluntary Youth Militia (*Dobrovol'naia Molodezhnaia Druzhina*). One of the Youth Militia's declared goals was to assist police in combatting crime, patrolling the streets and guarding the public events of the movement. According to accounts in the Russian media, numerous Militia people were members of the prone-to-violence soccer fans' organizations such as the Gallant Steeds (fans of CSKA Moscow football team[50]), and the Gladiators (FC Spartak Moscow fans). Informal leaders of these groups, such as Aleksey Mitryushin, Roman Verbitsky and Vasily Stepanov (also known as *Vasia-Killer*), were among the Nashi leaders.[51] At the 2007 Seliger camp, a role play imitating a coloured revolution scenario, ended in violence and the beating up of the 'orangists', played by members of two other small pro-Putin youth organizations, New People and Young Russia.[52]

The movement members were also allegedly behind numerous acts of physical violence against the Kremlin's opponents. The first evidence of Nashi's readiness to use violence came from the movement's founding congress. During the event, Ilya Yashin, the leader of the pro-democracy, Yabloko party youth wing, was discovered spying on Nashi. He was forcefully expelled from the building and thrown out into a snowdrift. Several days later, on 18 April 2005, former chess world champion and one of the opposition leaders Garry Kasparov, labelled by Yakemenko as a 'fascist collaborator', was attacked and beaten up with a chessboard. Although Nashi denied any connection with the attack, Kasparov supporters were confident that Nashi was responsible for the violence.[53] In November 2010, Nashi was accused of severely beating a renowned journalist, Oleg Kashin, the author of numerous critical articles on Nashi and the Russian government more generally.[54]

Another Nashi target was the UK ambassador in Moscow, Sir Antony Brenton. Nashi's campaign against Brenton started in 2006 after the ambassador's participation at a conference organized by the oppositional 'Other Russia' movement. Nashi demanded that the ambassador apologize for the address he delivered at the conference. 'Brenton addressed the gathering of fascists. If he does not apologize, he has to leave our country', exclaimed Yakemenko.[55] After Nashi's demand was ignored, the movement initiated a series of rallies in front of the British embassy building and started personally intimidating the ambassador. At one point, the ambassador's bodyguard had to use physical force against a prominent Nashi activist, Tikhon Chumakov, who decided to take Sir Antony as his 'personal project'.[56] The movement's actions against the British ambassador led to a diplomatic crisis between the two countries when the British Foreign Office complained to their Russian counterparts about Nashi actions. As a result of this complaint, Russian Foreign Minister Sergei Lavrov personally urged Yakemenko to respect the law and the Vienna Convention. Nevertheless, after the meeting with Lavrov, Yakemenko assured the media that actions against Brenton would be continued as before.[57] Later the 'Brenton scheme' of constant surveillance and intimidation was applied by Nashi against one of Putin's most prominent critics, former Prime Minister Mikhail Kasyanov.

Nashi under Medvedev

Overall, from the Kremlin point of view Nashi can be seen as a success story of authoritarian learning and reaction. The Putin administration and its political consultants succeeded in creating a youth mass movement that replicated and implemented the major colour revolution, techniques aimed *against* the Russian opposition to ensure the smooth conduct of the 2007–2008 Duma and presidential elections and the transition of power to the designated successor, Dmitrii Medvedev. Moreover, the authorities, for the first time in post-Soviet Russian history, were able to create a numerous and devoted cohort of young regime supporters who have a vested interest in the preservation of the current system. After all, despite their admiration of Putin, Nashi claims that it will extend its support to any leader continuing the implementation of the 'Putin Plan'. It is true that Nashi has never had to display its loyalty in a time of need, and none can predict how the movement's rank and file would act against a real mass protest. This type of counterfactual analysis is beyond the scope of this article but evidently the lack of a need to confront such real challenges indicates the success of the Russian authorities' anti-Orange strategy, of which Nashi is an integral component.

Nashi activities also allowed some of the movement leaders and most prominent activists to reach high-ranking positions in the Russian political system. In October 2007, even prior to the Duma elections, Vasily Yakemenko was promoted by the Kremlin to head a recently established agency, the State Commission for Youth Affairs, thus becoming the youngest Cabinet member. Later, two Nashi activists became United Russia Duma members. Dozens of lower-level activists entered regional and municipal legislative assemblies. Arguably, for a movement that toyed with the idea of becoming the 'party of power', these results are rather disappointing. Nonetheless, Nashi clearly realized that (at least until 2008) the movement's main role was to provide the Kremlin with some sort of 'anti-Orange insurance'.[58]

Having completed their electoral and post-electoral missions, Nashi had to redefine the movement's role in the newly created political landscape and to cope with the departure of Yakemenko who was succeeded by Nikita Borovikov, a 27-year-old lawyer from Vladimir. One of Borovikov's first tasks was to assure the continuation of Nashi activities after the desired electoral outcome had been secured by the Kremlin. Nashi's mass events presented the Kremlin and its business allies with a significant financial burden, perceived as unnecessary after the United Russia and Medvedev victories. Moreover, the movement's vehemently anti-Western and militant rhetoric and actions fostered a negative image of Russia, its political system and Putin himself in the USA and Europe.

As a result, Nashi had no other choice but to adapt to the changing conditions on the ground. According to Borovikov, since the Orange threat is already non-existent, it is about time to concentrate on other social and political projects.[59] As the new Nashi leader bluntly puts it, 'the 1990s drove the Russian youths to the ghetto of social handicapness (*invalidnost'*), sentenced them to have a glamorous, narco-alcoholic or criminal future. Nowadays neither families nor schools can work with youths'.[60] Therefore, when the colour revolution threat is no longer around, such an educational and guiding role should be assumed by the restructured Nashi movement. At the same time, to be successful, pro-regime education has to be based on some ideological foundations. Developing such foundations became another main component of Russia's authoritarian survival strategies.

Intellectual responses to Orange Revolution: attempts to create new 'official' nationalism

Most studies of colour revolutions tend to focus on institutional and economic factors, such as the regime type, the freedom of the media, independent electoral monitoring, or the existence of united opposition and the business class willing to financially support it.[61] However, what the scholarship on colour revolutions tends to overlook is the importance of ideational and ideological factors, such as the 'return to Europe' civic nationalism, discussed by Kuzio.[62] Yet ideological factors do play an important role not only in colour revolutions,[63] but also in authoritarian reactions to the challenge of democratization. The following section demonstrates the ideological strategies of colour revolution prevention undertaken by the arguably non-ideological regime of Vladimir Putin.

There is a consensus among scholars that the Putin regime and its political party, United Russia, are profoundly non-ideological, despite the fact that the latter calls itself a 'conservative' party.[64] In the 2000 presidential campaign, Putin projected himself as a candidate without an ideological platform, to sharpen the contrast with his main rival, the Communist Party candidate Zyuganov. Throughout his two terms in office Putin, like authoritarian leaders elsewhere, emphasized achievements in the economic sphere and international politics as a major legitimizing strategy. Nevertheless, the defeat of the Kremlin's preferred candidate, Victor Yanukovich, in the Ukrainian presidential election and the Orange Revolution in that country required not only legislative and organizational efforts but also an ideological answer. As Pavlovsky stated shortly after the Orange Revolution, 'counter-revolutionary know-how', which contains an intellectual dimension, is necessary to prevent a similar event from taking place in Russia.[65]

In other words, in Pavlovsky's eyes Putin's regime clearly required a legitimizing ideological foundation capable of countering the democracy promotion efforts of the West, especially the United States.[66]

Articulating an anti-democratic official ideology, however, was problematic to the regime which was an heir to Yeltsin's government and was reluctant to completely discard its own self-proclaimed democratic credentials. The reason for that was simple: since the early 1990s the Communist Party and a variety of nationalist parties, movements and intellectuals articulated their own version of an authoritarian creed for Russia which delegitimized the entire post-communist experiment with democracy and a market economy. In other words, official ideology had to be both anti-democratic and sufficiently distinct from communist and nationalist versions of an authoritarian creed.

The first articulation of this emerging ideology was an article by the Chief Justice of the Russian Constitutional Court, Valery Zorkin, entitled 'Apology of the Westphalian System' (*Apologiya Vestfal'skoi sistemy*) published in the journal *Russia in Global Affairs (Rossiia v global'noi politike)* in its May–June 2004 issue and reprinted in an abridged form in the official mouthpiece of the Russian government, the newspaper *Rossiiskaya Gazeta*, on 13 July 2004.[67] While not referring explicitly to the colour revolution, Zorkin clearly had in mind Western democracies' support of NGOs and other civic groups engaged in democracy promotion. This support grossly violated what he perceived as the fundamental principle of national sovereignty established in the aftermath of the Peace of Westphalia (1648). Alluding to colour revolutions, Zorkin criticized Western arguments of limiting state sovereignty in the name of human rights, right of self-determination or any abstract principle. Abandoning the Westphalian principle of state sovereignty, he warned, would lead to chaos and the destruction of the international system, the system which the United Nations was established to protect.[68]

While Zorkin's argument attempted to ground the ideological opposition to coloured revolutions in principles of international law, Pavlovsky used his internet websites and print media to politically delegitimize democratic revolutions in Serbia, Georgia, and, especially, Ukraine.[69] In these publications the very principle of regime change through revolutionary means was condemned as illegitimate, financed by Western money and aimed at building puppet anti-Russian states on its borders, destroying the unique cultural identity of Eastern Europe and undermining the sovereign nature of political institutions in the region. In Russia, it was argued, a colour revolution would not solve such problems as crime, corruption or the presence of the oligarchs. In fact, such a revolution would not make Russia more democratic but fatally weaken the state and would be extremely violent. Therefore calls for an Orange-type revolution in Russia amounted to calls to bring back the weak state of the Yeltsin era and all its horrors. This suited perfectly the newly emerging state mythology which legitimized Putin's authoritarianism in the strengthening of the Russian state and restoring order after a decade of chaos, disorder and humiliation.[70]

The idea of Western support for a colour revolution as a threat to the sovereignty, territorial integrity and stability of Russia was further developed by Surkov, deputy head of presidential administration. He was entrusted by Putin to be chief organizer of the counter-revolutionary strategy, which was a cornerstone of post-Orange Russian official ideology. In the lecture he gave to the activists of United Russia on 7 February 2006, which was followed by a manifesto style article published on 20 November 2006, Surkov introduced the concept of 'sovereign democracy'.[71] As the term implied, it was a rejection of the principles of liberal democracy. The article's main argument asserted that Russia is not a Western country with liberal traditions which emphasize individual rights, but a country with traditions of collectivism and a strong state. The collective (that is, the nation) realizes its sovereign will through the strong state which protects the collective from having the wills of domestic oligarchs or foreign powers imposed upon it, like in the case of Orange-type revolutions. At the same time, Surkov tries to draw a line distinguishing this new official nationalism from the ideological creeds articulated by the communist and nationalist opposition which he calls 'national isolationists'. Russia, argues Surkov, is historically and culturally a part of Europe and will remain so in the future. Attempts to realize communist and nationalist visions for Russia would ultimately lead to a failed Soviet-type bureaucratized and uncompetitive state with deadly ethnic conflicts spreading across the country.[72] Immediately upon the publication of Surkov's essay, Pavlovsky began vigorously to promote the ideas it articulated through his internet and print media outlets.[73] Even academic centres were set up in order to give the idea a scholarly foundation and support.[74]

In effect, the concept of 'sovereign democracy' became the core of the new official state ideology aimed at providing ideological foundations for the democracy preventing strategies of the regime. At the same time, the ideological opposition to colour revolutions and democratization was articulated by Russian nationalist intellectuals with various degrees of connection to the ruling elite. Thus, Konstantin Krylov, in a series of articles on the Orange Revolution, written as the events in Ukraine were unfolding, presented the revolution as driven by hate of Russia rather than hate of the authoritarian regime.[75] The Orange Revolution slogan of embracing Europe was essentially hiding its true essence, namely total surrender of Ukraine to the West, claimed Krylov. Russia, the argument went, has to be passionately hated by the revolutionaries since she is the main obstacle to such a surrender.[76]

Writing in late December 2004, Yury Krupnov called the new Ukraine an 'occupational democracy' achieved as a consequence of the coup d'état with support of foreign governments and international NGOs. The United States was said to be the main promoter of this project since it was an integral part of its plan to establish global hegemony, which requires surrounding Russia with hostile regimes. Krupnov goes even further, calling on Russia's leaders to counter this US action by orchestration of an overthrow of Ukrainian and Georgian regimes, which, in his view, would amount to helping both states to 'regain their independence'.[77]

Framing colour revolutions in terms of the Russian–Western geopolitical rivalry was further developed by Arkady Maler and especially by Aleksandr Dugin, prominent right-wing nationalist intellectuals. In Maler's view, civilizationally Ukraine is part of Russia. Hence Ukraine must be accepted by the West to be in the Russian sphere of influence. Therefore, Western interference in Ukrainian affairs is a blatant challenge to Russian national interests. Since Russia still is a nuclear superpower it should anchor its foreign policy in forcing the West to accept Russia as main arbiter in the domestic affairs of countries bordering Russia. In other words, Maler asserts Russia's exclusive right to accept or veto regime change in countries like Ukraine.[78]

Since the mid-1990s, Dugin has articulated his theory of international relations (geopolitics in his terms). His 1997 book, *Foundation of Geopolitics* (*Osnovy geopolitiki*), with its rabid anti-Westernism, was popular among Russian political and security elites.[79] The Orange Revolution gave Dugin an opportunity to expound his theory. In his articles, one of which was published in the Russian government's official newspaper, Dugin presented the events in Kyiv as yet another stage in the reorganization of the geopolitical space of Eurasia by the United States, whose ultimate goal was creation of a single geopolitical space capable of promoting American military and economic interests. Yushchenko's victory meant undermining Russia's influence in the post-Soviet space. Moreover, the methods used in Kyiv could be applied by the US and its allies in other post-Soviet countries, Russia included. In this way, the Orange Revolution was a grave threat to Russia as well. In other words, Dugin provides a geopolitical justification to Putin's repressive policies.[80]

Among the Russian nationalist indirect intellectual responses to colour revolutions a four-volume (2006–2010) project entitled Project Russia (*Proekt Rossiya*) stands out.[81] While the project authors officially remain anonymous, it was revealed that the books were written by a team from the so-called Institute for Strategic Security, a security services sponsored think tank. While the project does not address the issue of the coloured revolutions, it does challenge Surkov's conception of sovereign democracy which, as we showed above, was articulated in response to such revolutions.

Project Russia authors openly challenge Surkov's vision of Russia as a secular and European nation. Moreover, their opposition to the West is not articulated in geopolitical terms. They present the West as mired in moral corruption (gay marriages are given as a main example) and promoting profoundly anti-Russian and anti-Christian ideas of secular humanism. Russia should isolate itself from the West and rediscover its Orthodox roots as a path for national greatness. These types of ideas by themselves are not new and are common currency among the highly marginalized Russian nationalist intellectuals who articulate them on their websites or in small circulation books. However, the first volume of the project (2006) was distributed in the Duma, FSB (Federal Security Service) and the General Staff before appearing in the book stores, while the third volume has an official print run of 1,000,000 – an unprecedented figure for a non-fiction book in the post-communist era.[82] Moreover, all the volumes were lavishly produced and published by major Russian publishers. All this clearly suggests both major political sponsors and a substantial financial subsidy, since it is not likely that such a book would ever make a profit.

In 2012 the danger of a colour revolution in Russia has certainly passed. However, the institutions created in 2004–2006 are still in place. It was the realm of ideology where the changes were most pronounced. The sovereign democracy doctrine seems to have fallen out of vogue. Chelyabinsk University Center for Study of Constitutional and Legal Problems of Sovereign Democracy (see note 74) seems to be dormant if not shut down entirely since the institute's website has not been updated since 2008. The Institute of Contemporary Development (INSOR), the Medvedev-favoured think tank promotes ideas which clearly favour the adoption of Western-style democracy. INSOR plans and 'Project Russia' clearly suggest that the 'sovereign democracy' project no longer enjoys a hegemonic status within the ruling elite. Its fate apparently will follow many previous projects to create ideological legitimacy for the regime under threat, that is, the dustbin of history. At the same time, the Russian nationalist anti-democratic ideas, developed either directly or indirectly as a consequence of the Orange Revolution, constitute the easily available body of literature which the ruling elite could utilize and expound if it once again felt threatened.

Concluding remarks

In this article we presented the Russian government's reactions to colour revolutions in neighbouring, post-communist countries. As we showed, these events created an acute sense of threat among the Russian elites – a threat that had to be countered by a wide array of policies and measures, ranging from youth movement camps to electoral legislation reform to ideological debates over the nature of the Russian state. The choice of strategies pursued by the Kremlin was not accidental and focused on precisely the fields and policies that were instrumental to the success of regime changes in Serbia, Georgia and Ukraine, indicating the importance of authoritarian learning for the analysis of democratization and authoritarian backlashes.

Furthermore, as we demonstrated, the analysis of authoritarian states' anti-democratization and survival strategies should not be limited to the institutional and economic spheres only. Authoritarian states can and do invest substantial efforts in garnering popular support through the creation of youth movements or by building the ideological foundation of the regime. These factors and policies should be studied and analysed by the students of democratization and authoritarianism, and we hope that this analysis of the Russian case will contribute to a better understanding of how modern autocrats confront the challenge of democratization.

Notes

1. 'Ukraine: In Search of Plan B'; Bush, 'Putin's Biggest Blunder'.
2. For a detailed literature review see the Introduction to this special issue: Finkel and Brudny, 'No More Colour! Authoritarian Regimes and Colour Revolutions in Eurasia'.

3. McFaul, 'Transitions from Postcommunism'.
4. Kuzio, 'Democratic Breakthroughs and Revolutions in Five Postcommunist Countries'.
5. There is a significant debate about the nature of civil society in post-communist Russia. However, this debate is far beyond the scope of the current article. Here we operationalize the concept the 'civil society' by focusing on independent NGOs.
6. McFaul, 'Transitions from Postcommunism'.
7. Putin, 'Poslanie'.
8. Human Rights Watch, 'Russia: Amended Law Threatens NGOs'.
9. Obshchestvennaia Palata Rosiiskoi Federatsii, http://www.oprf.ru/ru/about/structure/.
10. According to the 1993 Russian electoral law, 225 members of the parliament were elected according to the proportional representation (PR) principle and an additional 225 in single member districts according to the 'first past the post' principle.
11. Stoner-Weiss, 'Comparing Oranges and Apples', 264, notes that in practice 'the KPRF has effectively ceased being an opposition party' as it votes with the government on most issues.
12. Ryabov, 'Moskva prinimaet vyzov'.
13. Hale and Colton, 'Russians and the Putin-Medvedev "Tandemocracy"'; Stoner-Weiss, 'Comparing Oranges and Apples', 267–8.
14. Stoner-Weiss, 'Comparing Oranges and Apples', 269.
15. McFaul, 'Transitions from Postcommunism'.
16. See, for example, Omel'chenko, 'Molodezh' dlia politikov, molodezh' dlia sebia'; Bransten, 'Russia: Nations' Youth are Apolitical and Materialistic'.
17. For the discussion of the role of young people in coloured revolutions, see Niko-layenko, 'The Revolt of the Post-Soviet Generation'.
18. Mendelson and Gerber, 'Soviet Nostalgia', 85.
19. Although the Russian *Pora* was very small numerically, it was nonetheless seen by the authorities as a real threat. In 2007, the movement leader Andrey Sidelnikov escaped Russia to the UK, where he was later granted political asylum. See: 'Lider Rosiiskogo dvizhenia "Pora" poluchil politicheskoe ubezhishe v Velikobritanii'.
20. Yakemenko was born in 1971 in Lyubertsi (Moscow oblast') where his father worked as chief constructor at the Kamov helicopters design bureau. After graduating from Moscow University of Management, Yakemenko worked in show business, helicopter leasing and publishing. In 2000 he joined President Putin's Executive Office but left the Kremlin after only three months to establish 'Marching Together'.
21. Galimova, 'Pod znakom unitaza'.
22. 'K chemu vlasti gotoviat "Nashih"'; 'Kratky kurs istorii dvizheniya "Nashi"'.
23. Nashi Manifesto, http://www.nashi.su/ideology; see also: http://nashi.su/manifest; http://www.nashi.su/manifest/comments.
24. *Agitator Edinoi Rossii.*
25. Democratic Antifascist Youth Movement Nashi, 'Nashi Manifesto'.
26. Ibid.
27. See, for example, Kachurovskaya, 'Kontseptsiya izmenilas''.
28. Precise data on Nashi membership is not available. According to Nashi's estimations, several months after the establishment of the movement, it could count on the support of 1000 members and almost 100,000 sympathizers. Source: Kashin, 'Vasiliy Yake-menko: v chem-to ia pohozh na Khodorkovskogo'.
29. Mendelson and Gerber, 'Us and Them'.
30. Romanov and Samarina, 'Ne prospat' stranu'.
31. 'Dvizhenie 'Nashi' vozvestilo o pobede Putina'.
32. Buribaev, 'My ne otryadi shturmovikov'; Kashin, 'Vasiliy Yakemenko'.
33. See, for example, 'Nashisty' v gorode'.

34. 'Timur' i ego commandos'; 'V dosku nash'; Vasiunin, 'Pryanik na budushchee'.
35. Kachurovskaya, 'Paren' iz "nashego" ozera'.
36. Shleinov, 'Den'gi "Nashikh"'. In Russian rubles the amount is 450 million.
37. Vasiunin, 'Pryanik na budushchee'.
38. Kashin, 'Vasily Yakemenko'.
39. Stepanenko, 'How Ukrainians View Their Orange Revolution'; see also Brystina and Golovakha, 'The Folklore of the Orange Revolution'.
40. During the Orange Revolution several weddings of pro-Yushchenko protesters took place at Kyiv's Maidan Square, the centre of mass protests.
41. Buribaev, '"Vkruchivat" Lampochki v MGU do 18.00'.
42. Goldstein, *The Role of Digital Networked Technologies in the Ukrainian Orange Revolution*; Kuj, 'Internet use in Ukraine's Orange Revolution'.
43. The impact of publicizing electoral fraud on mass protests during the colour revolutions is discussed in Tucker, 'Enough!'.
44. Trimaste, 'Dolzhni li nablyudateli zdorovat'sya s izbiratelyami'.
45. On pro-government youth movements see Levintova, and Butterfield, 'History Education and Historical Remembrance in Contemporary Russia'.
46. Bykov, 'Elitka na sklone'; Yakuba, 'Kreatiff bez pozitiva'; see also Levintova and Butterfield, 'History Education and Historical Remembrance in Contemporary Russia'.
47. Yakuba, 'Kreatiff bez pozitiva'. Additional information on the Higher School of Management can be found at: http://www.vshu.ru/.
48. Nashi. 'Proekt "Obuchenie za Rubezhom' http://www.nashi.su/news/20560. Unfortunately, we were unable to get reliable data on how many Nashi members actually went to study in the West.
49. Kozenko, 'Nashi natyanuli odeyalo na Vladimira Putina'; 'Malen'kie "Mishki" prosyat Putina stat' megasupermedvedem'.
50. The acronym CSKA (*Tsentralny Sportinvny Klub Armii*) stands for the Central Sport Club of the Army.
51. See, for example, Buribaev, 'My ne otryadi shturmovikov'; Romanov, 'Bredovoe poboishche'.
52. Kostenko and Romanov, 'Terrarium edinomishlennikov'.
53. Buribaev, 'My ne otryadi shturmovikov'; Kashin, 'Protiv Garri Kasparova sdelali khod doskoi'.
54. Zakharov, 'Bez suda i dostoinstva'.
55. Savina, 'Sergei Lavrov provel peregovory s Nashimi'.
56. Ibid.
57. Ibid.
58. Kachurovskaya, 'Kontseptsiya izmenilas'.
59. Novikov, '"Nashisty" scchhitaiut sebya zolotymi mozgami'.
60. Ibid.
61. For the review of scholarship on colour revolutions please see the Introduction to this special issue: Finkel and Brudny, 'No More Colour! Authoritarian Regimes and Colour Revolutions in Eurasia'.
62. Kuzio, 'Democratic Breakthroughs and Revolutions in Five Postcommunist Countries'.
63. Brudny and Finkel, 'Why Ukraine Is Not Russia'.
64. It is not surprising therefore that in several monographs dedicated to Putin and his regime the word 'ideology' is missing from the index, see: Sakwa, *Putin: Russia's Choice*; Shevtsova, *Russia – Lost in Transition*.
65. *Nezavisimaya gazeta*, December 7, 2004.

66. Pavlovsky's subsequent activities, founding in 2005 the 'Europe' (Evropa) publishing house and revamping intellectual internet journal *Russky Zhurnal* (founded 1997), clearly aimed to create the appropriate ideological forums where such ideology could be articulated and debated.
67. Zorkin, 'Apologiya Vestfal'skoi systemy'. The regime viewed this article as very important and on 22 August 2006 reprinted it once more in *Rossiiskaya Gazeta*: http://www.rg.ru/2006/08/22/zorjkin-statjya.html
68. In 2010 Zorkin explicitly called the ruling of the European Court of Human Rights which declared that the rights of the Russian opposition parties during the 2003 elections were violated as aiding potential coloured revolutions and undermining the principle of national sovereignty, see: Zorkin, 'Predel ustupchivosti'.
69. Pavlovsky more than any other Kremlin affiliated consultant understood the importance of a presence in cyberspace. Through his consulting firm, Foundation for Effective Politics, he created a variety of internet websites. Some focused on political news (Strana.ru, smi.ru, Utro.ru), others published a high-brow intellectual commentary on current events (*Russky zhurnal*). His most important print outlet is Europe (Evropa) Publishing House which publishes a variety of books on politics and history by Russian and foreign authors. On Europe Publishing House publication policies see Laruelle, *In the Name of the Nation*, 139–42.
70. Ivanov, *Antirevlutsioner*; Ivanov, 'Antirevlutsioner: Pochemu Rossii ne nuzhna "oranzhevaya revolutsiya"; Kholmogorov, *Zashchitit li Rossiya Ukrainu?*; Mirzoev, *Gibel' prava*; Pavlovsky, *Oranzhevaya revolutsiya*.
71. Surkov, 'Natsionalizatsiya budushchego'. Surkov's lecture appeared on the United Russia website two weeks after the event and its extensive summaries subsequently appeared in Russia's major newspapers and internet outlets generating an intense political debate.
72. Surkov, 'Suverenitet – eto politichesky sinonim konkurentosposobnosti'.
73. Chernyshev, *Rossiya suverennaya*; Garadzha, *Suverenitet*; Orlov, *Suverennaya demokratiya*; Polyakov, *PRO suverennuyu demokratiyu*.
74. University of Chelyabinsk, a major regional university in the Ural Mountain region, created a centre entitled Center for Study of Constitutional and Legal Problems of Sovereign Democracy. Such an initiative could have come either from Surkov or a local governor and regional United Russia office.
75. At the time, Krylov was editor-in-chief of *Spetsnaz Rossii*, the publication of Special Forces veterans.
76. Krylov, 'Udovol'stvie bunta'; Krylov, 'Oranzhevaya natsia'.
77. Krupnov, 'Ukraina poluchila okkupatsionnuyu demokratiyu'.
78. Maler, 'Sem' shagov k imperii'.
79. Dugin, *Osnovy geopolitiki*. On the book, see Dunlop, 'Aleksandr Dugin's *Foundations of Geopolitics*'.
80. Dugin, 'Viktor Yushchenko kak zerkalo rossiiskoi geopolitiki'; Dugin, 'Razval Rossii nachat na Ukraine'.
81. *Proekt Rossiya*. The project also has an official website, see: http://www.proektrussia.ru.
82. Senderov, 'Proekt Rossiya i vokrug nego'. The first and second volumes also had very large print runs for political books: 50,000 (volume 1) and 60,000 (volume 2).

Notes on contributors

Evgeny Finkel is a PhD candidate, Department of Political Science, University of Wisconsin-Madison, and a Research Fellow, Program on Order, Conflict, and Violence, Yale University, USA. His articles have been published and are forthcoming in *Comparative Politics*, *East European Politics and Societies* (with Y. Brudny), *Global Society*, and several other journals.

Yitzhak M. Brudny is the Jay and Leonie Darwin Chair in Russian Studies, The Hebrew University of Jerusalem, Israel. He is the author of *Reinventing Russia: Russian Nationalism and the Soviet State, 1953–1991* (Harvard University Press, 1998), and the principal editor of *Restructuring Post-Communist Russia* (Cambridge University Press, 2004). His articles on Russia and the former Soviet Union have appeared in numerous journals and edited volumes.

References

Agitator 'Edinoi Rossii': Voprosi, Otbeti, Politicheskie Poniatiia. Moskva: Evropa, 2006.
Bransten, Jeremy. 'Russia: Nations' Youth are Apolitical and Materialistic'. *Radio Free Europe/Radio Liberty*, November 7, 2011. http://www.rferl.org/content/article/1097925.html.
Brudny, Yitzhak, and Evgeny Finkel. 'Why Ukraine is not Russia: Hegemonic National Identity and Democracy in Russia and Ukraine'. *East European Politics and Societies* 25, no. 4: 813–833.
Brystina, O., and I. Golovakha, 'The Folklore of the Orange Revolution'. *Folklorica* 10 (2005): 1–17.
Buribaev, Aidar. 'My ne otryady shturmovikov'. *Gazeta*, October 3, 2005.
Buribaev, Aidar. '"Vkruchivat" Lampochki v MGU do 18.00'. *Gazeta*, November 3, 2005.
Bush, Jason. 'Putin's Biggest Blunder'. *Bloomberg Businessweek*, December 13, 2004. http://www.businessweek.com/magazine/content/04_50/b3912076_mz054.htm.
Bykov, Dmitry. 'Elitka na sklone'. *Sobesednik*, July 25, 2007.
Chernyshev, Sergei. *Rossiya suverennaya*. Moscow: Evropa, 2007.
Democratic Antifascist Youth Movement Nashi. 'Nashi Manifesto'. http://www.nashi.su/manifest.
Democratic Antifascit Youth Movement Nashi. 'Proekt "Obuchenie za Rubezhom'. http://www.nashi.su/news/20560.
Dugin, Aleksandr. *Osnovy Geopolitiki: geopoliticheskoe budushchee Rossii*. Mosva: Arktogeia, 1997.
Dugin, Aleksandr. 'Razval Rossii nachat na Ukraine'. *Rossiya*, January 27, 2005. http://www.evrazia.org/modules.php?name=News&file=article&sid=2192.
Dugin, Aleksandr. 'Viktor Yushchenko kak zerkalo rossiiskoi geopolitiki'. *Rossiiskaya Gazeta*, January 26, 2005.
Dunlop, John B. 'Aleksandr Dugin's *Foundations of Geopolitics*'. *Demokratizatsiya* 12 (2004): 41–57.
'Dvizhenie 'Nashi' vozvestilo o pobede Putina'. *NewsRu*, November 30, 2007. http://www.newsru.com/russia/30nov2007/nashii.html.
Finkel, Evgeny, and Yitzhak M. Brudny. 'No More Colour! Authoritarian Regimes and Colour Revolutions in Eurasia'. Democratization 19, no. 1 (2012): 1–14.
Galimova, Natal'ya. 'Pod znakom unitaza'. *Moskovskii Komsomolets*, September 10, 2002.
Hale, Henry, and Timothy Colton. 'Russians and the Putin-Medvedev "Tandemocracy": A Survey-Based Portrait of the 2007–08 Election Season'. *Problems of Post-Communism* 57 (2009): 3–20.
Human Rights Watch. 'Russia: Amended Law Threatens NGOs'. http://www.hrw.org/en/news/2005/12/27/russia-amended-law-threatens-ngos.
Ivanov, Vitaly. 'Antirevlutsioner'. *Russky zhurnal*, January 14, 2005. http://www.russ.ru/politics/docs/antirevolyucioner.
Ivanov, Vitaly. *Antirevlutsioner: Pochemu Rossii ne nuzhna 'oranzhevaya revolutsiya*. Moscow: Evropa, 2006.
Garadzha, Nikita, ed. *Suverenitet*. Moscow: Evropa, 2006.

Goldstein, Joshua. *The Role of Digital Networked Technologies in the Ukrainian Orange Revolution*. Cambridge, MA: Berkman Center Research Publication, 2007.

'K chemu vlasti gotoviat "Nashih"'. *Birzha*, July 26, 2005.

Kachurovskaya, Anna. 'Kontseptsiya izmenilas'. *Kommersant*, August 5, 2007.

Kachurovskaya, Anna. 'Paren' iz 'nashego' ozera'. *Kommersant*, June 30, 2007.

Kashin, Oleg. 'Protiv Garri Kasparova sdelali khod doskoi'. *Kommersant*, April 18, 2005.

Kashin, Oleg. 'Vasily Yakemenko: v chem-to ya pokhozh na Khodorkovskogo'. *Kommersant*, July 11, 2005.

Kholmogorov, Egor. *Zashchitit li Rossiya Ukrainu?* Moscow: Evropa, 2006.

Kostenko, Natal'ya, and Igor Romanov. 'Terrarium Edinomishlennikov'. *Nezavisimaia Gazeta*, July 30, 2007.

Kozenko, Andrei. 'Nashi natyanuli odeyalo na Vladimira Putina'. *Kommersant*, October 8, 2007.

'Kratky kurs istorii dvizheniya "Nashi"'. *Kommersant*, January 29, 2008.

Krupnov, Yurii. 'Ukraina poluchila okkupatsionnuyu demokratiyu'. *Rosbalt*, December 28, 2004. http://www.rosbalt.ru/2004/12/28/190954.html.

Krylov, Konstantin. '"Oranzhevaya natsia": psikhiatrichesky portret'. *APN.ru*, December 31, 2004. http://www.apn.ru/publications/article1240.htm.

Krylov, Konstantin. 'Udovol'stvie bunta'. *APN.ru*, November 30, 2004. http://www.apn.ru/publications/article1199.htm.

Kuj, Myroslaw. 'Internet use in Ukraine's Orange Revolution'. *Business Horizons* 49 (2006): 71–80.

Kuzio, Taras. 'Democratic Breakthroughs and Revolutions in Five Postcommunist Countries: Comparative Perspectives on the Fourth Wave'. *Demokratizatsiya* 16 (2008): 97–109.

Laruelle, Marlène. *In the Name of the Nation*. New York: Palgrave Macmillan, 2009.

Levintova, Ekaterina, and Jim Butterfield. 'History Education and Historical Remembrance in Contemporary Russia: Sources of Political Attitudes of Pro-Kremlin Youth'. *Communist and Post-Communist Studies* 43 (2009): 1–28.

'Lider Rosiiskogo dvizhenia "Pora" poluchil politicheskoe ubezhishe v Velikobritanii'. *Lenta.Ru*, April 7, 2008. http://lenta.ru/news/2008/07/04/sidelnikov/.

'Malen'kie "Mishki" prosyat Putina stat' megasupermedvedem i podderzhivayut ego kal'koi so stalinskikh lozungov'. *NewsRu*, December 6, 2007. http://www.newsru.com/russia/06dec2007/mishki.html.

Maler, Arkadii. 'Sem' shagov k imperii'. *Apn.ru*, December 20, 2004. http://www.apn.ru/publications/article1222.htm.

McFaul, Michael. 'Transitions from Postcommunism'. *Journal of Democracy* 16 (2005): 5–19.

Mendelson, Sarah, and Ted Gerber. 'Soviet Nostalgia: An Impediment to Russian Democratization'. *The Washington Quarterly* 29 (2005): 83–96.

Mendelson, Sarah, and Ted Gerber. 'Us and Them: Anti-American Views of the Putin Generation'. *The Washington Quarterly* 31 (2008): 131–50.

Mirzoev, Sergei. *Gibel' prava: legitimnost' v 'oranzhevykh revolyutsiyakh*. Moscow: Evropa, 2006.

'Nashisty' v gorode'. *Psokvskaia gubernia*, July 13, 2005.

Nikolayenko, Olena. 'The Revolt of the Post-Soviet Generation: Youth Movements in Serbia, Georgia, and Ukraine'. *Comparative Politics* 39 (2007): 169–88.

Novikov, Konstantin. '"Nashisty" schchitaiut sebya zolotymi mozgami'. *Moskovskiy Komsomolets*, December 26, 2007.

Omel'chenko, Elena. 'Molodezh' dlia politikov, molodezh' dlia sebia'. *Polit. Ru*, June 15, 2006. http://www.polit.ru/article/2006/06/15/youth/.

Orlov, Dmitrii, ed. *Suverennaya demokratiya*. Moscow: Evropa, 2006.

Polyakov, Gleb, ed. *Oranzhevaya revolutsiya*. Moscow: Evropa, 2006.

Polyakov, Leonid, ed. *PRO suverennuyu demokratiyu*. Moscow: Evropa, 2007.

Proekt Rossiya, vol. 1. Moscow: Olma Press, 2007; vol. 2, Moscow: Eksmo, 2007; vol. 3, Moscow: Eksmo, 2009.

Putin, Vladimir. 'Poslanie Federal'nomu Sobraniyu Rossiiskoi Federatsii', May 26, 2004. http://archive.kremlin.ru/text/appears/2004/05/71501.shtml.

Romanov, Igor, and Aleksandra Samarina. 'Ne prospat' stranu'. *Nezavisimaia Gazeta*, March 26, 2007.

Romanov, Mikhail. 'Bredovoe poboishche'. *Moskovskiy Komsomolets*, August 31, 2005.

Ryabov, Andrei. 'Moskva prinimaet vyzov "tsvetnykh revolutsiy"'. *Pro et Contra* 19 (2005): 18–27.

Sakwa, Richard. *Putin: Russia's Choice*. London: Routledge, 2004.

Savina, Ekaterina. 'Sergei Lavrov provel peregovory s "Nashimi"'. *Kommersant*, January 18, 2007.

Senderov, Valeriy. 'Proekt "Rossiya" i vokrug nego'. *Voprosy filosofii* 2 (2010): 52–9. http://vphil.ru/index.php?option=com_content&task=view&id=100&Itemid=44.

Shevtsova, Lilia. *Russia – Lost in Transition: The Yeltsin and Putin Legacies*. Washington, DC: Carnegie Endowment for International Peace, 2007.

Shleinov, Roman. 'Den'gi "Nashikh"'. *Vedomosti*, November 29, 2011.

Stepanenko, Viktor. 'How Ukrainians View Their Orange Revolution: Public Opinion and the National Peculiarities of Citizenry Political Activities'. *Demokratizatsiya* 13 (2005): 595–616.

Stoner-Weiss, Kathryn. 'Comparing Oranges and Apples: The Internal and External Dimensions of Russia's Turn Away from Democracy'. In *Democracy and Authoritarianism in the Postcommunist World*, ed. Valerie Bunce, Michael McFaul, and Kathryn Stoner-Weiss, 253–73. New York: Cambridge University Press, 2010.

Surkov, Vladislav. 'Natsionalizatsiya budushchego: paragrafy pro suverennuyu demokratiyu'. *Ekspert*, November 20, 2006.

Surkov, Vladislav. 'Suverenitet – eto politichesky sinonim konkurentnosposobnosti'. http://www.kreml.org/media/111622794.

'"Timur" i ego commandos'. *Tribuna*, July 16, 2005.

Trimaste, Mariya-Luiza. 'Dolzhni li nablyudateli zdorovat'sya s izbiratelyami'. *Kommersant*, November 10, 2005.

Tucker, Joshua. 'Enough! Electoral Fraud, Collective Action Problems, and Post-Communist Colored Revolutions'. *Perspectives on Politics* 5 (2007): 537–53.

'Ukraine: In Search of Plan B'. *The Economist*, December 2, 2004. http://www.economist.com/node/3446520.

'V dosku nash'. *Vremia Novostei*, October 11, 2007.

Vasiunin, Il'ia. 'Pryanik na budushchee'. *Novaia Gazeta*, July 30, 2007.

Yakuba, Aleksandr. 'Kreatiff bez pozitiva'. *Rossbalt*, July 28, 2007.

Zakharov, Mikhail. 'Bez suda i dostoinstva'. *Polit.Ru,* June 21, 2011. http://www.polit.ru/article/2011/06/21/kashin_vs_yakemen/.

Zorkin, Valery D. 'Apologiya Vestfal'skoi systemy'. *Rossiya v global'noi politike* 3 (2004). http://www.globalaffairs.ru/number/n_3223.

Zorkin, Valery D. 'Predel ustupchivosti'. *Rossiiskaya Gazeta*, October 29, 2010. http://www.rg.ru/2010/10/29/zorkin.html.

Questioning democracy promotion: Belarus' response to the 'colour revolutions'

Elena Korosteleva

Centre for European Studies, Department of International Politics, Aberystwyth University, Aberystwyth, UK

The article focuses on the aftermath of the colour revolutions by analysing and questioning the *real success*, as often depicted by the West, of democracy promotion in the East European region. First of all, the article challenges the conventional logic of democracy promotion – even when backed by moral reasoning and resource availability – as sufficient and adequate for instigating democratic change in non-liberal regimes. By examining the case of Belarus it further contends that authoritarian regimes effectively learn to resist and counteract foreign-led democracy promotion, and often do so *legitimately*, with a minimal use of force. The article concludes that in order to exercise democracy promotion (if such a thing is possible at all) a far deeper understanding of autocratic narratives is needed, associated with a much closer look at societal norms and values, as well as an individual country's geopolitical resources and strategies.

There will be no revolution in Belarus ... Those who entice *democratisation* in the former Soviet Union are yet to rip off the fruit of their actions ...[1]

The early 2000s witnessed a series of events which later became popularized as 'colour revolutions'.[2] These public protests, which often adopted a colour as a symbol, included the 'Rose Revolution' in Georgia (2003), 'Orange Revolution' in Ukraine (2004) and the 'Tulip Revolution' in Kyrgyzstan (2005).[3] They were arguably successful in overthrowing previous authoritarian regimes and facilitating democratic breakthroughs.[4] Moreover, in their strikingly similar patterns, and involvement of Western non-governmental organizations (NGOs) as part of the international diffusion process, they all centred on elections as the key mechanism for challenging the incumbency.

The 'second generation' of similar events (2005–2009), however, was unambiguously less successful. In 2005–2006 revolutionary attempts were made across a number of states of the Former Soviet Union (Russia, Azerbaijan, Uzbekistan, Kazakhstan and Belarus), with comparable events initiated and equally failing elsewhere.[5] Many of these undertakings were effectively thwarted before they occurred, and others were sweepingly suppressed, with a minimal use of force. This necessarily raises a question – which also opens up a wider debate on 'democracy promotion' in the region – whether the autocratic regimes have learned to resist and even counteract externally promoted 'electoral revolutions'.

There is no straightforward answer to this question. As some scholars observe,[6] for many autocratic regimes witnessing what were widely perceived as feigned revolutionary activities in their neighbourhood, the urgency to learn to prevent their subversive effect became *realpolitik* thus necessitating moderately oppressive tactics concomitant with open hostility to 'rapacious Western interests'.[7] However, regimes' learning is only one side of the story, which would be incomplete without contextualizing each 'non-colour' case with the purpose of understanding the real (far deeper) reasons behind the failed (foreign-led) revolutionary enticement. Belarus as 'the last dictatorship in Europe' serves as a curious testimony to these uncanny logics of 'democracy promotion' and 'autocratic diffusion'[8] revealing its own and *not-so-authoritarian* narrative with which the 'dictatorship' withstood its electoral turmoil in 2006.[9]

On both the day itself and the day after the presidential election in March 2006, protestors took their discontent to the streets of Minsk, thus closely following the *Democratic Revolutionary Handbook*.[10] Prior to this, many young revolutionaries travelled as far afield as Serbia and Ukraine to learn about the strategies and tactics of regime subversion to be applied in their own home. This consequently resulted in a 10,000-strong public protest on the day of the election,[11] a five-day camp resistance under physically and emotionally strenuous conditions, occasional clashes with riot police, and over 1000 arrests in the aftermath of the event.[12] In other words, the prerequisites to galvanize an 'electoral revolution' were evidently present in Belarus, but somehow failed to develop into a wider mass mobilization, despite the fact that the majority of Belarusians (70%), according to an IISEPS opinion poll,[13] were aware of and even discussed the event with their close friends and relations. This surprising public withdrawal from allegedly a 'people's event' is even more surprising when we consider the relatively moderate use of violence by authorities (including their actions prior to and during the event),[14] and the feeble and often embarrassing attempts of the state media to conceal the reality.[15] In other words, contrary to the anticipated draconian measures of Lukashenko's dictatorship, only limited (and largely non-violent) state interference was used to counteract insurgencies.

In the light of the revolutionary 'contagion' and seemingly propitious conditions for popular mobilization, why did the Belarusians not rise up against the 'outpost of tyranny'? Evidently, the country was as far away from a 'tipping point' of political change as a 'revolutionary situation' could be without its constitutive elements: a people's desire to rise and governors' inability to rule.[16] Interestingly, this kind of 'controversy' of allegedly people's revolutions is not solely attributable to the 'exceptional' case of Belarus; instead, it appears to be broadly illustrative of far deeper problems related to 'democracy promotion' and 'autocratic resilience' in the region.[17] In this article I limit myself to an analysis of nuances of the 2006 attempt at democracy promotion in Belarus. I focus on efforts by the anti-regime opposition, encouraged by the West. I also seek to explain the government's response to it. In what follows, I will first discuss the limitations of the precarious 'international diffusion' model that has explicitly dominated the debate on 'colour revolutions', and will offer some counter-points premised on Lane's argument of 'revolutionary coup d'état'.[18] In the second part of this article, I will examine Way's theory of structural factors[19] in order to evaluate the Belarusian response to colour revolutions in more detail. The 'structural factors' perspective, here interpreted more broadly, is not only essential for understanding the reasons of success/failure of the recent attempt at 'international diffusion' in Eastern Europe, but also for far deeper understanding of why democratization by Western design may not necessarily succeed in the region, despite the perceived leverage of or linkage with the West.[20] Finally (and by way of conclusion) I will discuss the relevance of legitimacy that underpins Lukashenko's regime thus alluding to a possible counterintuitive 'balance' between publicly perceived societal needs and values, and respective government performance, the understanding of which somewhat shifts the focus of 'democracy promotion' from the impatient 'when' to the improbable 'if', thus questioning whether external democracy promotion may succeed in Eastern Europe and elsewhere by similar means.

International diffusion or revolutionary coup d'état?

Much of the recent literature written on colour revolutions focuses on 'international diffusion' as a mechanism of emulating successful narratives of 'democracy promotion' in the region – through training and sharing ideas and resources to direct involvement – with the intention to overthrow existing autocratic regimes.[21] This scholarship has been particularly influential in debating successful international diffusion (after the trials in Southern Europe in the late 1990s) in the recent 'colour' cases of Georgia, Ukraine and Kyrgyzstan. Yet it appears far less comprehensive for dealing with those less victorious stories that by far dominate the 'second tide' of the 'colour revolutions' from 2005 onwards, and therefore needs closer examination in order to understand why some 'revolutions' fail and 'how Western policy misses the mark'.[22]

According to Bunce and Wolchik, 'diffusion can be defined as a process wherein new ideas, institutions, policies, models or repertoires of behaviour spread geographically ... whether within a given state or across states'.[23] In the case of Eastern Europe, it refers to 'an electoral model of democratisation' that was developed in Bulgaria, Romania and Slovakia between 1996 and 1998, and in Serbia in 2000, whereby trained opposition activists use fraudulent elections to mobilize popular support to defeat weak autocratic incumbents.

By aiming to introduce 'democracy from below', all these revolutionary activities shared a common strategy: targeting the removal of incumbency through mass protests occurring within a constitutional framework (non-violent), focusing on allegedly fraudulent electoral procedures and drawing on young and enthusiastic activists to form the core for mobilizing larger crowds by conventional and other means, including popular entertainment and modern technology (use of mobile phones, internet and media resources).[24]

Furthermore, as Bunce and Wolchik assert,[25] in order to make international diffusion 'available for possible export', a set of three factors should be met. First of all, potential revolutionaries need to closely follow the electoral model, which offers a range of strategies and tactics as to how to topple the incumbent regime[26]; second, the importing countries should have similar conditions – 'put succinctly, common contexts and common identities'; and finally, there should exist 'collaborative networks' that 'cross the boundaries' and 'provide incentives for actors on both sides of the diffusion process to embrace transplantation'.[27]

The relevance of the third factor for 'democracy promotion' in the region, and especially for the occurrence of 'the colour revolutions', should not be underestimated,[28] as it has essentially – through the provision of logistical, intellectual and financial resources – been the driving force of international diffusion in Eastern Europe. Open and unabashed exposure of Western involvement and sponsorship – being part of these 'collaborative networks' – were indisputably a key feature of regional democracy promotion. International NGOs and aid organizations were particularly instrumental for the promotion and organization of large-scale entertainment events including payments to the attendees themselves.[29] As Way contends:

> Transnational networks of previously successful activists, with assistance from the US Agency for International Development (USAID) and other organisations as well as from experts in non-violent protest such as Gene Sharp, are credited with stimulating transitions in countries that lacked sufficient prerequisites for revolution and where the fall of autocrats was 'not predicated by most analysts'.[30]

Drawing on the scale and arguable success of the first electoral revolutions in Georgia, Ukraine and Kyrgyzstan, and their repetitive character, some scholars even suggested conceptualizing them as an instance of modular development premised on the imitation or indeed emulation of 'the prior successful example of others'.[31] In Beissinger's interpretation, for example, all these revolutionary activities should not be viewed as independent cases, 'but rather [as] an interrelated modular phenomenon in which opposition groups borrowed frames, strategies, repertoires, and even logos from previously successful efforts and gained inspiration from the acts of others'.[32] He further insists that if all structural advantages of the electoral revolutions are taken into account there may be further anticipation of electoral uprisings in the region based on the electoral cycles of the existing regimes.[33]

Yet there are a number of reasons to believe that modular diffusion has run its course in the region, and even more, that its allegedly successful first trials clearly failed to produce any noticeable change of regime, let alone to achieve democratization.[34] On reflection, it becomes apparent that while these 'revolutions' may have been legitimated in democratic terms by involving some 'staged' mass activities, they should be more appropriately termed not as 'people's events', but instead as 'revolutionary coup d'état'[35] aided by Western sponsorship. These 'colour cases', as Lane asserts further, 'were more than palace putsches but they were not classical revolutions',[36] either in their intentions or their outcome. They did involve some mass mobilization but they did not produce any system/regime change. Instead, what seems to have occurred is the instalment of new political incumbents instigated through the agency of mass popular support and Western orchestration.[37]

These electoral revolutions, especially those of the second (2005–2009) generation, which Chaulia suitably depicted as 'political convulsions'[38] have evidently failed to take into account domestic circumstances (including the precarious legitimacy) of some existing autocracies, and instead focused on maximizing 'electoral opportunities' in a situation when oppositional forces explicitly struggled or indeed were unable to mobilize public support for a legitimate transfer of power. As David Lane qualifies it further:

> What is portrayed in the media as 'people's power' is in reality an elite manipulated demonstration. While the masses may be captivated by euphoric revolutionary ideology, they are in political terms instrumentalities of indigenous counter elites, often encouraged by foreigners with their own agendas. If successful, rather than such revolutions leading to significant socio-political change, a circulation of elites follows the ousting of former rulers or their cooption into a new elite structure.[39]

This is precisely what happened as a result of the first 'wave' of colour takeovers: not a regime change but a change of governing elite in countries like Georgia, Ukraine and Kyrgyzstan now being popularly associated with anarchy, corruption and new forms of authoritarianism.[40] On the contrary, the 'second generation' of colour changeovers has managed to maintain the existing status quo thus resisting (with a minimal use of force) the temptation of externally orchestrated revolutions. Belarus offers a particularly striking example of how the 'revolutionary contagion' failed to mobilize the masses, and exposes the need to explore the roots of public 'inertia' with reference to regime legitimacy and societal values – the principal focus of this article.

Interestingly, in many cases of 'revolutionary coup d'état' of the second generation especially – that is, involving mass protest but no system change per se[41] – a single crucial element was clearly missing – that of 'domestic receptivity'.[42] Without considering each case individually it is difficult to generalize whether 'lacking [legitimate] domestic partners'[43] was essentially due to pre-emptive actions by the autocratic regimes, or more broadly, due to the indigenous conditions (including structural and psychological predispositions of the population) unsuitable for making revolutions. In either circumstance, a simple wisdom related to the promotion of internal change through manipulation of societal norms and values – Nye's formula[44] – which was placed at the heart of the US-led 'colour revolutions' in Eastern Europe[45] was evidently wrong-handled here. In his earlier work Nye explicitly claimed that only those 'countries that are closest to global norms of liberalism, pluralism, and autonomy; those with the most access to multiple channels of communication; and those whose credibility is enhanced by their domestic and international performance'[46] are likely to gain from international diffusion, in undertaking their (r)evolutionary change. The countries of the second generation of 'colour democratic breakthroughs', no matter how advantageous their electoral opportunities may have been, evidently failed to meet these criteria thus underlining the importance of contextualizing 'democracy promotion' for each given case, and considering structural factors propitious or otherwise for undertaking regime change with external assistance. In the meantime, following the commentary of *RIA-Novosti*, one needs to emphasize that 'presidential elections in Belarus, and their aftermath, showed that "orange" technologies may be applicable even in Belarusian conditions, but they may not necessarily be effective'.[47]

Structural factors: regime's learning curve

Contrary to the wisdom of '*external* democracy promotion', Way argues that 'diffusion may explain *fewer* aspects of recent postcommunist revolutions than is sometimes argued'.[48] What matters instead are the structural factors that lay foundations for any possible change to occur, and which may eventually develop into a revolutionary situation, with de-legitimation of the incumbent authority. Experiencing international 'contagion' on one's doorstep and having domestic revolutionaries trained in accordance with the *Democratic Revolutionary Handbook*[49] are not sufficient 'ingredients' to initiate a revolution *à la carte*. Way asserts that 'revolutions have often failed even when oppositions have adopted the "right" strategies from abroad. The most striking case is Belarus, which garnered serious attention and input from Serb, Slovak, Ukrainian, and other activists in the run-up to the 2006 presidential elections'.[50] He emphasized that 'Lukashenka's opponents seemed to do everything they were supposed to and arguably followed the "model" much more faithfully [than their counterparts]. Yet no large-scale support materialized, and Lukashenka never came close to being unseated'.[51]

Instead, as Way authoritatively contends, it is the structural factors that play a far more decisive role in explaining 'why some postcommunist authoritarian regimes have been more vulnerable than others to opposition threats'.[52] In particular, Way singles out two broad categories of structural factors that may explain the dynamics of recent electoral turnovers: (i) the strength of a country's ties with the West; and (ii) the strength of the incumbent regime's autocratic party or state. Evidently, it was the 'lame-duck' effect of the incumbency combined with actively exercised Western leverage over the country that led to the toppling of the previous autocratic regimes in Georgia and Ukraine, under the well-organized activities of the opposition. In countries where the leadership enjoys solid structural support including psychological predispositions of the population (for example, Belarus), little can be done externally, in order to stage full scale mobilization and revolutionary change:

> Lukashenka's success at remaining in power has less to do with any particular strategies adopted in response to postcommunist revolutions than with his already overwhelming domination over the opposition.[53]

In other words, although revolution may have been attempted in Belarus in 2006, arguably at the behest of the West, the endeavour clearly yielded no 'revolutionary situation' there, thus highlighting the relevance of structural factors propitious (or otherwise) for democratization.

Pre-emptive authoritarianism

In Belarus' case, limited linkage with the West (partly instigated by the West itself)[54] and long-term pre-emptive actions of Lukashenko's government made the 'colour revolution' in Belarus destined to fail. The concept of 'pre-emptive authoritarianism' was well developed by Vital Silitski[55] to underline the regime's learning ability to survive by adopting preventative measures to combat the democratic contagion. Over the 15 years of its struggle for survival Lukashenko's regime has naturally perfected the policy of pre-emption and, more importantly, is constantly learning to survive by emulating consensus between the regime's performance and perceived societal needs.[56] There is a plethora of instruments that the regime can deploy – from institutional through to cultural, ideological, tactical and other structural tools – in order to enhance its survival skills and public satisfaction, while also learning to strike first.

It is correct to insist that over the years Lukashenko's regime has mastered an unlimited grip on power by actively utilizing principles and instruments of pre-emption, and prepared well to meet the challenges of regional democratic con-tagion. In brief,[57] *institutionally*, to ensure legality and stability of his authority, Lukashenko has (i) re-written the constitution thus acquiring unlimited powers (including legislative), and removing restrictions on his stay in office; (ii) elimi-nated noncompliant elements of society, either by legally limiting the scope for their activities, through fear/intimidation, or by removing them physically from the scene (as in the infamous political disappearances of 1999–2001), thus enhan-cing the perceived efficacy of his government; (iii) installed new structural pillars (presidential vertical; police/armed forces) to exercise minimal coercion when necessary; and (iv) altered the format of other institutions (parliament; educational establishments; civil society; etc.) to act in unison with presidential propaganda. *Culturally*, he has (i) defeated the nationalism of the Belarusian Popular Front, which was a driving force for independence in the neighbouring Baltic states, becoming associated instead with a new type of nationalism building on a post-transitional identity and the relative economic stability of the country; (ii) removed from circulation any symbolic reminders of the pre-Soviet identity (flag, literature, the use of Belarusian language for teaching); and instead (iii) promoted Soviet/state patriotism and its relevant symbolic manifestations to boost public nostalgia for the Soviet 'nanny' state; and (iv) inculcated public awareness of Lukashenko's Belarus, vividly embodied by the slogans of his election campaigns 'For Belarus' (2001) and 'For *Independent* Belarus' (2006) which in the eyes of many is an oasis of stability, security and equal opportunities. *Ideologically*, he has (i) launched a concept of egalitarian state nationalism drawing on 'three essential pillars: Belarus uniqueness, unity and sovereignty'[58]; (ii) re-introduced ideological education and propaganda in workplaces; (iii) actively promoted the rise of BPSM (Belaruski Republikanski Sayuz Moladzi – Belarusian Republican Union of Youth) by making its membership a tacit requirement for entry to high education; and (iv) supported the activities of *Belaya Rus*, a popular social movement staffed with Lukashenko's supporters, as a potential foundation for building the Party of Power, as/where necessary. *Tactically*, not only has Lukashenko (i) literally and otherwise decapitated, discredited and demobilized the opposition by forcing them into their self-exile or indeed ghettoizing them into a manageable compound; he has also (ii) learned to legally, militarily and ideologically quell public unrest by initiating a number of laws that would thwart public mobilization in the making.[59] Finally, *international* pre-emption has included Lukashenko's joining the non-aligned states[60] in 2006 to withstand the pressure of the West, and continuously seeking Russia's (and the Commonwealth of Independent States' (CIS)) political backing[61] in order to ensure his 'international' legitimacy. In other words, by learning to act first, largely owing to the country's relative economic stability and popular legitimacy of the president, Lukashenko's regime has developed an enviable immunity to democratic change, associated with the wave of coloured revolutions in the neighbourhood.[62]

Anti-revolutionary measures

However, this is not to contend that Lukashenko's regime did not take any immediate precautionary measures in order to ensure that the government would survive the potential turmoil of colour revolutions. On the contrary, actions to prevent 'orange contagion' in Belarus were well calculated and painstakingly followed through, thus turning Lukashenko's statement that 'there will be no rose, orange, or banana revolution in Belarus'[63] into a categorical imperative for the government to act promptly and to be in full control of the situation. Early precautionary measures included intensified state propaganda through 'countless reports, documentaries, propaganda broadcasts, and newspaper articles to explain to the population the official take on the revolutions'.[64] Particularly influential in setting the popular anti-revolutionary mood were TV broadcasts including controversial documentaries *Spiritual War* and *Conspirology* by Yury

Azarionok, portraying the battle between the president and the opposition 'bought out by the West'. More subtle productions included a series of documentaries *Belarus: The Look from Outside* and *Fifteen* reviewing social and economic developments in the former Soviet Union and beyond, and praising the achievements of Lukashenko's government.[65] Pop-propaganda[66] also intensified in the form of mass concerts and other entertainment (street parades, sports events, harvest festivals) delivering images of green-and-red 'flag-waving' happy crowds and official establishment faces mingling with commoners to counteract the effect of orange or any other revolutionary colour used in the neighbourhood to entice the public: for example, a technique also effectively deployed by Nazarbaev in Kazakhstan to counteract revolution.[67]

Furthermore, early precautions also included some 'hard measures', for example, by putting a considerable part of the Belarusian army onto a full security alert. In particular, following the Kyrgyz events, in March 2005, the president requested full military mobilization of the 28 battalion in Baranovichi (near Minsk), and additionally recalled 2000 reserve troops into military action.[68]

Security forces also intensified their input in the struggle against the colour revolution. Notably, in December 2005 the KGB, which still functions under the same infamous name in Belarus, issued a document titled 'Analytical report on colour revolutions: a possible scenario for Belarus', prepared for dissemination in the House of Representatives for the MPs to 'work' with their respective constituencies in order to prevent the occurrence of unrest. As KGB chairman General Stephan Sukhorenko commented on 2 December 2005: 'We have sufficient information to disseminate to our deputies, so that they can prepare their electors and inform them of *our understanding* of the situation'.[69] The analytical report contained detailed information on how colour revolutions occurred in the region (paying particular attention to Ukraine and Kyrgyzstan), who organized them and how precisely they were staged in order to overthrow existing governments. According to the report, a revolution would be staged to follow four crucial steps in order to achieve leadership replacement: from facilitating popular perception of incumbency as tyrannical to exposing elections as fraudulent and demanding justice by taking people's protest to the streets. The report also offered some details of the possible toppling of Lukashenko's regime and what precautionary measures needed be taken in order to prevent such activities.[70]

On the eve of the presidential election, on 19 March 2006, every mobile phone user in Minsk received a text message cautioning against attending demonstrations organized by the opposition, and suggesting that all participants of unlawful protests would be 'severely battered'.[71] A day earlier General Sukhovenko publicly announced that all participants of unauthorized public actions during or after the election would be charged under the Terrorist Act and could be subject to 20 years imprisonment. He further insisted that the KGB discovered a secret plot involving the opposition staging protests against the president and even possible detonation of four schools in the capital during/after the election.[72]

The official propaganda went into full swing on the day of the election and thereafter: the official media distributed fabricated images of homosexuals and drug addicts, and even alleged that contagious diseases were spreading in October Square where the tents were staged.[73] The spin continued after the crackdown on the demonstrators: the official media broadcast pictures of riot policemen and official TV crews violently beaten by opposition supporters and hospitalized with severe head and chest injuries. Furthermore, according to Wilson,[74] 'Lukashenko's "technologists" added the anti-Polish element and successfully demonised Milinkevich [the then leader of the united opposition] as a stooge of the Vatican and Warsaw kresy[75] – politics, as well as the USA. Milinkevich's popularity in foreign capitals was therefore a double-edged sword.'

On the day of the election, in order to handle the prospect of civilian disquiet, Lukashenko recalled to full alert 110,000 paramilitary forces (especially to handle the aftermath of the election), including OMON, a special force branch, which were further supplemented by a significant number of reserves, and a newly established special police force led by Colonel Dmitry Pavlichenko, who was allegedly involved in commanding 'death squads' aimed at murdering Lukashenko's prominent opponents. Furthermore, as reported by other sources,[76] Lukashenko's personal bodyguard force was activated to include about 200 enlisted men, 'specially trained and equipped with cutting edge technology',[77] and selected on grounds of personal loyalty to the president. Additionally, a powerful and highly secretive SWAT team, 'Alma', belonging to the Ministry of Interior and paramilitary quick reaction squad SOBR were on full alert to counteract any insurgence. None of the above forces, however, was deployed (or even seen on the streets), except for Colonel Dmitry Pavlichenko's squad used to disband the demonstration of a few thousand people led by Kozulin during Freedom Day on 25 March 2006. Nevertheless, protestors still faced paramilitary batons and the threat of rubber bullets, allegedly fired at some by Pavlichenko's brigade from carabines C-23 'Selezen' designed for shooting with rubber bullets and gas.[78]

This was the only occasion where the state used moderate force to counteract civic unrest. There were other 'localized' and small-scale clashes with the paramilitary police, however, generally speaking, public demonstrations (including the disbursement of the tent city) were handled in a moderately peaceful manner by the authorities and paramilitary forces (some of which – especially the Pavlichenko squad – were known for their extreme brutality and violence).

This relatively mild and controlled response from the authorities to hitherto unprecedented (for Belarus) levels of public protest was quite unexpected, thus taking the opposition by surprise. The Russian media subsequently commented that 'Batska's [Nation's Father] opponents awaited brutal oppression of the protests: they had been warned about this in advance ... However, there was an impression that neither Kozulin, nor Milinkevich was ready for this peaceful reaction, and could not handle the crowds sensibly'.[79] Apparently, 'militia behaved reservedly, no OMON forces were seen on the square, and although threatened, no armoured military vehicles with water guns were deployed either'.[80] Some observers noted that despite Batska's quite emotional personality,[81] the authorities stayed in control of the 'revolutionary situation' in Belarus by integrating all their resources (from military readiness to the effective use of state propaganda) into a coordinated response to thwart political unrest in the making:

> Belarus has demonstrated a relatively new phenomenon for the post-soviet space – how to counteract a planned but unaccomplished revolution...The state and civil society in Belarus were too robust to be subverted by the political crisis developing on its doorsteps.[82]

Therefore, there was nothing surprising in Lukashenko's 'elegant and convincing' victory in presidential election[83] and his peaceful curbing of the planned but failed electoral revolution in the country.

What was surprising instead was the limited use of coercion and violence in these clearly volatile and nerve-racking circumstances for the autocratic leadership in the region. One commentator noted: 'In order to defeat Lukashenko, his opponents need to learn to win heart and minds not only of intelligentsia, business-men and students, but also of someone like tetia Natasha...[who said] "Of course I voted for Lukashenko. Because we are now used to him. He is not new, and life has actually become more stable with him."'[84]

Why was an authoritarian response NOT necessary in Belarus?

Accounting for domestic structural factors thus not only elicits some general explanation of why revolutions fail or succeed in the region and beyond, but also suggests the need to 'contextualize' democracy promotion in order to under-stand the regime's endurance and its logic for survival in each 'non-colour' case.

There is little doubt that Lukashenko's government has used all its resources to build a regime, which many would describe as 'legitimate', that is, enjoying extensive public support.[85] Through autocratic suppression, institutional means of prevention, government economic performance, active propaganda and a growing sense of cultural identity amongst the Belarusians – identity mastered by the president – Lukashenko has managed to achieve an enviable balance between his government and the Belarusians at large, expressed through public endorsement of his regime. People now evaluate his and others' performance (that of home-grown opposition and of governments in their neighbourhood) through the actions (and the outcome these actions entail – usually of order and stability) of their own president, with lasting and largely negative perceptions of any external or internal challenges for the incumbency.[86] It would be absolutely true to say that the specificity of Lukashenko's regime lies with (i) his own actions that he clearly directed to safeguard his authority over the years, including achieving relative economic stability in the country; and more crucially, (ii) with his own electorate which proved to be so malleable for responding to Lukashenko's leadership, and thus generating the most enduring feature of his regime – its genuine legitimacy: 'rule is legitimate when its subjects believe it to be so'.[87] As our 2011 post-election nationwide survey indicates, Lukashenko still remains popular (44% – four times greater than all other candidates) among the general population – that is, despite the bloody aftermath of the December 2010 presidential election, and the imprisonment of almost all the presidential candidates.[88]

In this section I will briefly explore what makes Lukashenko's regime legitimate – the people/president bond, which naturally reduces the need for the regime to utilize state coercion extensively. More broadly, I will also examine the normative foundations of the Belarusian society that have made Lukashenko's phenomenon possible and even flourishing in Belarusian conditions.

Regime's legitimacy

Lukashenko is and will remain absolutely legitimate if people continue to identify with him and appreciate his relatively successful social and economic policies directed at supporting communal well-being, security and stability.[89] Popular perception that, in a situation of total collapse, the country could only be saved by the president – rather than any other existing or possible agency – clearly makes the regime unwaveringly stable.

Belarus, like many other countries, has been hit hard by the economic crisis, but the effects of the global economic downturn have not yet fully resonated with the society at large, and many still feel stable and secure under Lukashenko's leadership.[90] Over a third of the polled population still believe that the state of the economy in Belarus is sound; with another 43% feeling neutral towards the overall economic performance of their country.[91] Over two thirds of the population state that their family income is relatively stable (67%) and a healthy plurality observe (46%) that it has not changed in the past year, with another 24% even declaring a slight improvement.

On balance, more people believe (over 60%) that the country is stable and developing in the right direction (as against 24% who think otherwise). Overall, about 40% of the respondents perceive their president's actions as complete or rather satisfactory, with another third feeling neutral or hesitant, which serves as a clear sign of the continuity of the president's legitimacy in Belarus in 2011.

Furthermore, if one were to choose between economic well-being and democracy/independence, well-being comes first: almost 70% (as against 22%) concur with the importance of the former. Therefore, people's positive preferences for Lukashenko come as no surprise: due to the relative efficacy of his regime and his convincing political discourse, he continues to remain the sole alternative on the Belarusian political landscape.

Why do people vote for Lukashenko? In 2008[92] they simply believed that he was successful in restoring order in society (66.3%), in building an independent and economically viable state (64.5%), in promoting collaboration within the CIS (60.1%), in not letting the 'oligarchs' rule the country (59.7%), and in fighting crime (58.9%) and corruption (49.6%). In comparison with Soviet times, people (08/2006) also see the incumbent authority as 'close to the people' (30.4%), less bureaucratic (25.5%), strong and reliable (23.6%) as well as lawful (23.2%).

Moreover, people seem to identify with their president *knowingly* – that is, despite being aware of government corruption, allegations of political murder, media manipulation and the absolute power the president has (including being above the law) in the country. This conscious choice of the Belarusians remains a mystery to many students of politics. How can Belarusians *knowingly* identify and support Lukashenko's regime – in many eyes, an oppressive, murderous, and by many accounts, a stupefying order?

Common sense and logic suggest that indeed what Belarusians seem to treasure most is their personal security, given the legacies of the past instability and hardship – personal security above newly attained sovereignty and personal freedoms and rights. This is duly reflected in their 'strategic choice' of leadership. Belarusians 'have bread and butter' daily on the table, they are in full employment with regularly paid wages and pensions;[93] they are lavishly entertained by the state, and cared for through various (although limited) social benefits. They have made their choice of leadership because this government does not abuse/harass them individually, and because they know that in the absence of any eligible alternative, Lukashenko is their best bet.

Being different?

There is however more to this 'strategic choice' of leadership. This kind of preference for strong, orderly and authoritarian government seems common for many East European transient states vulnerable to change and desiring stability, and has far deeper roots – going well beyond pre-emptive actions of the regime itself – in society.[94] As our research indicates,[95] many countries of the former Soviet Union demonstrate an enduring proclivity for strong leadership and adherence to other-than-liberal values – those of community, tolerance, cultural heritage, etc. as opposed to democracy, lawfulness and human rights – which invariably make them *different* and so less susceptible to values and ideals of the liberal democracy, as practised by the West.

Interestingly, the normative disjunction between the West and the former Soviet Union[96] is not simply an intellectual contestation, or a projected discourse of autocratic governments in an attempt to justify their authoritarian policies. As the absolute majority of the respondents in many case studies indicated, this is deeply rooted in public perceptions whereby people clearly and uncompromisingly differentiate between Western values – of market economy, human rights, democracy and lawfulness – and their own values – of peace, tolerance, respect for cultural heritage and religion.[97]

This naturally leads to questioning the overall logic of democracy promotion by the West, which is often premised on the normative *acquis* of *liberal* democracies and their respective vested interests.[98] As Lane contends: 'Western interests are involved in these processes – in support of groups, in Margaret Thatcher's terms, "with whom we can do business", or from a geo-strategic point of view, to change allegiances in favour of the West'.[99] The logical questions are (i) that of mutual reciprocity and indeed receptivity – that is, whether there is any common normative denominator between the aiding and the receiving sides – and (ii) whether one set of arguably more virtuous values can be successfully installed in those societies which for generations have followed a different (and often contested) path of democratic development – the path premised on different values and in many cases evincing a legitimate consensus between the people and their government.

A new scholarship is now emerging to contest the concept of liberal democracy and democracy promotion per se,[100] which insists on exposing not only the positive but also the negative forms and practices of democracy, and on the need to pluralize and contextualize democracy in each given case. It is to be hoped that this will engender a better understanding of why some transition countries may resist generous and gratuitous aid, and may even find some Western efforts offensive in their attempt to change what may be *externally* seen as 'rogue' or an 'outpost of tyranny', but internally, for what it is worth, is a perceivably legitimate order for many people in the other-than-liberal states.

Conclusions

In this article the experience of the colour revolutions in Eastern Europe, and Belarus in particular, has been examined. In the light of the continuing political turmoil and in some cases, an increased authoritarian clampdown on genuine non-confrontational forms of civic activities in the region, we have questioned the real success of the first colour revolutions in bringing about political change, let alone democratization. The all-colour endeavours in Georgia, Ukraine and Kyrgyzstan, and later on in many more countries of the former Soviet Union, may have been democratic in their mobilization, but they evidently failed to wield any system change and thus can be more suitably theorized as 'revolutionary coup d'état', intending leadership replacement with some public support to ensure legitimacy of the 'new order'. 'These revolutionary coup d'états ... involve the rise of different elite groups, clans or families, which seek to redistribute the assets of the previous regime'[101] and are duly promoted by the West, as those 'whom we can do business with'.[102]

The colour revolutions clearly demonstrated that international diffusion of the foreign-led revolutionary experience in the region, even if underpinned by an impressive financial backing and enthusiastic training of the revolutionaries, is an insufficient and inadequate tool to instigate change in Eastern Europe.[103] A careful account of domestic structural factors is needed in order to understand why so many colour revolutions, of the second generation (2005–2009) especially, have failed to materialize into democratic breakthroughs. Furthermore, it has been insisted that both pluralization of the meaning of democracy and the contextualization of democracy promotion in each given case is essential in order to evaluate the readiness for and the willingness of change by a particular regime, and what kind of change in actual fact is desired.

Belarus has undermined the Western 'logic' of democracy promotion premised on templates and sponsorship, and by many accounts, offered a relatively conventional authoritarian 'response' to the attempted revolution on its doorsteps. The regime has evidently learned (through long- and short-term measures) how to defend itself and, more remarkably, it has developed skills of how to do so *legitimately*, without resorting to extensive coercion, so often anticipated from the 'outposts of tyranny'. The article has argued that Belarusian authorities, by undertaking certain immediate precautionary measures during the presidential election in March 2006, managed to maintain the status quo in a relatively peaceful and non-aggressive manner.[104] Effective learning by regimes, however, is only one side of the story, which would be incomplete without analysis of the internal (domestic) conditions that created the propitious environment for the survival and endurance of the Lukashenko regime.

It has been argued that the incumbency in Belarus is unmistakably premised on the precarious legitimacy that gives Lukashenko's regime an enviable immunity and had effectively conditioned public withdrawal from the attempts at electoral mobilization during elections. The origin of this legitimacy is many-fold and not least dependent on the efficacy of the regime and its deliverables. However, the essential part of the governing consensus has nevertheless been deeply rooted in the historical/traditional values of the society itself, the manifestation of which has been so perplexingly well epitomized by Lukashenko himself. Therefore, in order to exercise democracy promotion effectively (if such a thing is at all possible) a far deeper understanding of autocratic narratives is needed, concomitant with a much closer analysis of local societal norms and values as well as of a country's geopolitical resources and strategies.

Acknowledgement

I wish to record my gratitude to the ESRC (RES-061-25-0001) for the financial support of my project, and the anonymous referees for their comments on the earlier version of this article. I also would like to dedicate this article to the memory of my colleague and friend, Vital Silitski, whose untimely death left us utterly bereft.

Notes

1. Lukashenko, 'V Belarusi Budut Sokhraneny'.
2. The years 2010 and 2011 have witnessed new uprisings in the EU Southern Neighbourhood (Tunisia, Egypt, Libya, Jordan, Syria, Yemen, and others), which could be classed as a third generation of the new-type ('colour') revolutions, analysis of which, due to the limits of space, is beyond the scope of this article.
3. The 'Bulldozer Revolution' in Serbia (2000) is perhaps one of the few exceptions here.

4. Kuzio, *Aspects of the Orange Revolution VI*; *Journal of Democracy*, 'Debating the Color Revolutions'; Diamond, *The Spirit of Democracy*; D'Anieri, 'Explaining the Success and Failure of Post-Communist Revolutions'; Simecka, 'Diffusion and Civil Society Mobilisation in Coloured Revolutions'.

5. This included 'Cedar Revolution' in Lebanon (2005), 'Purple Revolution' in Iraq (2005), 'Carnation Revolution' in Armenia (2007), and a 'Twitter Revolution' in Moldova (2009).

6. Lane, 'Coloured Revolution as a Political Phenomenon'; White and McAllistair, 'Rethinking the "Orange Revolution"'; Beachain, 'Roses and Tulips: Dynamics of Regime Change in Georgia and Kyrgyzstan'; Wilson, 'Belarus Between "Coloured Revolution" and "Counter-Revolutionary Technology"'.

7. Lane, 'Coloured Revolution as a Political Phenomenon', 132.

8. This term is used in opposition to the 'international diffusion' of democratic break-throughs. For more on 'international diffusion' see Bunce and Wolchik, 'Getting Real about the "Real Causes"'; Heathershaw, 'Rethinking the International Diffusion of Coloured Revolutions'.

9. The focus of this article is the 2006 failed revolutionary attempt in Belarus. The events of the December 2010 elections and their analysis are beyond the scope of this article.

10. Rakhmanova, *Democratic Revolutionary Handbook*, a documentary which seeks to reveal the mechanics as well as the controversies of *modular (colour) revolutions* in Eastern Europe. For more information see a critical appraisal of the film at http://icarusfilms.com/new2007/demo.html.

11. The numbers varied depending on the source of reporting from 10,000 to 35,000. See for example, OSCE/ODIHR, *Republic of Belarus*; Zarakhovich, 'V Belarusi – Revolutsiya?'.

12. As the OSCE reported, in Minsk alone the number of individuals sentenced in a single day exceeded a record-breaking 200. For more information see OSCE/ODIHR, *Republic of Belarus*, 25.

13. Independent Institute for Socio-Economic and Political Studies, polls, http://www.iiseps.org/poll06.html

14. Intimidation was deployed by authorities, but it was comparably moderate and mainly covert. Large-scale violence was absent. For more information see Martino-vich, 'Protokoly Chekistskikh Mudretsov'; Zarakhovich, 'V Belarusi – Revolut-siya?'; 'Ulada Baittsa Kastusia Kalinouskaga'; 'Khto Lepsh Zasvoiy Vuroki Pamaranchavai Revalyutsii?'.

15. Silitski, 'Pamyatats', shto Dyktatury Ruinyyuttsa'; Chavusau, 'Zhdani i nadzei Kastrychnitskai Ploschy'.

16. Lenin, 'May Day Action by the Revolutionary Proletariat'.

17. For more discussion see the special issue of the *Journal of Communist Studies and Transition Politics* 25 (2009); Lankina and Getachew, 'A Geographic Incremental Theory of Democratization'; Burnell, 'Political Strategies of External Support for Democratization'; Carothers, 'The Backlash against Democracy Promotion'.

18. Lane, 'Coloured Revolution as a Political Phenomenon'.

19. Way, 'The Real Causes of the Color Revolutions'.

20. Levitsky and Way, 'Linkage versus Leverage'; Way and Levitsky, 'The Dynamics of Autocratic Coercion after the Cold War'.

21. Kuzio, *Aspects of the Orange Revolution VI*; *Journal of Democracy*, 'Debating the Color Revolutions'.

22. Play on words using Gregory Ioffe's title of the book, *Understanding Belarus and How Western Foreign Policy Misses the Mark*.

23. Bunce and Wolchik, 'International Diffusion and Postcommunist Electoral Revolutions'; Kuzio, *Aspects of the Orange Revolution VI*, 10–11.

24. For more information see special issue 'Rethinking the "Coloured Revolutions"', *Journal of Communist Studies and Transition Politics*.

25. Bunce and Wolchik, 'International Diffusion and Postcommunist Electoral Revolutions'.

26. Rakhmanova, *Democratic Revolutionary Handbook*, offers a comprehensive guide as to how the colour revolutions were organized in Eastern Europe.

27. Bunce and Wolchik, 'International Diffusion and Postcommunist Electoral Revolutions'.

28. A more illustrious debate concerning the role of territoriality and the role of geographical proximity has been raised by Tomila Lankina and Lullit Getachew in their seminal article 'A Geographic Incremental Theory of Democratization'. There they argue about the importance of a geographical incremental process for the pace of democratization, facilitated by the regional exposure to the external environment and its gradual adaptation to the norms and standards necessary for cooperation.

29. For more information and examples, view Tatjana Rakhmanova's documentary *Democratic Revolutionary Handbook* (2006), and references to evidence in Lane and White, *Rethinking the 'Coloured Revolutions'*.

30. Way, 'The Real Causes of the Color Revolutions', 56.

31. For more information see Beissinger, 'Structure and Example in Module Political Phenomena'; Hale, 'Regime Cycles'.

32. Beissinger, 'Structure and Example in Module Political Phenomena', 263.

33. Ibid., 272.

34. A number of successive events counteract the alleged success of colour revolutions in the region: violent outbreaks in Georgia throughout 2008–2010, government instability and permanent crisis in Ukraine since 2004; 'precarious democracy' and authoritarian trends in Kyrgyzstan especially in 2008–2009.

35. Lane, 'Coloured Revolution as a Political Phenomenon'. The article offers ample evidence to substantiate the reference to 'revolutionary coup d'état' in the case of the 'colour revolutions'.

36. Ibid., 118–19.

37. Ibid., 119.

38. Chaulia, 'Democratisation, NGOs and "Colour Revolutions"'.

39. Lane, 'Coloured Revolution as a Political Phenomenon', 116–17.

40. 'Georgia: Sliding Towards Authoritarianism?'; Brill Olcott, 'The New Political System in Kyrgyzstan'; Walker and Goehring, 'Petro-Authoritarianism and Eurasia's New Divides'.

41. For more analysis of this term refer to Lane, 'Coloured Revolution as a Political Phenomenon'.

42. Bunce and Wolchik, 'International Diffusion and Postcommunist Electoral Revolutions', 31.

43. Ibid.

44. Nye, *Soft Power*.

45. For further explanation of this claim refer to Rakhmanova's *Democratic Revolutionary Handbook*.

46. Nye, 'Why Military Power is No Longer Enough', quoted in Lane, 'Coloured Revolution as a Political Phenomenon', 115.

47. Philippov, '"Oranzhevye" tekhologii v Belorussii primenimy, no neeffectivny'.

48. Way, 'The Real Causes of the Color Revolutions', 57, emphasis added.

49. Rakhmanova, *Democratic Revolutionary Handbook* .

50. Way, 'The Real Causes of the Color Revolutions', 57.
51. Ibid., 58–9.
52. Ibid., 60.
53. Ibid., 65.
54. For more discussion see Korosteleva, 'Was There a Quiet Revolution?'; Korosteleva, 'The Limits of the EU Governance'; Korosteleva, 'Is Belarus a Demagogical Democracy?'.
55. Silitsky, 'Preempting Democracy'; Silitski, 'Pamyatats', shto Dyktatury Ruinyyuttsa'.
56. That is, when the regime manipulates public needs to legitimize its (poor) perform-ance: in particular, when the president ordered the cutting of some public subsidies he immediately offered respective justifications (from ideological to institutional) to allay public anxiety.
57. For more extensive discussion, see Silicki, 'Belarus'; White, Korosteleva, and Low-enhardt, *Postcommunist Belarus*.
58. Leshchenko, 'The National Ideology and the Basis of Lukashenka Regime in Belarus'; Marples, 'Color Revolutions'; Marples, *The Lukashenko Phenomenon*.
59. This first of all includes legislative anti-revolution provisions (Law of Defamation of state officials; Law on Counteraction of Extremism; Law on Some Changes and Amendments into the Criminal Code Increasing Responsibility for Crime against Individuals and State Security; Changes and amendments related to some issues of financing terrorism; decrees on responsibility of acting on behalf of unregistered organizations, or criminalizing training and other preparations that may lead to the violation social order, etc). See Pontis Foundation, 'Anti-Revolution Legislation'.
60. The non-aligned states movement (NAM) is an association of about 118 developing states to represent the interests of the developing world. For more information see http://news.bbc.co.uk/1/hi/2798187.stm.
61. Bajmukhametov, 'Apraudanne Raseiai zhorstkastsi Belaruskikh uladau vygliadae prosta zhakhliva'.
62. For closer analysis of 'authoritarian pre-emption' refer to Silitsky's 'Preempting Democracy'.
63. Lukashenko, 'V Belarusi Budut Sokhraneny Mir, Spokoistvie I Stabil'nost'.
64. Silicki, 'Belarus', 78.
65. Ibid.
66. Pop-propaganda is a technical term to describe a government's actions which target the wider population through pop-concerts, pop-entertainment etc.
67. Rakhmanova, *Democratic Revolutionary Handbook*.
68. Martinovich, 'Revolyutsii ne budet'.
69. Martinovich, 'Protokoly Chekistskikh Mudretsov', emphasis added.
70. Ibid.
71. Zarakhovich, 'V Belarusi – Revolutsiya?'.
72. Ibid.
73. Silicki, 'Belarus'.
74. Wilson, 'Belarus Between', 95.
75. 'Kresy' means 'borderland', here referring to the Polish-owned period of Belarus' history.
76. Burger, 'The Divergence between Declaratory and Action Policy'.
77. Ibid., 34.
78. Center for Political Education, 'Belarus After Election'.
79. Logvinovich, 'Aleksandru Lukashenko stalo tesno v Belorussii'.
80. Ibid.
81. Matikevich, *Nashestvie*; Sheremet and Kalinikina, *Sluchainyi President*; Feduta, *Lukashenko*.

82. Philippov, '"Oranzhevye" tekhologii v Belorussii primenimy, no neeffectivny'.
83. Nobody doubted Lukashenko's victory in elections either in 2006 or 2010, even if they were fraud-free and absolutely transparent. For more information see http:// www.charter97.org/bel/news.
84. Logvinovich, 'Aleksandru Lukashenko stalo tesno v Belorussii'.
85. For full discussion of 'legitimacy' see Clark, 'Legitimacy in a Global Order', 79.
86. 'People' in this context means general public opinion, as evidenced from nation-wide opinion polls (March–April 2011).
87. Max Weber, quoted in Clark, 'Legitimacy in a Global Order'.
88. The survey was conducted during March 2011 by the Centre for Political Research, Belarusian State University, under the ESRC-funded project (RES-061-25-0001). For more information see the project website and synopsis of findings at http:// www.aber.ac.uk/en/interpol/research/research-projects/europeanising-securitising-outsiders.
89. For more discussion of the economic factor see Korosteleva, 'When Time Goes Backwards'; Ioffe, *Understanding Belarus and How Western Foreign Policy Misses the Mark*.
90. This is even despite the recent terrorist attack that took place in Minsk (11 April 2011) during rush hour at the busiest interlinking underground station of the city, leaving 14 dead and over 200 injured. The author witnessed the aftermath of the event.
91. The data is quoted from the 2011 post-election survey conducted in Belarus under the ESRC-funded project 'Europeanising or securitising the outsiders' (RES-061-25-0001).
92. For more information see http://www.iiseps.org/arhdata.html, which is also corroborated by the findings of our survey, available as a synopsis from http://www.aber.ac.uk/en/interpol/research/research-pojects/europeanising-securitising-outsiders.
93. For more discussion of Belarus' economic 'miracle' and the prospects of its sustainability see Korosteleva, 'Belarus' Foreign Policy at the Time of Crisis'; Zlotnikov, 'The Belarusian Economic Miracle'; Yeremeyeva, 'The Impact of the Global Financial Crisis on Belarusian Economy'.
94. For more discussion of 'differences', especially values-based, see Korosteleva, *Eastern Partnership*.
95. For more information visit the project's website http://www.aber.ac.uk/en/interpol/research/research-projects/europeanising-securitising-outsiders.
96. The normative disjunction is far broader than is suggested here, and embraces all non-liberal democracies. In this article, however, Belarus, Russia, Ukraine and Moldova are used as the case studies of the project to substantiate the point.
97. For more information see Korosteleva, *Eastern Partnership*. Case studies included interviews with politicians, focus groups and nation-wide surveys. A synopsis of research findings can be found at http://www.aber.ac.uk/en/interpol/research/research-projects/europeanising-securitising-outsiders/.
98. The West's projection or anticipation of the adoption of liberal democracy elsewhere in the world irrespective of particular societal values, perceptions and traditions, is succinctly summarized in David Collier and Steven Levitsky's article, where they classify all 'other forms' of democracy as those with 'missing attributes' of the liberal model. For more information see 'Democracy with Adjectives'.
99. Lane, 'Coloured Revolution as a Political Phenomenon', 132.
100. Kurki, 'Democracy and Conceptual Contestability'; Hobson, 'Democracy as Civilisation'; Biryukov and Sergeyev, 'The Idea of Democracy in the West and in the East'; Duncan, *Democratic Theory and Practice*.
101. Lane, 'Coloured Revolution as a Political Phenomenon', 132.
102. Ibid., fn. 56.

103. Please see fn. 29 for further information. Note that 'unpacking Western support' was not the purpose of the article. Instead, the focus was on why Lukashenko's regime survived the colour revolutions relatively unchallenged.
104. The December 2010 presidential election and especially its aftermath, however, offer a somewhat different picture of authorities' response to the public uprising – more violent, more brutal and spontaneous. The analysis of recent events in Belarus, however, is beyond the scope of this article.

Notes on contributor

Elena Korosteleva is Jean Monnet Chair in European Politics and Director of the Centre for European Studies, Department of International Politics, Aberystwyth University. She has published in the field of ENP, democracy promotion and democratization in Eastern Europe. Her recent book, *The EU and its Eastern Neighbours: Towards a More Ambitious Partnership?* (Routledge, 2012) is a result of her large ESRC-funded project 'Europeanising or Securitising the "Outsiders"? Assessing the EU's Partnership-Building Approach with Eastern Europe' (RES-061-25-0001).

Bibliography

Bajmukhametov, Sergei. 'Apraudanne Raseiai zhorstkastsi Belaruskikh uladau vygliadae prosta zhakhliva'. *Russian Bazaar*, April 11, 2008. http://www.charter97.org/en/news/2008/4/11/5683.

Beachain, Donnacha. 'Roses and Tulips: Dynamics of Regime Change in Georgia and Kyrgyzstan'. *Journal of Communist Studies and Transition Politics* 25, nos. 2–3 (2009): 199–226.

Beissinger, Mark. 'Structure and Example in Module Political Phenomena: The Diffusion of Bulldozer/Rose/Orange/Tulip Revolutions'. *Perspectives on Politics* 5, no. 2 (2007): 259–76.

Biryukov, Nikolai, and Viktor Sergeyev. 'The Idea of Democracy in the West and in the East'. In *Defining and Measuring Democracy*, ed. David Beetham, 182–99. London: Sage, 1994.

Brill Olcott, Martha. 'The New Political System in Kyrgyzstan: In Search of Sustainability'. December 12, 2008. http://www.carnegieendowment.org/events/?fa=eventDetail&id=1235.

Bunce, Valerie, and Sharon Wolchik. 'Getting Real about the "Real Causes"'. *Journal of Democracy* 20, no. 1 (2009): 69–73.

Bunce, Valerie, and Sharon Wolchik. 'International Diffusion and Postcommunist Electoral Revolutions'. *Communist and Post-Communist Studies* 39, no. 3 (2006): 283–304.

Burger, Ethan. 'The Divergence between Declaratory and Action Policy: US Non-Recognition of the Results of the Belarusian March 2006 Presidential Election'. In *The Geopolitical Place of Belarus in Europe and the World*, ed. Valer Bulhakau, 21–43. Warsaw: Wyzsza Szkola Handlu i Prawa, 2006.

Burnell, Peter. 'Political Strategies of External Support for Democratization'. *Foreign Policy Analysis* 1 (2005): 361–84.

Carothers, Thomas. 'The Backlash against Democracy Promotion'. *Foreign Affairs* (2006): 55–68.

Center for Political Education. 'Belarus After Election: The Naked Dictator', April 13, 2006.

Chaulia, Shreeram. 'Democratisation, NGOs and "Colour Revolutions"'. *Open Democracy*, January 19, 2006. http://www.opendemocracy.net/globalization-institutions_government/colour_revolutions_3196.jsp.

Chavusau, Yury. 'Zhdani i nadzei Kastrychnitskai Ploschy'. *Arche* 6 (2006). http://arche.bymedia.net/2006-6/cavusau606.htm.

Clark, Ian. 'Legitimacy in a Global Order'. *Review of International Studies* 29, no. 1 (2003): 75–95.

Collier, David, and Steven Levitsky. 'Democracy with Adjectives: Conceptual Innovation in Comparative Research'. *World Politics* 49, no. 3 (1997): 430–51.

D'Anieri, Paul. 'Explaining the Success and Failure of Post-Communist Revolutions'. *Communist and Post-Communist Studies* 39, no. 3 (2006): 331–50.

'Debating the Color Revolutions'. *Journal of Democracy* (Special Issue) 20, no. 1 (2009).

Democratic Revolutionary Handbook. Directed by Tatjana Rakhmanova. France, 2006.

Diamond, Larry. *The Spirit of Democracy: The Struggle to Build Free Societies Throughout the World*. Basingstoke: Palgrave Macmillan, 2008.

Duncan, Graham, ed. *Democratic Theory and Practice*. Cambridge: Cambridge University Press, 1983.

Feduta, Alexander. *Lukashenko: Politicheskaya Biographiya*. Moscow: Referendum, 2005.

'Georgia: Sliding Towards Authoritarianism?'. *Europe Report No. 189*, December 19, 2007. http://www.crisisgroup.org/home/index.cfm?id=5233&l=1.

Hale, Henry. 'Regime Cycles: Democracy, Autocracy, and Revolution in Post-Soviet Eurasia'. *World Politics* 58, no. 1 (2005): 133–65.

Heathershaw, John. 'Rethinking the International Diffusion of Coloured Revolutions: A Study of the Power of Representation in Kyrgyzstan'. *Journal of Communist Studies and Transition Politics* 25, nos. 2–3 (2009): 297–323.

Hobson, Christopher. 'Democracy as Civilisation'. *Global Society* 22, no. 1 (2008): 75–95.

Ioffe, Gregory. *Understanding Belarus and How Western Foreign Policy Misses the Mark*. New York: Rowman and Littlefield, 2008.

'Khto Lepsh Zasvoiy Vuroki Pamaranchavai Revalyutsii?'. *Nasha Niva*, April 10, 2006. http://nn.by/?c=ar&i=1368.

Korosteleva, Elena. 'Belarus' Foreign Policy at the Time of Crisis'. *Journal of Communist Studies and Transition Politics* 27, nos. 3–4 (2011): 566–86.

Korosteleva, Elena, ed. *Eastern Partnership: A New Opportunity for Neighbours?* London: Routledge, 2011.

Korosteleva, Elena. 'Is Belarus a Demagogical Democracy?'. *Cambridge Review for International Affairs* 16, no. 3 (2003): 525–35.

Korosteleva, Elena. 'The Limits of the EU Governance: Belarus' Response to the European Neighbourhood Policy'. *Contemporary Politics* 15, no. 2 (2009): 229–45.

Korosteleva, Elena. 'Was There a Quiet Revolution? Belarus After the 2006 Presidential Election'. *Journal of Communist Studies and Transition Politics* 25, nos. 2–3 (2009): 324–46.

Korosteleva, Julia. 'When Time Goes Backwards, or Overviewing Transition Progress in Belarus'. Paper presented at the annual conference of the British Association of Slavonic and East European Studies, Cambridge University, March 30, 2007.

Kurki, Milja. 'Democracy and Conceptual Contestability: Towards Pluralisation and Contextualisation of Conceptions of Democracy in Democracy Promotion'. Paper presented at a Workshop on Conceptualising Democracy, European Research Council, Aberystwyth University, December 2008.

Kuzio, Taras. *Aspects of the Orange Revolution VI: Post-Communist Democratic Revolutions in Comparative Perspective*. Stuttgart: Ibidem-Verlag, 2007.

Lane, David. 'Coloured Revolution as a Political Phenomenon'. *Journal of Communist Studies and Transition Politics* 25, nos. 2–3 (2009): 113–35.

Lane, David and Stephen White, eds., *Rethinking the 'Coloured Revolutions'*. London: Routledge, 2010.

Lankina, Tamila, and Lullit Getachew. 'A Geographic Incremental Theory of Democratization: Territory, Aid, and Democracy in Post-Communist Regions'. *World Politics* 58, no. 4 (2006): 536–82.

Lenin, Vladimir. 'May Day Action by the Revolutionary Proletariat'. *Social-Democrat*, June 15, 1913, reprinted in *Lenin Collected Works*. Moscow: Progress Publishers, 1977, 19: 21–27.

Leshchenko, Natalja. 'The National Ideology and the Basis of Lukashenka Regime in Belarus'. *Europe-Asia Studies* 60, no. 8 (2008): 1419–33.

Levitsky, Steven, and Lucan Way. 'Linkage versus Leverage: Rethinking the International Dimension of Regime Change'. *Comparative Politics* 38, no. 4 (2006): 379–400.

Logvinovich, Aleksey. 'Aleksandru Lukashenko stalo tesno v Belorussii'. *Izvestiya*, March 21, 2006. http://izvestia.ru/world/article3091257.

Lukashenko, Alexander. 'V Belarusi Budut Sokhraneny Mir, Spokoistvie i Stabil'nost'. January 8, 2005. http://www.president.gov.by/press16874.html#doc.

Marples, David. 'Color Revolutions: The Belarus Case'. *Communist and Post-Communist Studies* 39, no. 3 (2006): 351–64.

Marples, David. *The Lukashenko Phenomenon*. Trondheim: Trondheim Studies on East European Cultures and Societies, 2007.

Martinovich, Viktor. 'Protokoly Chekistskikh Mudretsov'. *BelGazeta*, December 12, 2005. http://www.belgazeta.by/20051212.49/010030141.

Martinovich, Viktor. 'Revolyutsii ne budet'. *BelGazeta*, April, 4, 2005. http://www.belgazeta.by/20050404.13/010060142.

Matikevich, Vladimir. *Nashestvie*. Moscow: Iaza, 2004.

Nye, Joseph. *Soft Power: The Means to Success in World Politics*. New York: Public Affairs, 2004.

Nye, Joseph. 'Why Military Power is No Longer Enough'. *The Guardian*, March 31, 2002. http://www.guardian.co.uk/world/2002/mar/31/1.

OSCE/ODIHR. *Republic of Belarus: Presidential Election*. Warsaw: OSCE/ODIHR Election Observation Mission Report, 2006.

Philippov, Yury. '"Oranzhevye" tekhologii v Belorussii primenimy, no neeffectivny'. *RIA-Novosti*, March 21, 2006. http://www.rian.ru/analytics/20060321/44618306-print.html.

Pontis Foundation. 'Anti-Revolution Legislation in Belarus: State is Good, Non-state is Illegal'. December 22, 2005. http://www.nadaciapontis.sk/.

Sheremet, Pavel, and Svetlana Kalinikina. *Sluchainyi President*. St Petersburg: Limbus Press, 2004.

Silicki, Vital. 'Belarus: Anatomy of Preemtive Authoritarianism'. In *The Geopolitical Place of Belarus in Europe and the World*, ed. Valer Bulhakau, 59–91. Warsaw: Wyzsza Szkola Handlu i Prawa, 2006.

Silitski, Vitali. 'Pamyatats', shto Dyktatury Ruinyyuttsa'. *Arche* 7–8 (2006). http://www.arche.bymedia.net/2006-7/silicki706.htm (especially fn. 35).

Silitsky, Vitali. 'Preempting Democracy: The Case of Belarus'. *Journal of Democracy* 16, no. 4 (2005): 83–97.

Simecka, Michal. 'Diffusion and Civil Society Mobilisation in Coloured Revolutions'. *CEU Political Science Journal* 4, no. 1 (2009): 1–30.

'Ulada Baittsa Kastusia Kalinouskaga'. *Khartyia97*, October 27, 2007. http://www.charter97.org/be/news/2007/10/27/1054/.

Walker, Christopher, and Jeannette Goehring. 'Petro-Authoritarianism and Eurasia's New Divides'. *Freedom House: Nations in Transit*. Rowman and Littlefield, 2008. http://www.freedomhouse.hu/images/fdh_galleries/NIT2008/NT-Overview%20Essay%20-final.pdf.

Way, Lucan. 'The Real Causes of the Color Revolutions'. *Journal of Democracy* 19, no. 3 (2008): 56–97.

Way, Lucan, and Steven Levitsky. 'The Dynamics of Autocratic Coercion after the Cold War'. *Communist and Post-Communist Studies* 39, no. 3 (2006): 387–410.
White, Stephen, Elena Korosteleva, and John Lowenhardt, eds. *Postcommunist Belarus*. Lanham, MD: Rowman & Littlefield, 2005.
White, Stephen, and Ian McAllistair. 'Rethinking the "Orange Revolution"'. *Journal of Communist Studies and Transition Politics* 25 (2009): 227–54.
Wilson, Andrew. 'Belarus Between "Coloured Revolution" and "Counter-Revolutionary Technology"'. In *The Geopolitical Place of Belarus in Europe and the World*, ed. Valer Bulhakau, 91–7. Warsaw: Wyzsza Szkola Handlu i Prawa, 2006.
Yeremeyeva, Irina. 'The Impact of the Global Financial Crisis on Belarusian Economy'. PEI Electronic Publications No. 23/2009, Turku School of Economics, Pan-European Institute, Finland, 2009. www.tse.fi/pei.
Zarakhovich, Yury. 'V Belarusi – Revolutsiya?'. *Time*, March 22, 2006. http://www.charter97.org/bel/news/2006/03/22/time.
Zlotnikov, Leonid. 'The Belarusian Economic Miracle – Illusions and Reality'. In *Back from the Cold? The EU and Belarus in 2009*, Chaillot Paper, No. 119, ed. Sabine Fischer, 65–79. Paris: Institute for Security Studies, November 2009.

Oil in the family: managing presidential succession in Azerbaijan

Scott Radnitz

Henry M. Jackson School of International Studies, University of Washington, Seattle, USA

This article argues that Azerbaijan did not display a backlash against the 'colour revolutions' in the post-Soviet space because the primary threat to the regime came from within, and not from below. Thanks to the overlap of power and property in Azerbaijan, the ruling elite's revenues from oil resources, and the failure of international actors to support the opposition, civil society did not pose a major challenge to the regime's dominance during the 'revolutionary' period in the mid-2000s. However, there was a risk that the regime could fragment due to factional in-fighting. President Heydar Aliyev had laboured to consolidate power throughout the 1990s after years of turmoil, and, although Azerbaijan was stable by 2003, his passing did not guarantee a smooth transition. Instead, his successor – his son, Ilham – had to carefully manage rival factions to maintain the political status quo. The article argues that scholars of post-Soviet politics, though usually drawn to formal political opposition as a source of potential change, should also pay attention to the divisions among those in power, and not take a unitary state for granted.

In October 2003, following several days of protests and crackdowns, Azerbaijan's authoritarian regime ended up as the domino that failed to start the others toppling, passing to Georgia the role of 'revolutionary' vanguard in the post-Soviet region. Prior to the October election, a strong case could have been made that Azerbaijan would be likely to experience a peaceful regime change from below. The country, born out of political turmoil (in 1918 as well as 1991), was in the midst of a sensitive transfer of power to a new president. It had a small, motivated community of civil society activists, at least in the capital, Baku, and the party of the incumbent, outgoing President Heydar Aliyev, was to engage in a massive campaign of election fraud to facilitate his son Ilham's rise to power. Yet a 'colour revolution' did not materialize. Azerbaijan smoothly continued on its path toward authoritarian consolidation, and to this day has faced minimal resistance toward that goal.

When surveying the landscape of popular mobilization and the backlash, most scholars have paid attention to the most visible and inspirational of forces for change – civil society organizations, charismatic politicians, youth and ordinary people seeking justice – and framed the issue as a struggle of regime versus opposition.[1] Yet not all countries are the same, and the threats posed to autocrats from below can vary widely. There is not sufficient space here to assess the relative strengths of regimes and oppositions in post-Soviet states in comparative fashion, although I allude to some of those cases. Instead, in this article I use the case of Azerbaijan to argue that the greatest threat to the stability of non-democratic regimes may lie not in organized political opposition but in a challenge from within the regime itself. As such, the conventional objects of analysis of the colour revolutions, that is, civil society actors[2] who are visible, vocal and usually eager to share their aspirations with reporters and researchers, may be less important than the less transparent, informal mechanisms by which an incumbent maintains cohesion within his ruling coalition. In such a milieu, when a moment of opportunity arises at the commanding heights of political power, aggrieved or ambitious elites in the coalition may be tempted to make a bid for power, perhaps using existing oppositions as allies. If the actors who control the levers of state power can reach an agreement – or more precisely, if the president can deter defections and maintain loyalty in the coalition – then the ruler faces a significantly weaker threat.[3] If he cannot, the coalition may be at risk of fragmentation.

A ruler who is able to correctly discern the predominant threats to his power can economize resources to address the most critical threats to his regime without overreacting. In Azerbaijan, the leadership correctly discerned that it faced a greater challenge from the splintering of the ruling coalition than from a popular anti-authoritarian movement – such as occurred in the broader post-Soviet region – and expended resources judiciously to head it off. Thus, what may appear to be an Azeri 'backlash' against wave-like revolutionary forces when viewed in a regional context may be better understood as manifestations of a continuing movement toward authoritarian consolidation in Azerbaijan, which was neither hastened nor retarded by events in Georgia, Ukraine or Kyrgyzstan.

This article analyses Azerbaijan as a case of a pre-empted potential putsch by the shoring up of power internally during a trying period of leadership succession, rather than as an escape from deposition by its (feeble and disorganized) opposition. I first provide relevant background to the lead-up to Azerbaijan's critical 2003 and 2005 elections, detailing the gradual process of state-strengthening and consolidation of power that took place in the 1990s. I then analyse how the incumbent managed the transfer of power to his son and how the heir apparent secured continuity among his father's coterie. Despite the turmoil that followed the two elections, that strategy proved a success, in part thanks to lack of Western pressure and the availability of oil rents. I discuss actions the president's circle took during the period of apparent revolutionary upheaval across post-Soviet space and question whether a causal link can be drawn between regional events and self-serving measures taken by the Aliyev regime. Finally, I use the case of

Azerbaijan as a way to broaden the scope of inquiry into the colour revolutions and backlashes, and to contribute to the study of attempted and failed challenges to authoritarianism more generally.

In the course of researching for this article, in summer 2009 I conducted interviews with 12 Azerbaijani scholars, analysts and activists in Baku. These include longtime observers of domestic politics and several people who have served in the government. The interviews were conducted in Russian or English and lasted 45 to 60 minutes on average. On two occasions I re-interviewed the same source with follow-up questions. Because many of the topics we discussed are sensitive, in this article I refer to sources' professions rather than use their names.

Azerbaijan's quest for stability

The first part of Azerbaijan's first decade as an independent state was spent fighting to defend its territory and attempting to build a state. Unlike the euphoric Baltic States or Ukraine, which emerged from perestroika looking toward a better future, Azerbaijan left the Soviet Union mired in a bloody fratricidal conflict with Armenian secessionists in its autonomous republic Nagorno-Karabakh (1988–1994). By 1992, a nationalist and pro-democracy movement, the Popular Front of Azerbaijan (PFA) and its leader, President Abulfaz Elchibey, were running the country and leading the war effort. As the leading advocates for independence, they enjoyed popular support but they also lacked the experience or organizational skill to channel it effectively into military success. As Azerbaijan continued to suffer significant human and territorial losses and Armenia gained ground, Elchibey faced insurrection from a rogue militia leader. In order to stave off disaster, militarily and politically, Elchibey made the critical decision to invite Heydar Aliyev to the capital as head of parliament. Elchibey later fled and Aliyev engineered a coup to oust him. Aliyev, the country's leading power broker – a former leader of the republic, head of the KGB, and member of the Politburo – ended the country's tentative steps toward democracy but brought about a chance for stability when he became president.

Aliyev, like his Georgian counterpart, Eduard Shevardnadze, who also came to power following years of turmoil, promoted stability over national assertion, and made state-building and regime consolidation the overriding objective of his remaining years in power. Unlike the PFA, a party of liberal intellectuals and nationalists who sought a break with the Soviet past (having based its legitimacy on harkening back to Azerbaijan's short-lived period of democracy and independence earlier in the century),[4] Aliyev utilized the informal networks he had cultivated, and employed the methods he had honed, over a career of service to the Soviet state.[5] Aliyev replaced the ministers of foreign affairs, defense and internal affairs with associates from his past and staffed the corresponding ministries with loyalists. He averted several coup attempts from rogue elements of the security services and removed cabinet members whose allegiances were suspect. He cut Azerbaijan's military losses in Nagorno-Karabakh by agreeing to a cease-fire with Armenia in 1994, and brought about a restoration of state services to relieve hardship at home.[6]

Aliyev brought two critical advantages to the presidency. First was his access to a coterie of people who had been educated and socialized in the same Soviet institutions, to staff the bureaucracy. Unlike the ideological PFA, these officials were pragmatic and competent functionaries who shared a common working language. The second of Aliyev's advantages was the skills he honed over a career in Soviet politics and as head of the KGB, including the ability to anticipate threats and selectively but effectively use repression against his opponents.[7]

Aliyev, together with his brother Jalal and Ramiz Mehdiyev, the head of the presidential administration, held highly sought-after information on personnel and ensured that all transactions were routed through the president's office. Even low-level appointments within ministries had to be approved by the president.[8] Aliyev was assisted by a sophisticated intelligence apparatus that gathered *kompromat* (compromising material) on the officials working under him. As this collection of information was common knowledge, the threat of arrest and expropriation was a strong deterrent to disloyalty or insubordination, and helped ensure the compliance of subordinates. In cases where an official presented a challenge, Aliyev would preemptively strike, as he did in 1995 when the commander of the OMON (Special Forces) apparently planned to stage a coup. A special battalion comprised solely of troops from Aliyev's native region of Nakhichevan – a form of praetorian guard – was called up to defend the president, leading to a shootout that killed the mutineer.[9] Force was similarly used in purported coups in 1996 and 1998. Power remained concentrated around Aliyev until the end of his presidency.

The Aliyev regime ruled according to familiar (Soviet) methods from its inception, but it had to contend with residual pluralism from the PFA period and was forced to abide, at least superficially, by the international norms of democracy that were now hegemonic globally. This was especially the case while Azerbaijan was poor, war-torn, and reliant on Western aid. Azerbaijan held presidential elections in 1993 and 1998, and parliamentary elections in 1995 and 2000 with the participation of opposition parties. A moderately independent media developed in the mid-1990s and non-governmental organizations (NGOs) supported by the West opened in the country. At its peak, Azerbaijan earned a grudging 'partly free' rating from the non-partisan organization Freedom House until 1993 and again from 1997 to 2003, thanks to a tolerable civil liberties score.[10] There was some hope, not completely unfounded, that Azerbaijan could evolve into a pluralistic semi-democratic regime. However, this hope was not borne out.

The opposition to Aliyev was disadvantaged from the beginning. The new Azerbaijan Popular Front Party (APFP), which represented the Baku intelligentsia and absorbed activists from the PFA in 1997, advocated democratic reforms and an alternative to Aliyev's concentration of power. However, lacking funds – in part because the business community was supportive of Aliyev's *Yeni* (New) *Azerbaijan Party* (YAP) – and unable to distribute benefits to potential supporters, the opposition party could not compete well against the regime.[11] In the 1998 presidential elections, Aliyev defeated his opponent Etibar Mamedov 76.1% to 11.6%, although independent counts estimated that the margin of victory was narrower.[12] After the parliamentary elections of 2000, the opposition called a boycott in protest of government-imposed obstacles to its ability to run candidates, but with little discernible effect.

The regime's ability to fend off rivals was strengthened beginning in 1994, when Azerbaijan signed a 30-year production-sharing agreement with 10 of the world's major oil companies to develop fields that had been discovered in the late 1970s and early 1980s. The so-called Contract of the Century greased Azerbaijan's path out of weakness and fragility. Privatizing oil and gas fields to foreign companies rather than to domestic actors ensured that the state would benefit from foreign technical expertise without losing control of how the resulting revenues would be used, unlike in Russia, which privatized to domestic actors.[13] Having a guaranteed source of rents for the foreseeable future made the work of both state-building and regime consolidation far easier. By 2000, oil already comprised over 40% of government revenues.[14] By its 10-year anniversary in 2001, Azerbaijan no longer resembled the war-torn, fragmented and democratizing polity it had been. An increasingly confident, secure regime could throw its weight around domestically and internationally, including bucking Russia by acting as the source country for the Baku-Tbilisi-Ceyhan pipeline, a priority for US foreign policy.[15] With the aid of oil rents, Aliyev loyalists obtained control of privatized assets, ensuring that possession of economic resources would buttress political domination. Sustaining opposition to the ruling elite became even more difficult. By the beginning of Aliyev's second term in 1998, there was little doubt that he had consolidated power.

An inside job

Focusing only on the formal aspects of politics – political parties, legislatures and elections – may be the appropriate approach for understanding the dynamics of political development and change in many countries. However, in a setting where informality predominated, as it did in the Soviet Union, and where democracy was introduced only recently and lacks indigenous roots, a focus on formal institutions may distract from more important features of politics.[16] In Azerbaijan, a salient axis of politics that has the potential to shape major political developments is that of regional affiliation.[17] Internal opposition on the basis of this cleavage was of great concern to Aliyev. It also presented the greatest threat to his son Ilham during the presidential succession, rather than mobilization by civil society, which seemed to be endangering other post-Soviet regimes.

Two factions, representing the Azerbaijani region of Nakhichevan and descendants of immigrants from Armenia (so-called Yeraz, or Yerevan Azeris), respectively, were considered the most influential. Once an independent khanate, Nakhichevan was claimed by both the Armenian and Azeri Soviet Socialist

Republics after the Bolshevik Revolution and ultimately granted autonomous status within the Azeri SSR. Detached from the rest of Azerbaijan, in the post-Soviet era it became an enclave accessible only by air, and its isolation contributed to the development of a distinct identity. Nakhichevani migrants to Baku retained strong ties of solidarity years after resettling[18] and Aliyev, who was born in Nakhichevan, drew from those networks to shore up his regime.[19] These appointees, once in power, utilized their common background to maintain a dominant position within Aliyev's ruling coalition.

The Yeraz also developed a distinct identity. Azeri migrants from Armenia came to Azerbaijan in three waves: 1904–1905 after a series of pogroms, after World War II, and during the war in Nagorno-Karabakh. As a minority living in Armenia, they had developed a sense of self-awareness, which translated into mutual support when many migrated to Baku. Aliyev, whose father had been born in Armenia, also brought representatives of Yeraz into the government as a source of trusted subordinates.[20] Aliyev relied heavily on the loyalty of these two contingents, which in turn were able to block the entry of other factions into the system.

In order to govern, the president balanced between competing factions by remaining above them. As appointees and their subordinates were chosen on the basis of close personal connections to Aliyev, they owed their livelihoods to him and faced uncertain prospects under a different leader. The president stood at the apex of a pyramid in which information and resources flowed upward, and decisions and orders were sent down. Aliyev spent much of his time regulating the distribution of power between factions and defusing potential rivalries before they devolved. When it was announced in 2003 that Aliyev had contracted cancer, the complex system that he had created and nurtured as the basis of Azerbaijan's stability came under threat.

Surviving the succession

Though it may appear inevitable in hindsight, the collapse of a regime as a result of mass mobilization is not a foregone conclusion; many factors must congeal for the opposition to succeed.[21] States possess control over the means of violence, are better equipped than grassroots movements to act collectively and are able to disseminate propaganda on a massive scale. Regimes can thus counter the effectiveness of 'people power' tactics by taking certain measures: cutting off media access to demonstrations, co-opting and selectively harassing members of the opposition, paying the security forces sufficient salaries and cracking down early to deter future activism. Furthermore, states that are capable of subsisting without external aid can endure outside criticism more easily than ones that are dependent. The Aliyev regime had both the means and the will to endure. However, an unanticipated event called into question its apparent resilience.

Before any regional revolutions had occurred (with the exception of Serbia in 2000, though not considered by many a model for Azerbaijan to emulate),[22]

Azerbaijan experienced its first succession in a decade. Heydar Aliyev, who had already suffered a heart attack during the run-up to the 1998 election, prepared for his impending passing by stepping down before the presidential election, leaving his son Ilham to run in his place. He had appointed Ilham prime minister two months earlier, having presciently passed a referendum in 2002 transferring authority, in the case of the president's death, to the prime minister rather than to the speaker of parliament.[23] He had begun grooming his son for the post even earlier by appointing him as the vice-president of the State Oil Company of Azerbaijan (SOCAR) in 1994 and later the head of the National Olympic Committee. This effort to ensure a smooth – and self-serving – transition masked political conflicts taking place behind the scenes.[24] Although the elder Aliyev had managed to suppress conflict between competing factions in his government, there was no way to ensure that elites would remain loyal in conditions of uncertainty during the transfer of power. Most of Heydar's advisors rallied around Ilham, thanks to Heydar's deliberate passing of his torch and the paucity of rival claimants.[25] In 2003, the short time between Aliyev's promotion and the election left little opportunity for his opponents to coalesce around a different candidate. Ilham also reputedly gave personal assurances to his father's officials that he would leave them in their posts and refrain from disrupting their informal power centers.[26] Heydar Aliyev's death was announced on 12 December 2003.

Despite giving assurances, the younger Aliyev faced internal threats. Throughout Heydar Aliyev's tenure, a subset of elites sharing the Yeraz identity had resented the favouritism they perceived Aliyev showed toward Nakhichevanis. Two leaders of this faction, Ali Insanov, who was also the Health Minister, and Farhad Aliyev, the Minister of Economic Development (responsible for privatization), reputedly refused to recognize Aliyev's inheritance and sought a better deal for Yeraz elites.[27] They were arrested in 2005, along with three other government officials and charged with conspiring with exiled oppositionist Rasul Guliyev to launch a coup against the president. Between 2003 and 2006, Aliyev made several less dramatic replacements to the staff he inherited, while leaving in place critical power-brokers, such as his father's confidant, Mehdiyev.[28] The ministers' arrests, though likely on fabricated charges, had a claim to populist legitimacy – like most officials they had become wealthy by virtue of the access their ministerial posts conferred. They were reputed to be unpopular, except by those who relied on them for access to resources.[29] That the arrests took place two weeks prior to the elections suggested that the regime was sending a signal to elites who hoped to use the elections to build an anti-Aliyev bloc.

The 2003 presidential election, while instigating a drama that unfolded behind closed doors, also produced a reaction on the streets. The opposition objected when it was declared that the younger Aliyev had won in the first round with 76.8% of the vote in an election that the Organization for Security and Cooperation in Europe (OSCE) diplomatically stated 'fell short of international standards in several respects'.[30] A coalition of local NGOs conducted a parallel vote count with a limited budget, but it was sufficient to cover 60% of precincts.[31] Its tabulations contradicted the official announcement, coming out instead in favour of opposition candidate Isa Gambar.[32] On the evening the election results were announced, up to 10,000 supporters of Gambar gathered in Azadlig (Freedom) Square in the center of Baku.[33] The government, anticipating opposition protests, deployed soldiers and riot police to the scene, where they proceeded to violently disperse the demonstrators. In the several days following the election, one person was killed by the security forces, over 300 were injured, and 400 were arrested, including Gambar, who was charged with instigating the violence and released almost one month later.[34]

The Aliyev regime deployed rhetoric to defend its actions after the crackdown, arguing to the international community for the need for stability: 'The radical wing of the opposition has again demonstrated its essence. . .Azerbaijan is a strong state and is capable of defending itself. . . .[Opposition] leaders and those who provoked people into acting will be brought to book.'[35] By the time the Georgian revolution occurred, culminating in Shevardnadze's resignation on 23 November, the new Azeri president had dealt with the post-election demonstrations and secured international recognition of his 'victory'.[36]

Several explanations have been offered for the failure of the opposition to effectively challenge the regime despite the ostensibly weak position of the victor. Many claim that the international community, particularly the US, failed to support the opposition, having already decided to throw its weight behind Aliyev in the interests of stability and to preserve Western oil interests.[37] Another argument focuses on the tendency of revolutions to follow regime splintering, noting how the succession from father to son ensured that elites would rally around the chosen heir rather than pursue their individual interests.[38] A different approach highlights the failure of the business community to support opposition demonstrators, since it was not independent of the regime.[39] Finally, there is the fact that the security forces remained loyal to the regime and followed orders to use force against protesters, rather than defect to the opposition as many officers did in Georgia and Ukraine.[40] Each of these explanations reveals an important part of the story, suggesting that Azerbaijan's regime stability was in some sense overdetermined. The upshot was that a potential revolution failed to materialize; instead of undermining the status quo, the election reinforced it.

Backlash or coincidence?

The authors in this special issue, following on arguments about demonstration effects and international diffusion,[41] consider the proposition that non-democratic regimes used various tactics to pre-empt domestic mass protests after observing successful bottom-up challenges in states with otherwise similar characteristics. To confirm the occurrence of an authoritarian backlash, it is necessary to demonstrate, at the very least, that protests in one state were followed by crackdowns in another. Certainly, repression against the opposition was used in Azerbaijan between 2003 and 2005, consistent with this requirement. However, that is not sufficient to support the 'backlash' argument. One must also show that a revolutionary event *caused* a regime to become more repressive than it was before. Unlike other case studies of this special issue, Azerbaijan does not meet this second test. In fact, close attention to the timing of Azerbaijan's major public crackdown on the opposition in 2003 reveals that the causality was reversed; the crackdown *preceded*, rather than *followed*, successful mass mobilization elsewhere. Instead of precipitating a wave of revolutions, Azerbaijan could just as well be seen as the crest of a wave of repression against pro-democracy demonstrations that had begun in China (1989), gained inspiration from Vladimir Putin's emasculating of Russia's opposition, and migrated to Belarus (2001) and Armenia (2003). If we can imagine Azerbaijan establishing a demonstration effect for Georgian activists to absorb, it would be to fear their government, not to challenge it. Yet this example clearly failed to make an impression, as the opposition in Georgia enjoyed more favourable conditions than in Azerbaijan, and took advantage of them.[42] In the aftermath of the 2003 Rose Revolution, the Aliyev regime continued its suppression of civil society, which persisted even after the most intense revolutionary fervour in the region had subsided. The timing of its repressive measures strongly suggests that these moves were not a response to events in Georgia, Ukraine, or Kyrgyzstan, but rather the continuation of a long-term approach to managing the opposition.

Following the Rose Revolution, the Aliyev regime took several measures against civil society and the media, but nothing beyond what it was already doing before 2003. It continued to make life difficult for the opposition by intimidating critics and spreading propaganda through the state-run media. The government detained many journalists in the aftermath of the 2003 demonstrations and temporarily shut down the popular opposition newspaper *Yeni Musavat* in 2004 and 2005.[43] In February 2005, two journalists for the opposition newspaper *Azadlig* were beaten and had compromising material revealed to the public, presumably in revenge for publishing anti-Aliyev material.[44] In March, the editor of a prominent opposition magazine, *Monitor*, Elmar Husseinov, was assassinated.[45] The government also launched a campaign to discredit a nascent youth movement, *Yeni Fikir*, which had been emulating Georgia's *Kmara* and Ukraine's *Pora*.[46]

Aliyev responded to the wave of regime change in the region rhetorically as well, making the case that evolution, not revolution, would be the appropriate mode of change, as had other anxious leaders in the region.[47] He tried to discredit the opposition and its tactics before the 2005 parliamentary election, saying, 'It is a deliberate attempt of the opposition to create violence, to be beaten by police, and then to demonstrate that there's no democracy in Azerbaijan...Their goal became to be shown by various TV channels and to find their names in the world press and to try to present Azerbaijan as a country where freedom of assembly is not provided.'[48] He also argued that Azerbaijan's booming economy – growing at an astounding rate of 26.5% in 2005 – made it less susceptible to a revolution than Georgia or Ukraine.[49] The government instructed its diplomats abroad to condemn the revolutions at every turn.[50]

The 2005 parliamentary elections were a second chance for Aliyev's opponents to challenge the regime, this time using the revolutionary template. Although exit polls provided no smoking gun proving fraud, the opposition and foreign observers documented pervasive falsification in favour of the ruling YAP.[51] The opposition, led by Kerimli, staged a sit-in in Baku.[52] As in 2003, a short but brutal crackdown put an end to street demonstrations, preventing a drawn-out struggle in which the opposition could occupy the square, generate media attention and encourage ordinary people to join. YAP garnered 56 of 125 seats in parliament, to the opposition's eight.[53] A large number of MPs who won as independent candidates were supporters of Aliyev, thus giving the president a comfortable majority in parliament. In protest, the opposition MPs who won their elections rejected the results and refused to accept their seats.[54]

After the 2005 elections, the government continued to constrain civil society – even after the revolutionary wave had subsided and other autocracies were see-mingly loosening restrictions they had imposed in the period of concern. In 2007, the government announced the creation of a 'Council for State Support of NGOs', which would rival foreign sources by providing grants to support – and co-opt – domestic NGOs. It awarded about $2 million in 2008 and $2.5 million in 2009.[55] In 2007, a critical reporter at *Zerkalo* was arrested and also charged with slander against victims of the Karabakh conflict, although his real sin appeared to be criticizing the Aliyev regime. The same year, Ganimat Zahidov, the editor of *Azadlig* who had been set up in 2005, was arrested for 'hooliganism' and sentenced to four years in prison.[56] In 2009, parliament proposed a bill which would have limited foreign funding of NGOs, and required NGOs to set up branches in one-third of the regions of the country. It withdrew the most stringent parts of the proposal only after a barrage of international criticism. In July 2009, two young bloggers who had produced a video mocking President Aliyev and posted it on YouTube were arrested and charged with 'hooliganism'. A 2010 law prohibited journalists from taking images of people without their permission.[57] These recent moves against civil society evince a pattern of continuous harassment and co-optation even though the regime was already quite secure, and not a pointed crackdown following the Rose Revolution.

The secrets of its success

Ultimately, the absence of a serious threat from below, obviating the need for a 'backlash', can be attributed to the security of Azerbaijan's regime, a surprising outcome given its turbulent early years of independence. As the above argument demonstrates, the foremost medium-term factor ensuring its security was the consolidation of the ruling elite, which shared common methods of governing and benefitted materially from its control of the state. This gave it a stake in preser-ving the status quo, including supporting the president, which also meant that further democratic and economic reforms were not in its interests. The principal actors on Aliyev's team, once installed, remained in place for over a decade, including Ramiz Mehdiyev (1994–present); Ramil Usubov, minister of internal affairs (1994–present); Namik Abbasov, minister of national security (1994–2004); Safar Abiyev, minister of defence (1995–present); and Natik Aliyev, head of SOCAR (1993–2005, until his promotion to minister of industry and energy).[58] The stabilization of the cadre and the demonstrative closing of ranks around the president in the mid-1990s provided stability, deterred challengers and created barriers for the liberal opposition to make inroads.[59]

The second factor that enabled the ruling elite to maintain power was the concentration of economic resources in the regime's hands. Although Azerbaijan undertook moderate economic reforms in the early 1990s, as the Aliyev regime consolidated power it also re-established partial state control over the economy.[60] As Azerbaijan gradually came to resemble a 'petrostate', oil revenues distorted the economy by concentrating economic growth at the top and reducing the space for private commerce. This change placed a greater amount of resources at the disposal of the regime to distribute as patronage, which further enabled it to maintain political control.[61] The oil sector also provided the putative middle class and ambitious young people with lucrative employment opportunities and a stake in preserving the system, reducing the incentive to engage in pro-democracy activism.

At the same time, the shrinking share of the economy in private hands precluded the emergence of a business elite autonomous of the regime – a potential ally of the opposition in a bottom-up challenge and a critical component of Georgia, Ukraine and Kyrgyzstan's revolutions.[62] Wealthy elites who did not support the regime were considered threats. Some, like the ultra-wealthy Rasul Guliyev, who was once head of the state oil refinery, were forced into exile.[63]

A third advantage for the Aliyev regime was the tacit yet undeniable support it received from the West. Whereas the US spent $41 million on support for civil society in Serbia and $65 million in Ukraine in the years immediately preceding their revolutions,[64] mostly through quasi-NGOs such as the National Democratic Institute (NDI) and International Republican Institute (IRI), it spent only a small fraction of that in Azerbaijan. Azerbaijan, despite its increasingly undemocratic trajectory, avoided much of the criticism from the West directed at authoritarian states such as Belarus and Uzbekistan.[65] As the source point of one million barrels of oil per day flowing to Europe, the site of the largest energy contract signed since the end of the Cold War, and an ally sharing the West's goal of reducing Russia's influence in Eurasia, Azerbaijan was accorded special status that allowed it to avoid criticism.[66] When the regime was caught falsifying election results in its favour – twice – it was rebuked by the OSCE but suffered only a mild reproach from individual Western governments. The opposition, no less sincere or motivated than the opposition in Georgia, did not enjoy the same level of support from abroad. And with no hope of joining the European Union or NATO, the external tug that stimulated reform in the Baltic states, Ukraine and Georgia, was barely felt in Azerbaijan.[67]

The consolidation of power around a small number of people eventually generated its own countervailing forces in the form of resentment by those excluded from the system, but that was not sufficient to cause a revolution. Ordinary citizens developed justifiably burning grievances in response to widespread corruption and the low quality of public services despite the immense wealth of their country. People in rural areas lack clean water and suffer from high unemployment, leading many to migrate abroad in search of work, while 'oligarchs' drive around Baku in shiny Mercedes Benzes and invest in multi-million-dollar condominiums overlooking the Caspian Sea. In the 2003 and 2005 elections, voters expressed their dissatisfaction at an unjust system, but to little avail. Authoritarian regimes can survive long after they lose popular support. The Aliyev regime controls the instruments of coercion, the media and the revenues from oil with which to buy off potential rivals. Ordinary citizens face a collective action problem in ordinary situations, but the barriers are much more severe in the face of such an overwhelming imbalance of resources. A succession is one occasion that might reveal a split within the regime, giving opposition actors a chance to contest for power with the help of elite allies, but the Aliyev family endured. The elder Aliyev's careful preparation and skillful management of personnel ensured that his regime would survive its greatest challenge after his death and preserve his legacy.

The importance of these factors can be seen in the contrary case of Georgia. There, although Shevardnadze's restoration brought a modicum of stability to a country wracked by civil war, the regime was never able to centralize power and weaken rivals to the same extent as Aliyev. In part because of the greater fragmentation of the state, Shevardnadze was forced to cut more deals and cede more authority to other actors in the early years of his reign. Although he gradually restored the coercive power of the state, he was unable to reestablish control over critical parts of the economy, which enabled actors outside his coalition (and potential opponents) to wield power autonomous of the regime. When opposition politicians – who had once served under Shevardnadze – capitalized on mass grievances by mobilizing crowds to protest, the president watched as his coalition fragmented and his allies turned against him.[68]

Lessons for authoritarian backlash: states and regimes

In analysing post-Soviet states, it is useful to understand how their institutional inheritances shape their politics, in ways that differ fundamentally from the West European states that often act as the baseline for analysis in political science. Where perestroika-era reformers failed to gain or hold onto power following the Soviet collapse, the new order would operate much like the old one, only with Soviet-era elites now enjoying the trappings of statehood. These leaders built states and ruling coalitions by tapping into their personal and professional networks, and employed informal means to regulate power. Official posts were divided according to the logic of intra-elite bargaining, as a result of which the beneficiaries used the bureaucracy to pursue their own interests with little accountability to society. Analysis of how incumbents respond to the threat of mobilization from below must keep in mind the logic according to which such a state functions. Precedents from consolidated democracies are likely to be misleading at best.

Azerbaijan's response to bottom-up demands for change in the region cannot be understood in isolation from the construction of the Azeri state. Aliyev's strengthening of the state from 1993 to 2003 involved building a coalition of loyalists and marginalizing forces outside the coalition. This consolidation of power made the regime more vulnerable to threats from inside the state than outside it. If enough elites rival to either of the Aliyevs were to connive against him, they could launch a coup. The challenge for the younger Aliyev when Heydar became ill was to prevent defection by elites in the coalition who were at risk of mobilizing against him.[69] Ilham, having secured the support of critical allies, made a pre-emptive move against potential challengers. Subsequently, he became confident enough to replace parts of his father's team with members of his own network.

As this article has demonstrated, Azerbaijan's reaction to the colour revolutions cannot be considered a backlash. This is not to say it was permissive of opposition – on the contrary, the regime cracked down on protests even *before* Georgia's Rose Revolution took place. But once the 'wave' began, the regime was well positioned: it enjoyed a lopsided balance of power and faced a weak civil society. Insofar as NGOs were the driving force behind other revolutions – a proposition still being debated[70] – in Azerbaijan they did not pose a serious threat. The nature of the Azerbaijani state meant that the key to avoiding an outcome remotely like Georgia's – or a quieter, less 'democratic' transfer of power by coup – was to get its house in order. The Alievs did not need to speculate on what Shevardnadze should have done to confront NDI, the Soros Foundation, or *Kmara*, but could instead emulate Nursultan Nazarbaev in Kazakhstan, who had so reduced the space for autonomous citizen activity that he could be confident of surviving a rare protest outbreak. The Aliyevs were then free to focus on the more serious task – managing power among acquisitive and jealous elites in their ruling coalitions, which, while sometimes fractious, also served as efficient vehicles for ensuring the durability of the regime.[71]

Notes

1. For example, Åslund and McFaul, *Revolution in Orange*; Bunce and Wolchik, *Defeating Authoritarian Leaders*.
2. Ibid.
3. Bueno de Mesquita et al., *The Logic of Political Survival*; Slater, *Ordering Power*.
4. Azerbaijan was independent between 1918 and 1921, after which it was forcibly absorbed into the Soviet Union.
5. Willerton, *Patronage and Politics*, 194–222.
6. Since then, Armenia has occupied all of Nagorno-Karabakh and 14% of Azerbaijan's territory.
7. Willerton, *Patronage and Politics*.
8. Author's interview with Analyst, Baku, 24 July 2009; Politician, 14 August 2009. Names of sources are kept confidential for safety reasons.

9. Author's interviews with Analyst, Baku, 24 July 2009; Academic II, Baku, 5 August 2009.
10. http://www.freedomhouse.org/template.cfm?page=439. It also hovered on the border between 'anocracy' and 'autocracy' until 1998 according to the Polity Database. See http://www.systemicpeace.org/polity/aze2.htm.
11. Freizer, 'Dynasty and Democracy'; Alieva, 'Azerbaijan's Frustrating Elections'.
12. Cornell, 'Democratization Falters'.
13. Luong and Weinthal, 'Rethinking the Resource Curse'.
14. Wakeman-Linn, Mathieu, and van Selm, 'Oil Funds'. The country was projected to earn $160 billion from the contract by 2025. Schleifer, 'Azerbaijan Oil'.
15. Ismailzade and Rosner, *Russia's Energy Interests*, 22.
16. Ledeneva, *How Russia Really Works*.
17. Gusseynov, 'Aliev posle Aliyeva'; International Crisis Group, 'Azerbaijan: Turning'.
18. Fatullaev, 'Odna golova'; Swietochowski, 'Azerbaijan: Perspectives', 421; author's interviews in Baku: Analyst, 24 July 2009; Academic, 30 July 2009; Academic II, 5 August 2009; Journalist, 10 August 2009.
19. Gusseynov, 'Aliev posle Aliyeva'; Smirnov, 'Azerbaijan: The Transfer of Power'.
20. Gusseynov, 'Aliev posle Aliyeva'; International Crisis Group, 'Azerbaijan: Turning', 9; author's interviews with Politician, 20 July 2009; Analyst, 24 July 2009, Academic, 30 July 2009; Academic II, 5 August 2009; Journalist, 10 August 2009.
21. For some of these conditions, see McFaul, 'Transitions from Postcommunism'.
22. Beissinger, 'Structure and Example'; Way, 'Real Causes'.
23. Valiyev, 'Referendum in Azerbaijan'.
24. Data for the following section comes from interviews conducted by the author in Baku in July and August 2009 with journalists, academics, former politicians and independent analysts.
25. Hale, 'Regime Cycles'.
26. Author's interview, Journalist, Baku, 21 July 2009.
27. Sabarskiy, 'Okhota za prezidenta'.
28. The foreign minister was made ambassador to Poland, the speaker of parliament resigned, and the ministers of Communication and Youth were fired. Author's interview with Politician, Baku, 20 July 2009.
29. Peuch, 'Azerbaijan: Government in Control'; International Crisis Group, 'Azerbaijan's 2005 Elections', 10; author's interview with Analyst II, 12 August 2009.
30. OSCE, *International Election Observation Mission*.
31. Author's interview with NGO Leader, Baku, 6 August 2009.
32. Trilling and Mielnikiewicz, 'Unrest Rocks Baku'.
33. Valiyev, 'Parliamentary Elections in Azerbaijan', 21.
34. Human Rights Watch, *Crushing Dissent*.
35. 'Crackdown Deepens'.
36. Human Rights Watch, *Crushing Dissent*.
37. For example, Alieva, 'Azerbaijan's Frustrating Elections'. The fact that Heydar Aliyev was being treated in a Cleveland hospital during the election lent some support to this contention.
38. Hale, 'Regime Cycles'.
39. Radnitz, 'The Color of Money'.
40. D'Anieri, 'Explaining the Success'; Way, 'Real Causes'.
41. Elkins and Simmons, 'On Waves'.
42. Beissinger, 'Structure and Example'; Bunce and Wolchik, *Defeating Authoritarian Leaders*.
43. Committee to Protect Journalists, 'Cases 2004'.
44. Nazli, *Nations in Transit 2006*, 14.

45. The magazine was rumoured to have damaging information about the first lady. Author's interview with NGO Leader, Baku, 6 August 2009. Suspects living in Georgia were charged but never captured.
46. Valiyev, 'Parliamentary Elections in Azerbaijan', 24–5.
47. Author's interview with NGO Activist, Baku, 20 July 2009; Saudabayev 'The Kazakh Way.'
48. Holley, 'No Revolution Coming'.
49. Ibid.; http://data.un.org/CountryProfile.aspx?crName=Azerbaijan.
50. Author's interview with NGO Activist, Baku, 20 July, 2009.
51. Chivers, 'Crowd Protests Fraud'.
52. Socor, 'Kerimli Battle-Cry'.
53. Alieva, 'Azerbaijan's Frustrating Elections'.
54. Nichol, 'Azerbaijan's 2005 Legislative Election'; Abbasov and Muradova, 'New Azerbaijani Parliament Convenes'.
55. Human Rights House Network, 'Azerbaijan: Proposed Amendments to NGO Law'.
56. Yanusik, 'The Right Tool'.
57. Kazimov, 'New Azeri Law'.
58. The ability of these principals to bring about stability was aided by the fact that their authority extended back to the previous regime. For example, Mehdiyev had been in charge of ideology for the Azeri Communist Party, Usubov had been deputy chief of Internal Affairs in Nagorno-Karabakh and Minister of Internal Affairs in Nakhichevan in the 1980s, and Abbasov had been deputy chairman of the KGB in Azerbaijan. I thank an anonymous reviewer for pointing this out.
59. Levitsky and Way make a similar argument to account for the survival and demise of other post-Soviet regimes. See Levitsky and Way, *Competitive Authoritarianism.*
60. '...access to resources runs through the state, which functions as a network for the informal distribution of income. Private businesses exist, but the ruling clique keeps them dependent in ways that stop them from backing opposition movements.' Alieva, 'Azerbaijan's Frustrating Elections', 148.
61. Alieva, 'Azerbaijan's Frustrating Elections', 152.
62. Radnitz, 'The Color of Money'; Radnitz, *Weapons of the Wealthy.*
63. International Crisis Group, 'Azerbaijan: Turning'.
64. Beissinger, 'Promoting Democracy'.
65. International Crisis Group, 'Azerbaijan's 2005 Elections', 17.
66. *Azeri Times,* 'In 2010 Forecasts on Oil'.
67. Levitsky and Way, 'International Linkage'.
68. See Fairbanks, 'Georgia's Rose Revolution'; Wheatley, *Georgia from National Awakening.* On the dynamics of elite defection, see Hale, 'Democracy or Autocracy'.
69. Hale, 'Regime Cycles'.
70. Way, 'Real Causes'; Bunce and Wolchik, *Defeating Authoritarian Leaders.*
71. Saidazimova, 'Uzbekistan'; Kimmage, 'Kazakhstan'.

Notes on contributor

Scott Radnitz is Assistant Professor of International Studies at the University of Washington. His research deals with authoritarian politics, informal networks and identity, with an emphasis on Central Asia and the Caucasus. His book, *Weapons of the Wealthy: Predatory Regimes and Elite-led Protests in Central Asia,* was published by Cornell University Press in 2010. His articles have appeared in journals including *Comparative Politics, Comparative Political Studies, Journal of Democracy, Nationalities Papers,* and *Europe-Asia Studies.*

Bibliography

Abbasov Rufat, and Mina Muradova. 'New Azerbaijani Parliament Convenes, but Opposition Stays Away'. *EurasiaNet*, October 31, 2005. http://www.eurasianet.org/azerbaijan/news/parliament_20051202.html.

Alieva, Leila. 'Azerbaijan's Frustrating Elections'. *Journal of Democracy* 17 (2006): 147–60.

Åslund, Anders, and Michael McFaul. *Revolution in Orange: The Origins of Ukraine's Democratic Breakthrough*. Washington, DC: Carnegie Endowment, 2006.

Beissinger, Mark R. 'Promoting Democracy: Is Exporting Revolution a Constructive Strategy?'. *Dissent* 53 (2006): 84–9.

Beissinger, Mark R. 'Structure and Example in Modular Political Phenomena: The Diffusion of Bulldozer/Rose/Orange/Tulip Revolutions'. *Perspectives on Politics* 5 (2007): 259–76.

Bueno de Mesquita, Bruce, Alastair Smith, Randolph M. Siverson, and James D. Morrow. *The Logic of Political Survival*. Cambridge, MA: MIT Press, 2005.

Bunce, Valerie, and Sharon Wolchik. *Defeating Authoritarian Leaders in Postcommunist Countries*. New York: Cambridge University Press, 2011.

Chivers, C.J. 'Crowd Protests Fraud in Azerbaijan Vote'. *New York Times*, November 10, 2005.

Committee to Protect Journalists. 2004 'Cases 2004: Europe and Central Asia: Azerbaijan'. http://www.cpj.org/cases04/europe_cases04/azer.html.

Cornell, Svante. 'Democratization Falters in Azerbaijan'. *Journal of Democracy* 12 (2001): 118–31.

'Crackdown Deepens in Azerbaijan as Schism Hits International Monitors'. *EurasiaNet*, October 20, 2003. http://www.eurasianet.org/departments/insight/articles/eav102003a.shtml.

D'Anieri, Paul. 'Explaining the Success and Failure of Post-communist Revolutions'. *Communist and Post-Communist Studies* 39 (2006): 331–50.

Elkins, Zachary, and Beth Simmons. 'On Waves, Clusters and Diffusion: A Conceptual Framework'. *Annals of the American Academy of Political and Social Science* 598 (2005): 33–51.

Fairbanks, Charles H. 'Georgia's Rose Revolution'. *Journal of Democracy* 15 (2004): 110–24.

Fatullaev, Eynulla. 'Odna golova – khorosho, a dve – plokho'. *Monitor (Azerbaijan)*, January, 21, 2003.

Freizer, Sabine. 'Dynasty and Democracy in Azerbaijan'. *Open Democracy*, December 5, 2003. http://www.opendemocracy.net/democracy-protest/article_1626.jsp.

Gusseynov, Vagif. 'Aliyev posle Aliyeva: nasledovanie vlasti kak sposob yeye uderjaniya'. *Nezavisimaya Gazeta*, March 19, 2004.

Hale, Henry E. 'Democracy or Autocracy on the March? The Colored Revolutions as Normal Dynamics of Patronal Presidentialism'. *Communist and Post-Communist Studies* 39 (2006): 305–29.

Hale, Henry E. 'Regime Cycles: Democracy, Autocracy, and Revolution in Post-Soviet Eurasia'. *World Politics* 58 (2005): 133–65.

Holley, David. 'No Revolution Coming, Azerbaijani Leader Says'. *Los Angeles Times*, October 19, 2005.

Human Rights House Network. 'Azerbaijan: Proposed Amendments to NGO Law Will Eliminate NGOs', June 12, 2009. http://humanrightshouse.org/Articles/11044.html.

Human Rights Watch. *Crushing Dissent: Repression, Violence and Azerbaijan's Elections*, January 22, 2004. http://www.hrw.org/en/node/12183/section/1.

'In 2010 Forecasts on Oil and Gas Production Confirmed in Azerbaijan'. *Azeri Times*, January 29, 2010.

International Crisis Group. 'Azerbaijan: Turning Over a New Leaf?'. May 13, 2004.

International Crisis Group. 'Azerbaijan's 2005 Elections: Lost Opportunity'. November 21, 2005.

Ismailzade, Fariz, and Kevin Rosner. *Russia's Energy Interests in Azerbaijan*. London: GMB Publishing Ltd, 2006.

Kazimov, Seymur. 'New Azeri Law Enrages Journalists'. *Institute of War and Peace Reporting*, February 19, 2010. http://iwpr.net/report-news/new-azeri-law-enrages-journalists.

Kimmage, Daniel. 'Kazakhstan: A Shaken System'. *Radio Free Europe/Radio Liberty*, March 3, 2006. http://www.rferl.org/content/article/1066325.html.

Ledeneva, Alena V. *How Russia Really Works*. Ithaca, NY: Cornell University Press, 2006.

Levitsky, Steven, and Lucan A. Way. *Competitive Authoritarianism: Hybrid Regimes after the Cold War*. New York: Cambridge University Press, 2010.

Levitsky, Steven, and Lucan Way. 'International Linkage and Democratization'. *Journal of Democracy* 16 (2005): 20–34.

Luong, Pauline Jones, and Erika Weinthal. 'Rethinking the Resource Curse: Ownership Structure, Institutional Capacity, and Domestic Constraints'. *Annual Review of Political Science* 9 (2006): 241–63.

McFaul, Michael. 'Transitions from Postcommunism'. *Journal of Democracy* 16 (2005): 5–19.

Nazli, Kaan. *Nations in Transit 2006: Azerbaijan*. Washington, DC: Freedom House, 2006.

Nichol, Jim. 'Azerbaijan's 2005 Legislative Election: Outcome and Implications for U.S. Interests'. *Congressional Research Service*, November 30, 2005.

Organization for Security and Cooperation in Europe (OSCE). *International Election Observation Mission, Presidential Election, Republic of Azerbaijan, Statement of Preliminary Findings and Conclusions*. October 15, 2003.

Peuch, Jean-Christophe. 'Azerbaijan: Government in Control as Opposition Falls Behind'. *Radio Free Europe/Radio Liberty*, October 24, 2005. http://www.rferl.org/content/article/1062357.html.

Radnitz, Scott. 'The Color of Money: Privatization, Economic Dispersion and the Post-Soviet "Revolutions"'. *Comparative Politics* 43 (2010): 127–46.

Radnitz, Scott. *Weapons of the Wealthy: Predatory Regimes and Elite-Led Protests in Central Asia*. Ithaca, NY: Cornell University Press, 2010.

Sabarskiy, Elnur. 'Okhota za prezidenta'. *Monitor (Azerbaijan)*, March 13, 2004.

Saidazimova, Gulnoza. 'Uzbekistan: Islam Karimov vs. the Clans'. *EurasiaNet*, April 23, 2005. http://www.rferl.org/content/article/1058611.html.

Saudabayev, Kanat. 'The Kazakh Way to Democracy: Evolution, Not Revolution'. *Kazakhstan's Echo*, November 30, 2005. http://prosites-kazakhembus.homestead.com/echo22.html.

Schleifer, Yigal. 'Azerbaijan Oil: A Mixed Blessing'. *Christian Science Monitor*, December 30, 2005.

Slater, Dan. *Ordering Power: Contentious Politics and Authoritarian Leviathans in Southeast Asia*. New York: Cambridge University Press, 2010.

Smirnov, Sergei. 'Azerbaijan: The Transfer of Power'. *Central Asia and the Caucasus* 25 (2004).

Socor, Vladimir. 'Kerimli Battle-Cry Sparks Melee in Baku'. *Eurasia Daily Monitor*, November 28, 2005.

Swietochowski, Tadeusz. 'Azerbaijan: Perspectives from the Crossroads'. *Central Asian Survey* 18 (1999): 419–44.

Trilling, David, and Justyna Mielnikiewicz. 'Unrest Rocks Baku as Opposition Protests Azerbaijani Election Results'. *EurasiaNet*, October 16, 2003. http://www.eurasianet.org/departments/insight/articles/eav101603.shtml.

Valiyev, Anar. 'Referendum in Azerbaijan: Next Victory of the Azeri President'. *Central Asia-Caucasus Analyst*, September 11, 2002.

Valiyev, Anar M. 'Parliamentary Elections in Azerbaijan: A Failed Revolution'. *Problems of Post-Communism* 53 (2006): 17–35.

Wakeman-Linn, John, Paul Mathieu, and Bert van Selm. 'Oil Funds and Revenue Management in Transition Economies: The Cases of Azerbaijan and Kazakhstan'. *Working Paper, Earth Institute*. New York: Columbia University, 2003.

Way, Lucan A. 'The Real Causes of the Color Revolutions'. *Journal of Democracy* 19 (2008): 55–69.

Wheatley, Jonathan. *Georgia from National Awakening to Rose Revolution: Delayed Transition in the Former Soviet Union*. Aldershot: Ashgate, 2005.

Willerton, John P. *Patronage and Politics in the USSR*. New York: Cambridge University Press, 1992.

Yanusik, Alyaksandr. 'The Right Tool for the Job'. *Transitions Online*, November 9, 2009.

Coloured by revolution: the political economy of autocratic stability in Uzbekistan

Jennifer Murtazashvili

Graduate School of Public and International Affairs, University of Pittsburgh, PA, USA

Uzbekistan contains all the ingredients that observers have long argued would lead to not only regime change but civil war: economic, political and religious repression. Despite the presence of these factors, the autocratic regime in Uzbekistan has remained remarkably stable in the face of revolutions in neighbouring countries. This article suggests three complementary reasons why the regime has remained firm as others crumbled around it, including relatively strong economic performance, state capacity to repress revolutionary aspirations and government co-optation of local institutions. Understanding autocratic stability requires that we move beyond the 'agency-structure' debates that pervade the literature on post-communist institutional development toward a more encompassing explanation that recognizes how institutional and structural factors both liberate and constrain individual choices.

Introduction

The past 20 years have reminded us that revolutions are not 'dead'.[1] The coloured revolutions appeared to alter the political landscape in several post-communist countries at the dawn of the twenty-first century. Despite significant scholarly attention explaining *why* coloured revolutions occurred,[2] there has been less attention to states where regime change has *not* occurred. Historically, revolutions are such rare events with such stunning impact they inevitably receive extraordinary attention.[3] However, revolutions leading to regime change have seemingly become common place in the post-Soviet sphere: political mobilization has led to regime change in the vast majority of post-communist states since independence. The true anomaly in the post-Soviet sphere, it seems, is authoritarian stability, not revolution.

Instead of exploring the causes of political change or authoritarian reversals, this article investigates sources of political *stability* to understand why Uzbekistan has avoided political change since gaining independence in 1991 amid a sea of change in similarly repressive regimes. Failure to consider reasons that contribute to autocratic stability suggests a fundamental gap in our understanding of post-Soviet as well as authoritarian politics. With few exceptions, explanations of political stability and authoritarian outcomes in Uzbekistan have focused over-whelmingly on a single political variable: the willingness of a state to use coercive authority ruthlessly.[4] While use of repression is undeniably an important means used by governments to consolidate authority, the Uzbek government's reliance on economic policy and other incentives has not received nearly as much attention in studies of regime stability. President Islom Karimov's government, which has ruled Uzbekistan since independence in 1991, has expanded the capacity of the state to engage in repression, but has also used its capacity to distribute economic and social benefits to its population. The contribution in this article is to consider explicitly the role of economic and social incentives, along with the capacity to repress, as sources of authoritarian quiescence. Understanding the multi-dimensional aspects of state capacity in Uzbekistan helps to shed light on why the regime has succeeded to remain in power. By looking beyond repression as a means to explain stability, the incentive-based explanation provided here that relies on tools of political economy helps us understand that state capacity in Uzbekistan may be far greater than many analysts have acknowledged.

Uzbekistan is an important case to study because it has been one of the most stable authoritarian regimes in the world. It has maintained its stability as most other regimes in the former Soviet Union have undergone some kind of funda-mental regime change.[5] In particular, the Karimov government has not engaged in significant economic or political liberalization. Karimov, who has refused to allow competitive elections or meaningful political opposition, is one of the few leaders in the post-Soviet sphere who has not succumbed to the temptation of competitive authoritarianism as a means to gain legitimacy with the international community or from his own people. Economic liberalization has also lagged behind many of the post-Soviet successor states.[6] Despite this lack of economic or political liberalization the government has not weakened. Since 1991, the government has actually increased its grasp on some sectors of the economy. For example, some have argued that the number of state-owned collective farms in Uzbekistan has *grown* since independence.[7]

Stability has been the self-professed goal of the Karimov regime. The Uzbek term *barqarorliq* ('stability') appears on slogans on streets and in nearly every pre-sidential speech and official statement.[8] While the regime seems to have success-fully pursued this singular objective, this article considers the puzzle of how Karimov has maintained authoritarian control over the past 20 years. The expla-nation here emphasizes the role of diverse policy tools, including economic and social policy, which promote regime stability. In particular, I argue that the regime has not just relied on tools of repression, but has employed a well thought out policy of economic redistribution, state subsidies and social policies that has enabled it to stay in power.

In relation to other former Soviet Union states, the political science and economics literature regarding Uzbekistan is among the most limited.[9] It is likely this is due to the fact that the authoritarian government has made it difficult for researchers to visit,[10] and as a result it is difficult to collect primary data in the country. The single case study presented here, therefore, relies on existing secondary literature on Uzbekistan, as there are very few alternatives at the present time.

The article is organized as follows. In the next section, I analyse dominant explanations of political change in the former Soviet Union. The third section explores political economy explanations of authoritarian regimes to help explain stability in Uzbekistan. Such an approach is arguably more insightful for understanding the case of Uzbekistan than using dominant approaches which emphasize either social movements or social conflict. A political economy approach is particularly relevant because it considers repression (sticks) as well as economic inducements (carrots), and as such, it sheds light on other sources of regime stability that have remained neglected in the larger literature on Uzbekistan. Therefore, the fourth section empirically details what I term the political economy of authoritarianism in Uzbekistan by describing how public policies across three specific sectors have helped the government avert political change. The final section summarizes the argument.

Explanations for autocratic continuity and change

The collapse of the Soviet Union suggested an inevitable transition toward democracy.[11] This forecast, however, was inaccurate for Uzbekistan. The country is neither a democratizing country, nor is it a consolidating authoritarian regime as it has *always* maintained strong levels of authoritarianism. Uzbekistan is what Steven Levitsky describes as a 'full authoritarian regime: a regime in which no viable channels exist for opposition to contest legally for executive power'.[12]

Social scientists eventually realized that the collapse of the Soviet Union would not lead all of its former members on a journey to democracy. Henry Hale has noted the emergence of three subsequent schools of thought which reflect diverse political trajectories in former Soviet States.[13] One group has argued that more attention should be paid to authoritarian relapses.[14] A second group has focused on why some countries have been more successful in consolidating democracy.[15] And a third group explored 'hybrid regimes' that did not appear to be on a fixed path toward either authoritarianism or democracy.[16]

While these categories better reflect a diversity of experience in former Soviet states, the typology is incomplete. In particular, Uzbekistan does not fit nicely into any one of these categories: it never transitioned toward or away from democracy, nor has it flirted with hybrid arrangements: it has remained steadfastly authoritarian in the 20 years since it gained independence. We can describe this state of affairs as authoritarian resilience.

There are several perspectives that provide insight into authoritarian resilience in Uzbekistan. The first and perhaps most vocal perspective is offered by 'conflictologists', who view Uzbekistan as a 'failing' or 'weak state' due to the levels of effort with which the government is willing oppress potential opponents.[17] This perspective defines state weakness by sole reliance on coercion to maintain power. An implicit assumption in this approach is that revolutionary backlash is mechanically related to repression: individuals will rebel against repressive tactics by the state.[18] For example, shortly after the government brutally suppressed protests during the 2005 Andijon Uprising in Uzbekistan's eastern Ferghana Valley, the International Crisis Group wrote that 'anger and frustration with the regime are tangible everywhere in Uzbekistan, and the explosion point is dangerously near'.[19] In this view, repression is the fuel that feeds uprisings against authoritarian regimes.

Prior to 11 September 2001, books such as Ahmed Rashid's *Jihad*[20] and the Centre for Preventive Conflict's *Calming the Ferghana Valley,*[21] shaped popular and policy discourse on Uzbekistan – especially in policy circles. Both volumes focused on the potential for violent religious conflict in the region predicting that hungry masses, and in particular restless youth, would turn to radical Islam to address growing grievances. Given the tendency of the Karimov regime to repress Islamist movements,[22] growing citizen support of such groups would only lead to confrontation with the state. Predictions of the demise of the Karimov regime permeated academic and popular literature on Uzbekistan.[23] The Andijon uprising, for instance, featured many elements conflict scholars have long pointed out to be a toxic mix: Islam, the densely populated and Ferghana Valley, border incursions into Kyrgyzstan and anti-government protests. Yet the regime endured the Andijon uprising as well as other threats to its existence.

Surprisingly, conflict-oriented assessments of Uzbekistan rarely consider economic performance. When they do consider economic conditions, the sources of their data appear to be based on anecdotal evidence rather than on actual economic data, leading to a misrepresentation of the economic environment. Consider the following description of Uzbekistan from the *Foreign Policy and Fund for Peace,* The Failed States Index 2007:

> Uzbekistan's government continues to repress its people and to commit gross human rights violations, with no signs of letting up. Such tactics deter foreign investment in an already suffering economy. Economic reforms are needed, along with a significant effort to decrease corruption, in order to achieve high and sustainable growth and to lessen the uneven development which has been exacerbated by tight economic controls. Uzbekistan has the potential to improve its economy due to its natural resources, but the current government's repressive tactics and lack of economic reform, if not addressed, will continue to be an impediment to growth and long-term stability.[24]

Similarly, Rashid argues that violence in Central Asia is unavoidable as: 'rising levels of poverty and unemployment ... are now major concerns for the regime, but it appears to be doing little to tackle the issue ... 60 per cent of the population is now under 25 years old. These young people are jobless, restless, and hungry, and their numbers are growing'.[25] As a result of hunger and despair, young people turn to radical Islamist movements. Poverty combined with radical ideology is, thus, in his view, a recipe for revolt.

While it may be true that some young Uzbeks are undoubtedly 'jobless, restless, and hungry', and it may be true that their 'numbers are growing', economists and representatives from international financial institutions (IFIs) generally look upon Uzbekistan as a moderate economic success story, especially when viewed in terms of economic growth.[26] While the Government of Uzbekistan (GoU) is no doubt repressive of political voice and deters significant foreign direct investment[27] the limited economic data available indicates the Uzbek economy has done fairly well since independence, especially compared to most of its neighbours. Not only has the country experienced considerable economic growth over the past 20 years, growth has actually been evenly distributed.[28] Between 2001 and 2005, Uzbekistan maintained an average growth rate of 5.7% and the proportion of the population living in extreme poverty decreased.[29] While much of the economic data in Uzbekistan comes from official sources, researchers have found that measurement error alone could not account for the positive economic outcomes seen in Uzbekistan since independence.[30] As such, these economic numbers suggest that the regime may have been able to use economic policy to enhance its prospects for survival and the conflictology approach alone does not provide enough insight to explain Uzbekistan's situation.

A second approach to the study of political change in the former Soviet Union stresses the role social mobilization of individuals and groups, or what is often referred to as an 'agency' perspective to topple regimes.[31] The agency perspective stresses diffusion of democratic movements across borders, leadership of those movements, as well as mobilization strategies among opposition groups to explain regime change. In this view, the ability of groups to mobilize is emboldened by domestic political conditions that favour the growth of civil society organizations as well as flows of foreign aid to support democratic movements.[32] Collective action contributing to regime change is often argued to diffuse across borders allowing individuals in nearby states to learn from the examples of others.[33]

Agency perspectives in the social movement literature emphasize the role of 'civil society' as one of the fundamental agents of political change and suggests that institutional change occurs when civil society rises up to challenge regimes.[34] The agency perspective maintains a focus on individual action, but it does not provide a compelling an account of the incentives facing those individuals to participate in social movements. Rather, it is content to emphasize that change occurs when social movements arise without explaining precisely why individuals had incentives to participate in these movements. Moreover, agency perspectives, by focusing attention on opposition dynamics and political change, have been less concerned with cases of autocratic stability – and in particular have been less concerned with explaining the non-emergence of civil society or social movements.

A third approach to political change stresses macro-level policies – or 'structural' factors – that enable or constrain social mobilization.[35] According to Lucan Way, authoritarian stability 'is most affected by: 1) the strength of a country's ties to the West; and 2) the strength of the incumbent regime's autocratic party or state'.[36] Politics is thus 'the logical manifestations of particular institutional designs or social processes set into motion well before the events in question occurred'.[37] Unlike an agency approach that focuses on social mobilization, a structural approach is better equipped to explain authoritarian outcomes because it analyses tactics used by regimes to maintain authority rather than focusing primarily on activity by potential regime opponents.

Structural explanations provide clues as to how policies at the national level may encourage or prevent political change, but do not adequately consider dynamics of regime stability that extend beyond repression. Structural approaches focus primarily on coercive authority and ruling party cohesion (which could also be viewed as a consequence of repressive authority) as the primary explanatory variables that explain regime change.[38] In short, structural perspectives emphasize sticks rather than carrots.[39] In particular, structural approaches thus do not sufficiently emphasize the use of public policies to distribute economic and social benefits as a means to maintain regime stability. Furthermore, Way's particular explanation of authoritarian stability provides little traction in the case of Uzbekistan as the country maintained close ties with the West after independence until 2005 and in fact, hosted the first United States military installation on former Soviet territory.

Insights from political economy

Political economy perspectives provide an alternative approach to help us understand regime stability and instability. Political economists working from the rational choice tradition consider revolutions as an outcome jointly influenced by rulers and individuals.[40] Rulers are rational in the sense that they respond to incentives and want to remain in power.[41] Individuals are also assumed rational in the sense that they participate in (revolutionary) protests provided it benefits them personally, responding to rewards as well as punishments from the regime.[42] Unlike the perspectives discussed in the preceding section, which focus overwhelming attention on repressive tools as the primary means to explain regime stability, political economy approaches equally emphasize positive rewards provided by regimes, paying more attention to economic conditions and social policies used by regimes to maintain social order.

In particular, a political economy approach suggests it is important to look at three complementary explanations for autocratic stability. First, economic growth and economic equality are hypothesized to increase autocratic stability. One of the reasons people participate in a revolution to change a regime is because they expect greater wealth under new political institutions.[43] Economic growth, by increasing wealth, is expected to reduce the return to organized

violence. Income inequality may also play an important role in explaining movements against a regime. Most notably, Acemoglu and Robinson argue that income
distribution, not economic growth, govern incentives to revolt.[44] Increases in
income inequality thus are expected to increase the likelihood of rebellion
against an authoritarian regime as democracies redistribute wealth.[45]

A second explanation for political stability in authoritarian states is the political
capacity to repress dissent. This element is common among agency, structural, as
well as political economy approaches to regime stability. Yet, a political economy
approach stresses that the ability to repress movements is not just a signal of state
weakness, as is argued by the 'conflictology' scholars, but may signal state
strength. Individuals are less likely to participate in a revolution when they
are more likely to be punished, and punishment depends on state capacity.[46]
Consequently, capacity for repression is expected to influence autocratic stability:
repression, as a reflection of capacity, strengthens regime durability in the face of
pressure. Increased capacity of the state, including the capacity to repress, then,
diminishes incentives to rebel against the regime.[47]

Finally, rational leaders may be able to enhance their own stability by co-opting
groups through the implementation of specific social policies. Public policy
choices by the regime are a manifestation of institutional design. They do not
necessarily reflect 'agency' or 'structure' emphasized by the literature on political
change. Specifically, leaders may utilize public policies – policies other than
simple coercion or repression – to weaken ties between groups and individuals.
That is, policies that weaken social ties among groups may ultimately serve to
strengthen the regime,[48] because weakened social ties generally inhibit the
ability of groups to challenge the regime. Such policies may be 'affirmative' in
the sense that they provide goods and services to individuals and are likely to
stand in clear contrast to the 'negative' exhibition of state capacity manifested in
the use of repression.

Using social policy as an instrument to control the population should be particularly common in what Milan Svolik describes as an established dictatorship.[49]
Unlike contested dictatorships, in established dictatorships there are few threats
within the ruling class, thus enabling the leader broader policy discretion which
can stave off revolutionary pressure.[50] An established dictator is likely to have
far more leeway in policy-making and implementation than if he would face
substantial challenges from within leadership cadres.

Arguably, then, a political economy perspective provides a complementary
theoretical framework to existing approaches that may help us to better understand
the observed political stability in Uzbekistan. It points to a broader range of factors
and trade-offs available to leaders as well to as individuals who may be willing to
challenge authoritarian regimes. If political economy explanations are correct, then
we would expect to see the following factors present in Uzbekistan: higher levels of
economic growth and economic equality; state strength to repress dissent; and
social policies that weaken group ties. The next section explores these factors in
greater detail.

The political economy of Uzbekistan's stability

The analysis here, derived from insights into the political economy of regime change, provides a set of theoretically derived factors that explain why the Karimov regime in Uzbekistan has been able to stay in power for as long as it has. These factors highlight not only the repressive elements utilized by the regime, but also underline rewards provided to individuals in return for their quiescence. The bottom line is that the regime is unlikely to have endured utilizing tools of repression alone. There are other factors, such as above average economic performance and utilization of social policy, that paint a more nuanced picture of regime tactics in Uzbekistan.

Economic performance

Although Uzbekistan is typically viewed as one of the least liberal economies in the former-Soviet sphere, this characterization arguably reflects 'jaundiced views by the international financial institutions (IFIs)...and a conflation of political and economic considerations'.[51] While the pace of economic reforms has been slow, available data indicate that the Uzbek economy did not suffer negative shocks that befell other economies in the former Soviet Union.[52] Uzbekistan's growth performance in the first decade of independence was among the best of the former Soviet republics (see Table 1).[53] While some argue that increased control of the economy should lead to instability,[54] state control does not appear to have undermined economic growth. Despite the GoU rejection of economic reforms proposed by the IFIs, the state-controlled economy has appeared to grow. Analysts found that even when controlling for possible measurement errors, the Uzbek economy has suffered the smallest contraction and has been among the fastest to restart growth of any in the former Soviet Union.[55] Although Uzbekistan did experience a decline in GDP after the collapse of the Soviet Union, this decline was moderate compared to neighbouring countries. Despite impressive exports of oil and gas, neither of the neighbouring countries of Turkmenistan nor Kazakhstan had been able to recover the GDPs they had recorded in 1989 subsequent to the collapse of the Soviet Union.[56]

Table 1. Basic economic data for Central Asian states during the period of the Andijon uprising (2005).

Country	GNI/capita, 2004 @ ppp	Growth index, 2000 as % of 1990	Gini coefficient	% top 10% (2003)
Kazakhstan	6930	66	0.339	24.4
Kyrgyzstan	1860	66	0.303	27.9
Tajikistan	1160	33	0.326	25.6
Turkmenistan	1120[a]	61	0.408	31.7[b]
Uzbekistan	1860	98	0.268	22.0[c]

Source: 2006 World Development Indicators adapted from Spechler, 'Authoritarian Politics and Economic Reform in Uzbekistan'.
Notes: [a]2003 figure; [b]1998 figure; [c]2000 figure.

85

World Bank development indicators suggest that by 2000 the Uzbek economy had recovered 98% of its 1990 GDP levels, far surpassing other countries in the region.

Uzbekistan's economic growth suggests that Karimov's regime has been successful in its gradualist strategy, explicitly rejecting a 'big bang' approach to reform in the early 1990s out of a concern for the impact of liberalization on the poorest members of society.[57] An 'Uzbek model of development' evolved not as a series of ad hoc policies but rather a well-planned economic policy.[58] Since independence, Karimov has given countless speeches detailing the importance of 'stability' as the guarantor of both democracy and development. He has on several occasions explicitly stated that economic policies in Uzbekistan should mirror *dirigiste* regimes in Southeast Asia.[59] Accordingly, the government retained price controls on essential goods and services, pursued self-sufficiency in wages, and only partially privatized state-owned enterprises.[60] The government also moved to diversify its economy away from primary reliance on a cotton monoculture to other forms of agricultural outputs as well as a significant shift away from agriculture to service sector and other industries intensive in human capital.[61] It furthermore increased investment in the public sector, prioritizing infrastructure and industry in targeted sectors.[62]

Agricultural reforms have been gradual as well. Instead of opening the agricultural sector which employs a majority of the labour force to market forces, the government retained a highly regulated system of agricultural production to protect a population it viewed as vulnerable to market fluctuations.[63] As part of agricultural reforms, the government allowed villagers to increase the size of their household (private) plots over which the state retained no control, however the state retained firm control over inputs, credits and most land.[64] In addition, the state continued to heavily tax exports of resources including cotton (one of its largest sources of income), natural gas and gold.[65] From 1996 to 2003, the government engaged in heavy protection of domestic industry in order to gain self-sufficiency in wheat and energy production. When the government lifted most restrictions to trade in 2003, the country was far less reliant on income from cotton than it had been prior to the restrictions. By 2006, cotton was only 21% of export values down from 42% in 1999.[66]

The centralized structure of the economy is by no means optimal, but it has performed above expectations. In 2006, as the coloured revolutions were sweeping other countries in the region, Uzbekistan maintained the lowest level of income inequality in Central Asia, lower than both the other agriculturally dependent economies of Kyrgyzstan and Tajikistan (see Table 1). Furthermore, public opinion surveys in Uzbekistan illustrate that there is broader support for state ownership of industry in Uzbekistan than in any other former Soviet Republic.[67] Uzbek citizens appear to believe that the state should maintain a strong role in the economy.

Political repression

A second factor contributing to regime stability in Uzbekistan is the ability and willingness of the GoU to repress its people. As has been stated before, the GoU is one of the most repressive political regimes in the world.[68] In addition to possessing capacity to repress, the GoU has also been willing to use this capacity, imprisoning or forcing into exile many potential political adversaries. Uzbekistan's uniformly poor ratings on all human rights indices demonstrate the willingness of the regime to use force against its opposition and citizens.[69]

The ability to repress reflects Karimov's strength. Uzbekistan is a non-competitive autocracy, with Karimov facing few challenges by groups from within society or from within his own ranks. Karimov acceded to power after the fall of the Soviet Union by means of his position as General Secretary of the Communist Party of the then Uzbek Soviet Socialist Republic. When Uzbekistan became independent, there were no sustained challenges from within the government apparatus nor from within society.[70]

The government's preferred tactic of repression is torture. The United Nations Committee Against Torture has detailed 'widespread torture and ill-treatment' of individuals in pre-trial detention and has documented 'consistent allegations concerning routine use of torture and other cruel, inhuman or degrading treatment or punishment...to extract confessions' by law enforcement authorities.[71] Torture, as well as highly visible and violent suppression of protest movements, sends citizens a clear signal about the government's lack of tolerance for dissent. Beginning with the suppression of student movements at Tashkent State University in 1991, every organized political movement possibly signalling a challenge to the regime has been met with harsh repression by the regime. Specifically, government repression has led to the dismantling of two largely secular and political parties – *Erk* and *Birlik* – that emphasized democracy in the early days after independence. Not only were these groups effectively banned, but leaders and members were arrested on trumped-up criminal charges. Such oppression forced leaders of these parties into exile and harassment of members forced these movements to effectively disband. There has been no wide scale, publically organized political movement in the country since that time.

Repression has been the response not just to the more secular political groups, such as *Erk* and *Birlik*, but has been used with regularity against those seeking to establish Islamist political organizations in the country too. Beginning in 1992, groups with religious leanings such as the *Adolat* group of Jo'maboy Namangoni were violently suppressed by the regime. Repression forced the leadership of this group into exile in Tajikistan and then Afghanistan where they formed the Islamic Movement of Uzbekistan. Similarly, *Hezb-e Tahrir* – an Islamist group whose primary aim is the restoration of the Islamic Caliphate – has been forced underground.[72] Hezb-e Tahrir is most likely the largest organized political group in the country – despite being outlawed. This is in spite of the fact that most Uzbek citizens would most likely not support such a political strategy.[73] Repression has forced those who wish to challenge the regime underground regardless of their place on the ideological spectrum.[74]

Government use of repression increases an individual's costs of joining opposition movements, political organizations, or engaging in independent civil society groups. The highly repressive nature of Uzbekistan's regime also explains the highly fractured nature of the human rights and democracy movement in the country. Repression, in turn, reflects the non-competitive nature of Karimov's dictatorship.

Social co-optation and redistribution

A third factor that contributes to regime stability in Uzbekistan is state co-optation of social institutions. Rulers may use repression, but they can also more gently co-opt social institutions to divide and rule society. Karimov's regime balances repression of large-scale social movements with co-optation of everyday social institutions, such as *mahallas* (customary-based neighbourhood associations, see below). Co-optation of social institutions involves the state providing public goods in order to win the hearts and minds of the population and in the process the state gains a foothold in traditional social organizations.[75]

In the years since independence, the GoU has developed a host of social support organizations that seek to include community interests but that simultaneously serve as vehicles to enforce government directives.[76] These social programmes serve two distinct services: first, they enable the regime to maintain strict social control over its population; second, they enable the regime to engage in targeted redistribution to the population.

The GoU has engaged in redistribution across a wide variety of sectors. As part of its gradualist approach to reform, the Karimov government has retained higher levels of employment in the state sector for a longer period of time than other countries in the region,[77] and has been able to maintain health and education expenditures as part of the social safety-net.[78] Since 1991, the government has expanded its role in promoting social protection through the provision of targeted poverty alleviation as well as human capital formation.[79] It has also maintained high levels of investment in public education.[80] Literacy and enrolment rates in secondary schools have continued to rise since 1991 as a result of state investment.[81] Immediately after independence, the government engaged in a land privatization scheme whereby more than 10% of irrigated land in the country was given by the state to individual families, including some of the country's most productive land, to prevent social unrest.[82] Unlike many of its ex-Soviet counterparts, the GoU still maintains elaborate universal food and fuel subsidies that provide the entire population with access to grain and other foods at lower-than-market costs.

Perhaps the most notable effort of the state to penetrate social institutions and engage in redistribution is evident in its co-optation of *mahallas*, or customary-based neighbourhood associations. The state uses these social organizations to provide social welfare transfers to citizens in these communities.[83] Although the Soviet government was the first to formalize these previously informal groups in an attempt to co-opt them into the state apparatus, the Karimov government increased control over these associations in order to expand state capacity.[84] During the 1990s, the state brought *mahallas* more formally into the government fold. In the early years after independence, *mahallas* were used to maintain neighbourhood mosques, but by 1999 they were tasked to elect formal heads of these bodies (*rais*) to oversee the distribution of welfare, development of territory and sanitation, assistance in environmental matters, proposing changes to *mahalla* borders, distributing land plots, providing aid to poor families, taking an active role in law and order, mediating domestic disputes, providing or withholding divorce papers, and registering residency and religious activities, among other tasks.[85]

Tightened control over *mahallas* appears to have had two direct effects. First, it has increased the ability of the state to maintain a close eye on its citizens. The state appointed a *posbon* or 'defender of the people' in each *mahalla*, whose purpose was to report potential anti-state activities in communities. Typically, *posbons* look out for potential Islamic extremists or those who might otherwise engage in activity deemed subversive to state interests.[86] It is not unusual for *mahalla* leaders and *posbons* to aggressively inform on citizen behaviour to local government authorities.

Second, formalization of these bodies has given the government greater information about individual welfare needs so that it might better target assistance. By the early 1990s it became clear that the government could no longer afford to maintain the complete Soviet package of universal social benefits to all members of society. Instead of giving up completely on welfare transfers, the government used *mahallas* as agents to target the neediest in society. According to the logic of the government, as highly localized and legitimate forms of social organization, *mahalla* leaders and members would have the greatest sense of the most vulnerable among them. Available independent data demonstrate that the *mahalla* scheme has done an adequate job fulfilling this mandate. Using household survey data, researchers found that social welfare systems using *mahallas* to target vulnerable citizens have been effective: the *mahalla* scheme does deliver benefits to less prosperous households and may actually serve as a positive 'demonstration of the potential for "informally" run and flexible schemes of social assistance'.[87]

Although *mahalla* policies have come under severe criticism from human rights advocates, the approach taken by the GoU in communities illustrates the complex web of rewards and sanctions the regime uses to garner both support and generate fear among citizens at the local level. It is an example of how economic policy is used to redistribute resources in order to secure regime stability or even loyalty. The regime has co-opted this traditional structure to gain valuable information about potential threats to the regime, thus gaining traction in one of the most important networks of society. In the aftermath of the Andijon uprising the GoU used its control of *mahallas* to control the flow of information in and out of the city.[88] In present day Uzbekistan, *mahallas* no longer fully exist as customary, self-organized structures. Instead, many citizens view them as agents of state administration.

Conclusion

As coloured revolutions unfolded in the region, Uzbekistan's autocratic regime has managed to stay remarkably stable. The puzzle of Uzbekistan's stability is even more interesting given the fact that the Karimov government has also been able to withstand the challenge of the Andijon uprising. As the article has demonstrated, existing academic approaches within political science and economics are not able to provide sufficient explanations for the Uzbek case. The analysis provided here, which is based on a political economy approach suggests, instead, a more nuanced understanding of why the regime has endured, despite predictions of its demise. The regime has endured not just because it has been willing to engage in terrifically repressive acts – as many scholars and policy-makers have pointed out. The Karimov government has also been willing to complement this repression with social policy and redistribution. As a result, the Karimov government has behaved far more like a 'stationary bandit': a regime willing to forego some short-term gains in order to maintain its authority.[89]

Three factors in particular, all of which are underscored in political economy approaches to regime stability provide useful insights into the puzzling case of Uzbekistan. First, economic growth and relatively low inequality obviate against revolution. As Richard Pomfret has argued, 'the absence of reform may have just delayed rather than avoided decline, but gradual reform has been sufficient to provide the basis for modest but reasonably steady growth'.[90] Second, the non-competitive nature of the Uzbek dictatorship explains its autocratic stability, as Karimov's lack of competition increases his ability to use force selectively to crush his opposition. In this regard, Uzbekistan is a strong state among post-communist dictatorships. Third, economic policies that favour redistribution are reinforced by social policies that appear to – at least for now – enhance the stability of the regime. In the nearly 20 years since independence the Karimov government has created complex social policies designed to keep the regime in place.

Utilizing insights from a political economy perspective to explore regime stability in Uzbekistan, enables observers to take a more multifaceted approach to understanding why the regime has endured despite tremendous political change in most countries in the region. The picture that emerges from this analysis of Uzbekistan is that the state not only uses overt repression but also utilizes social and economic policies as instruments to control its population. Uzbekistan's autocratic stability, thus, should not only be explained by state aggression, but rather can be traced back to a much more multifaceted use of state capacity – both to punish and reward citizens – than analysts may have previously recognized.

Notes

1. Tilly, *European Revolutions*. I also draw upon Tilly's definition of a revolution, which is 'a forcible transfer of power over a state in the course of which at least two distinct blocs of contenders make incompatible claims to control the state, and some significant portion of the population subject to the state's jurisdiction acquiesces in the claims of each bloc' (Ibid., 8).
2. Kalandadze and Orenstein, 'Electoral Protests and Democratization Beyond the Color Revolutions'; Tucker, 'Enough!'; Way, 'The Real Causes of the Color Revolutions'.
3. King, Keohane, and Verba, *Designing Social Inquiry*; Tilly, *Revolutions and Collective Violence*; Tocqueville, *Democracy in America*.

4. Akbarzadeh, 'Uzbekistan and the United States'.
5. Freedom House, *Freedom in the World 2010*.
6. Spechler, 'The Political Economy of Reform in Central Asia'.
7. Ilkhamov, 'Shirkats, Dekhqon Farmers and Others'.
8. See Karimov, 'Uzbekistan on the Threshold of the Twenty-First Century'; and Levitin, 'Uzbekistan on a Historical Threshold'.
9. Frye, *Building States and Markets after Communism*, 230.
10. To illustrate, this researcher has been denied research visas to conduct field research in the country.
11. Fukuyama, *The End of History and the Last Man*.
12. Levitsky and Way, *Competitive Authoritarianism*, 6–7.
13. Hale, 'Regime Cycles'.
14. Fish, 'The Dynamics of Democratic Erosion'; Melvin, *Uzbekistan*; Roeder, 'Varieties of Post-Soviet Authoritarian Regimes'.
15. Hale, 'Regime Cycles'.
16. Diamond, 'Thinking about Hybrid Regimes'; Hale, 'Democracy or Autocracy on the March?'; Karl, 'The Hybrid Regimes of Central America'; Levitsky and Way, 'The Rise of Competitive Authoritarianism'; McMann, *Economic Autonomy and Democracy*; Robertson, 'Strikes and Labor Organization in Hybrid Regimes'; Shevtsova and Eckert, 'Russia's Hybrid Regime'; Spechler, 'Uzbekistan'.
17. Reeves, 'Locating Danger'.
18. McGlinchey, 'The Making of Militants'; Bakker, 'Repression, Political Violence and Terrorism'; Lewis, *The Temptations of Tyranny in Central Asia*.
19. International Crisis Group, 'Uzbekistan', 1.
20. Rashid, *Jihad*.
21. Rashid, *Jihad*; and Lubin et al., *Calming the Ferghana Valley*.
22. Khalid, *Islam after Communism*.
23. Johnson, *Oil, Islam, and Conflict*; McGlinchey, 'The Making of Militants'; Olcott, *Central Asia's Second Chance*; Olcott and Ziyaeva, 'Islam in Uzbekistan'.
24. *Foreign Policy*, 'The Failed States Index 2007'.
25. Rashid, *Jihad*, 81–2.
26. McKinley, *The Puzzling Success*.
27. Blackmon, 'Divergent Paths, Divergent Outcomes'.
28. Zettelmeyer, 'The Uzbek Growth Puzzle';
29. McKinley and Weeks, *A Proposed Strategy*.
30. Taube and Zettelmeyer, 'Output Decline and Recovery in Uzbekistan'.
31. Bunce and Wolchik, 'Getting Real about "Real Causes"'; Bunce, 'Rethinking Recent Democratization'; Bunce and Wolchik, 'Postcommunist Ambiguities'; Beissinger, 'Structure and Example in Modular Political Phenomena'.
32. Bunce and Wolchik, 'Favorable Conditions and Electoral Revolutions'.
33. Beissinger, 'Structure and Example in Modular Political Phenomena'; Gleditsch, *All International Politics Is Local*; Lake and Rothchild, *The International Spread of Ethnic Conflict*; Weyland, 'The Diffusion of Revolution'.
34. Kuran, *Private Truths, Public Lies*.
35. Way, 'The Real Causes of the Color Revolutions'; Way, 'A Reply to My Critics'.
36. Way, 'The Real Causes of the Color Revolutions', 60.
37. Beissinger, *Nationalist Mobilization and the Collapse of the Soviet State*, 8.
38. Way, 'State Power and Autocratic Stability'.
39. Way, 'Authoritarian State Building', 65.
40. See Acemoglu and Robinson, *Economic Origins of Dictatorship and Democracy*; de Mesquita et al., *The Logic of Political Survival*; Wintrobe, *The Political Economy of Dictatorship*.

41. Of course, they may make mistakes, choosing policies that unwittingly lead to bad outcomes for them. See Acemoglu, 'Why Not a Political Coase Theorem?'.
42. Kuran, *Private Truths, Public Lies.*
43. Ibid.
44. Acemoglu and Robinson, *Economic Origins of Dictatorship and Democracy.*
45. Mueller, *Public Choice III.*
46. Davenport, 'State Repression and Political Order'.
47. Della Porta, *Social Movements, Political Violence, and the State.*
48. Boix, *Democracy and Redistribution.*
49. Svolik, 'Power Sharing and Leadership Dynamics in Authoritarian Regimes'.
50. Wintrobe, *The Political Economy of Dictatorship.*
51. Pomfret, *The Central Asian Economies Since Independence*, 7.
52. Economic data on Uzbekistan is scarce and researchers have called into question its reliability. However, some economists have concluded that despite data problems evidence demonstrates the country has experienced limited inflation, maintained stable GDP, and enhanced economic growth independence (see Pomfret and Anderson, *Uzbekistan*, 9). Taube and Zettlemeyer conclude that measurement error alone could not account for lack of decline in the Uzbek economy after independence.
53. Cornia, *Growth and Poverty Reduction in Uzbekistan in the Next Decade*, 7.
54. Ilkhamov, 'The Limits of Centralization'.
55. Taube and Zettlemeyer, *Output Decline and Recovery in Uzbekistan.*
56. Spechler, 'Authoritarian Politics and Economic Reform in Uzbekistan', 186.
57. Pomfret and Anderson, *Uzbekistan*, 29.
58. See Karimov, 'Uzbekistan on the Threshold of the Twenty-First Century'.
59. Pomfret, 'Agrarian Reform in Uzbekistan?'.
60. Spechler, 'Uzbekistan', 295.
61. Cornia, *Growth and Poverty Reduction*, 24.
62. Luong and Weinthal, *Oil Is Not a Curse*, 104.
63. Spoor, 'Agricultural Restructuring and Trends in Rural Inequalities in Central Asia'.
64. Ibid.
65. Rudenko, Lamers, and Grote, 'Can Uzbek Farmers Get More for their Cotton?'.
66. Spechler and Spechler, 'Uzbekistan among the Great Powers', 358.
67. Luong and Weinthal, *Oil Is Not a Curse*, 110.
68. Freedom House, *Freedom in the World 2010.*
69. Ibid. See also Human Rights Watch, *World Report 2011.*
70. Collins, *Clan Politics and Regime Transition in Central Asia.*
71. United Nations Committee Against Torture, *UN Committee*, 2.
72. Rashid, *Jihad.*
73. Khalid, *Islam after Communism*; McGlinchey, 'Autocrats, Islamists, and the Rise of Radicalism in Central Asia'.
74. McGlinchey, 'The Making of Militants'.
75. de Mesquita and Smith, 'Political Survival and Endogenous Institutional Change'.
76. Kandiyoti, 'Post-Soviet Institutional Design'.
77. Ruziev, Ghosh, and Dow, 'The Uzbek Puzzle Revisited'.
78. Pomfret and Anderson, *Uzbekistan.*
79. Luong and Weinthal, *Oil Is Not a Curse*, 102.
80. Kissane, 'Education in Central Asia'.
81. Cornia, *Growth and Poverty Reduction in Uzbekistan in the Next Decade*, 81.
82. Abdullaev et al., 'Agricultural Water Use and Trade in Uzbekistan', 48.
83. Coudouel and Marnie, 'From Universal to Targeted Social Assistance'.
84. Sievers, 'Uzbekistan's Mahalla'.
85. Kamp, 'Between Women and the State'.

86. Human Rights Watch, *From House to House*.
87. Micklewright, Marnie, and Coudouel, *Targeting Social Assistance in a Transition Economy*, iii–iv.
88. Kimmage, 'Uzbekistan: Voices From Andijon'.
89. Olson, *Power and Prosperity*.
90. Pomfret, 'Central Asia since the Dissolution of the Soviet Union', 332.

Note on contributor

Jennifer Murtazashvili is an assistant professor of public and international affairs at the University of Pittsburgh, USA.

Bibliography

Abdullaev, Iskandar, Charlotte De Fraiture, Mark Giordano, Murat Yakubov, and Aziz Rasulov. 'Agricultural Water Use and Trade in Uzbekistan: Situation and Potential Impacts of Market Liberalization'. *International Journal of Water Resources Development* 25, no. 1 (2009): 47–63.

Acemoglu, Daron. 'Why Not a Political Coase Theorem? Social Conflict, Commitment, and Politics'. *Journal of Comparative Economics* 31, no. 4 (2003): 620–52.

Acemoglu, Daron, and James A. Robinson. *Economic Origins of Dictatorship and Democracy*. New York: Cambridge University Press, 2006.

Akbarzadeh, Shahram. '*Uzbekistan and the United States: Authoritarianism, Islamism and Washington's New Security Agenda*'. New York: Zed Books, 2005.

Bakker, Edwin. 'Repression, 'Political Violence and Terrorism: The Case of Uzbekistan'. *Helsinki Monitor* 17, no. 2 (2006): 108–18.

Beissinger, Mark R. *Nationalist Mobilization and the Collapse of the Soviet State*. New York: Cambridge University Press, 2002.

Beissinger, Mark R. 'Structure and Example in Modular Political Phenomena: The Diffusion of Bulldozer/Rose/Orange/Tulip Revolutions'. *Perspectives on Politics* 5, no. 2 (2007): 259–76.

Blackmon, Pamela, 'Divergent Paths, Divergent Outcomes: Linking Differences in Economic Reform to Levels of US Foreign Direct Investment and Business in Kazakhstan and Uzbekistan'. *Central Asian Survey* 26, no. 3 (2007): 355–72.

Boix, Carles. *Democracy and Redistribution*. New York: Cambridge University Press, 2003.

Bunce, Valerie. 'Rethinking Recent Democratization: Lessons from the Postcommunist Experience'. *World Politics* 55, no. 2 (2003): 167–92.

Bunce, Valerie, and Sharon L. Wolchik. 'Favorable Conditions and Electoral Revolutions'. *Journal of Democracy* 17, no. 4 (2006): 5–18.

Bunce, Valerie, and Sharon Wolchik. 'Getting Real About "Real Causes"'. *Journal of Democracy* 20, no. 1 (2008): 69–73.

Bunce, Valerie J., and Sharon L. Wolchik. 'Postcommunist Ambiguities'. *Journal of Democracy* 20, no. 3 (2009): 93–107.

Collins, Kathleen. *Clan Politics and Regime Transition in Central Asia*. New York: Cambridge University Press, 2006.

Cornia, Andrea Giovanni. *Growth and Poverty Reduction in Uzbekistan in the Next Decade*. Tashkent: United Nations Development Programme, September 2003.

Coudouel, Aline, and Sheila Marnie. 'From Universal to Targeted Social Assistance: An Assessment of the Uzbek Experience'. *MOCT-MOST: Economic Policy in Transitional Economies* 9, no. 4 (1999): 443–58.

Davenport, Christian. 'State Repression and Political Order'. *Annual Review of Political Science* 10, no. 1 (2007): 1–23.

de Mesquita, Bruce Bueno, and Alastair Smith. 'Political Survival and Endogenous Institutional Change'. *Comparative Political Studies* 42, no. 2 (2009): 167–97.

de Mesquita, Bruce Bueno, Alastair Smith, Randolph M. Siverson and James D. Morrow. *The Logic of Political Survival*. Cambridge, MA: MIT Press, 2003.

Della Porta, Donatella. *Social Movements, Political Violence, and the State: A Comparative Analysis of Italy and Germany*. New York: Cambridge University Press, 2006.

Diamond, Larry J. 'Thinking about Hybrid Regimes'. *Journal of Democracy* 13, no. 2 (2002): 21–35.

Fish, M. Steven. 'The Dynamics of Democratic Erosion'. In *Postcommunism and the Theory of Democracy*, ed. Richard Davis Anderson, M. Steven Fish, Steven E. Hanson, and Philip G. Roeder, 54–95. Princeton, NJ: Princeton University Press, 2001.

Foreign Policy and Fund for Peace. The Failed States Index 2007. Uzbekistan Country Report. Available at http://www.fundforpeace.org/global/?q=fsi-grid2007

Freedom House. *Freedom in the World 2010*. New York: Rowman and Littlefield Publishers, Inc., 2010.

Frye, Timothy. *Building States and Markets after Communism: The Perils of Polarized Democracy*. New York: Cambridge University Press, 2010.

Fukuyama, Francis. *The End of History and the Last Man*. New York: Free Press, 1993.

Gleditsch, Kristian Skrede. *All International Politics Is Local: The Diffusion of Conflict, Integration, and Democratization*. Ann Arbor, MI: University of Michigan Press, 2002.

Hale, Henry E. 'Democracy or Autocracy on the March? The Colored Revolutions as Normal Dynamics of Patronal Presidentialism'. *Communist and Post-Communist Studies* 39, no. 3 (2006): 305–29.

Hale, Henry E. 'Regime Cycles: Democracy, Autocracy, and Revolution in Post-Soviet Eurasia'. *World Politics* 58, no. 1 (2005): 133–65.

Human Rights Watch. *From House to House: Abuses by Mahalla Committees*. New York: Human Rights Watch, September 2003.

Human Rights Watch. *World Report*. New York: Human Rights Watch, 2011.

Ilkhamov, Alisher. 'Shirkats, Dekhqon Farmers and Others: Farm Restructuring in Uzbekistan'. *Central Asian Survey* 17, no. 4 (1998): 539–60.

Ilkhamov, Alisher. 'The Limits of Centralization: Regional Challenges in Uzbekistan'. In *The Transformation of Central Asia: States and Societies from Soviet Rule to Independence*, ed. Pauline Jones Luong, 159–81. Ithaca, NY: Cornell University Press, 2003.

International Crisis Group. 'Uzbekistan: The Andijon Uprising'. *Asia Briefing No. 38*. Bishkek/Brussles: International Crisis Group, May 25, 2005.

Johnson, Rob. *Oil, Islam, and Conflict: Central Asia since 1945*. London: Reaktion Books, 2007.

Kalandadze, Katya, and Mitchell A. Orenstein. 'Electoral Protests and Democratization beyond the Color Revolutions'. *Comparative Political Studies* 42, no. 11 (2009): 1403–25.

Kamp, Marianne. 'Between Women and the State: Mahalla Committees and Social Welfare in Uzbekistan.' In *The Transformation of Central Asia: States and Societies from Soviet Rule to Independence*, ed. Pauline Jones Luong, 29–58. Ithaca, NY: Cornell University Press, 2003.

Kandiyoti, Deniz. 'Post-Soviet Institutional Design and the Paradoxes of the 'Uzbek Path'. *Central Asian Survey* 26, no. 1 (2007): 31–48.

Karimov, Islam Abduganievich. *Uzbekistan on the Threshold of the Twenty-first Century: Challenges to Stability and Progress*. New York: Palgrave Macmillan, 1998.

Karl, Terry L. 'The Hybrid Regimes of Central America'. *Journal of Democracy* no. 6 (1995): 72–86.

Khalid, Adeeb. *Islam after Communism: Religion and Politics in Central Asia*. Berkeley, CA: University of California Press, 2007.

Kimmage, Daniel. 'Uzbekistan: Voices From Andijon'. *Radio Free Europe/Radio Liberty*, June 25, 2005. http://www.rferl.org/content/article/1059499.html.

King, Gary, Robert Owen Keohane, and Sidney Verba. *Designing Social Inquiry: Scientific Inference in Qualitative Research*. Princeton, NJ: Princeton University Press, 1994.

Kissane, Carolyn. 'Education in Central Asia: Transitional Challenges and Impacts'. In *The Politics of Transition in Central Asia and the Caucasus*, 226–49. New York: Routledge, 2009.

Kuran, Timur. *Private Truths, Public Lies: The Social Consequences of Preference Falsification*. Cambridge, MA: Harvard University Press, 1997.

Lake, David A., and Donald S. Rothchild, eds. *The International Spread of Ethnic Conflict: Fear, Diffusion, and Escalation*. Princeton, NJ: Princeton University Press, 1998.

Levitin, Leonid I. *Uzbekistan on a Historical Threshold: Critical Observations by a Supporter of President Karimov*. Cambridge: Granta, 2001.

Levitsky, Steven, and Lucan A. Way. *Competitive Authoritarianism: Hybrid Regimes After the Cold War*. New York: Cambridge University Press, 2010.

Levitsky, Steven, and Lucan Way. 'The Rise of Competitive Authoritarianism'. *Journal of Democracy* 13, no. 2 (2002): 51–65.

Lewis, David. *The Temptations of Tyranny in Central Asia*. New York: Columbia University Press, 2008.

Lubin, Nancy, Barnett R. Rubin, and Council on Foreign Relations and Century Foundation, Center for Preventive Action Ferghana Valley Working Group. *Calming the Ferghana Valley: Development and Dialogue in the Heart of Central Asia*. New York: Century Foundation Press, 2000.

Luong, Pauline Jones, and Erika Weinthal. *Oil Is Not a Curse: Ownership Structure and Institutions in Soviet Successor States*. New York: Cambridge University Press, 2010.

McGlinchey, Eric M. 'Autocrats, Islamists, and the Rise of Radicalism in Central Asia'. *Current History* 104, no. 684 (2005): 336–42.

McGlinchey, Eric M. 'The Making of Militants: The State and Islam in Central Asia'. *Comparative Studies of South Asia, Africa and the Middle East* 25, no. 3 (2005): 554–66.

McKinley, Terry. *The Puzzling Success of Uzbekistan's Heterodox Development*. Development Viewpoint. London: School of Oriental and African Studies, 2010. http://www.cer.uz/upload/iblock/a11/devviewpoint_eng.pdf.

McKinley, Terry, and John Weeks. *A Proposed Strategy for Growth, Employment and Poverty Reduction in Uzbekistan*. International Policy Centre for Inclusive Growth, October 2007. http://ideas.repec.org/p/ipc/cstudy/12.html.

McMann, Kelly. *Economic Autonomy and Democracy: Hybrid Regimes in Russia and Kyrgyzstan*. New York: Cambridge University Press, 2006.

Melvin, Neil J. *Uzbekistan: Transition to Authoritarianism*. New York: Routledge, 2000.

Micklewright, John, Sheila Marnie, and Aline Coudouel. 'Targeting Social Assistance in a Transition Economy: The Mahallas in Uzbekistan'. *Working Paper Series. UNICEF International Child Development Centre Innocenti Occasional Paper EPS No. 63*. UNICEF, 1999.

Mueller, Dennis C. *Public Choice III*, 3rd ed. New York: Cambridge University Press, 2003.

Olcott, Martha Brill. *Central Asia's Second Chance*. Washington, DC: Carnegie Endowment for International Peace, 2005.

Olcott, Martha Brill, and Diora Ziyaeva. 'Islam in Uzbekistan: Religious Education and State Ideology'. *Russia and Eurasia Program, Number 91*. Washington, DC: Carnegie Endowment for International Peace, July 2008.

Olson, Mancur. *Power and Prosperity: Outgrowing Communist and Capitalist Dictatorships*. New York: Basic Books, 2000.

Pierskalla, Jan Henryk. 'Protest, Deterrence, and Escalation: The Strategic Calculus of Government Repression'. *Journal of Conflict Resolution* 54, no. 1 (2010): 117–45.

Pomfret, Richard. 'Agrarian Reform in Uzbekistan: Why Has the Chinese Model Failed to Deliver?' *Economic Development and Cultural Change* 48, no. 2 (2000): 269–84.

Pomfret, Richard. 'Central Asia since the Dissolution of the Soviet Union: Economic Reforms and their Impact on State-Society Relations'. *Perspectives on Global Development and Technology* (2007).

Pomfret, Richard W.T. *The Central Asian Economies Since Independence*. Princeton, NJ: Princeton University Press, 2006.

Pomfret, Richard, and Kathryn Hart Anderson. *Uzbekistan: Welfare Impact of Slow Transition*. World Institute for Development Economics Research, 1997.

Rashid, Ahmed. *Jihad*. New Haven, CT: Yale University Press, 2002.

Reeves, Madeleine. 'Locating Danger: Konfliktologiia and the Search for Fixity in the Ferghana Valley Borderlands'. *Central Asian Survey* 24, no. 1 (2005): 67–81.

Robertson, G.B. 'Strikes and Labor Organization in Hybrid Regimes'. *American Political Science Review* 101, no. 4 (2007): 781–98.

Roeder, Philip G. 'Varieties of Post-Soviet Authoritarian Regimes'. *Post-Soviet Affairs* 10 (1994), 61–101.

Rudenko, Inna, John P.A. Lamers, and Ulrike Grote. 'Can Uzbek Farmers Get More for Their Cotton?'. *The European Journal of Development Research* 21, no. 2 (2009): 283–96.

Ruziev, Kobil, Dipak Ghosh, and Sheila C. Dow. 'The Uzbek Puzzle Revisited: An Analysis of Economic Performance in Uzbekistan Since 1991'. *Central Asian Survey* 26, no. 1 (2007): 7–30.

Shevtsova, L., and M.H. Eckert. 'Russia's Hybrid Regime'. *Journal of Democracy* 12, no. 4 (2001): 65–70.

Sievers, Eric W. 'Uzbekistan's Mahalla: From Soviet to Absolutist Residential Community Associations'. *Chicago-Kent Journal of International and Comparative Law* 2 (2002): 91–158.

Spechler, Martin C. 'Authoritarian Politics and Economic Reform in Uzbekistan: Past, Present and Prospects'. *Central Asian Survey* 26, no. 2 (2007): 185–202.

Spechler, Martin C. *The Political Economy of Reform in Central Asia: Uzbekistan under Authoritarianism*. New York: Routledge, 2008.

Spechler, Martin C. 'Uzbekistan: The Silk Road to Nowhere?' *Contemporary Economic Policy* 18, no. 3 (2000): 295–303.

Spechler, Dina Rome, and Martin C. Spechler. 'Uzbekistan among the Great Powers'. *Communist and Post-Communist Studies* 42, no. 3 (2009): 353–73.

Spoor, Max. 'Agricultural Restructuring and Trends in Rural Inequalities in Central Asia'. *Civil Society and Social Movements Programme Paper* 13 (2004).

Svolik, Milan W. 'Power Sharing and Leadership Dynamics in Authoritarian Regimes'. *American Journal of Political Science* 53, no. 2 (2009): 477–94.

Taube, Günther, and Jeromin Zettelmeyer. 'Output Decline and Recovery in Uzbekistan: Past Performance and Future Prospects'. *IMF Working Paper*. Washington, DC: International Monetary Fund, September 1998.

Tilly, Charles. *European Revolutions: 1492–1992*. New York: Wiley-Blackwell, 1996.

Tilly, Charles. *Revolutions and Collective Violence*. Ann Arbor, MI: Center for Research on Social Organizations, University of Michigan, May 1973.

Tocqueville, Alexis de. *Democracy in America*. New York: Library of America, 2004.

Tucker, Joshua A. 'Enough! Electoral Fraud, Collective Action Problems, and Post-Communist Colored Revolutions'. *Perspectives on Politics* 5, no. 3 (2007): 535–51.

United Nations Committee Against Torture. *UN Committee against Torture: Conclusions and Recommendations, Uzbekistan*. Geneva: United Nations Committee Against Torture, February 26, 2008.

Way, Lucan. 'A Reply to My Critics'. *Journal of Democracy* 20, no. 1 (2008): 90–7.

Way, Lucan. 'Authoritarian State Building and the Sources of Regime Competitiveness in the Fourth Wave: The Cases of Belarus, Moldova, Russia, and Ukraine'. *World Politics* 57, no. 2 (2005): 231–61.

Way, Lucan. 'The Real Causes of the Color Revolutions'. *Journal of Democracy* 19, no. 3 (2008): 55–69.

Way, Lucan. 'State Power and Autocratic Stability: Armenia and Georgia Compared'. In *The Politics of Transition in Central Asia and the Caucasus*, 103–23. New York: Routledge, 2009.

Weyland, Kurt. 'The Diffusion of Revolution: "1848" in Europe and Latin America'. *International Organization* 63, no. 3 (2009): 391–423.

Wintrobe, Ronald. *The Political Economy of Dictatorship*. New York: Cambridge University Press, 2000.

Zettelmeyer, Jeromin. 'The Uzbek Growth Puzzle'. *IMF Staff Papers* 46, no. 3 (1999): 274–92.

Tajikistan: authoritarian reaction in a postwar state

Lawrence P. Markowitz

Department of Political Science & Economics, Rowan University, Glassboro, NJ, USA

Why and how has Tajikistan responded to the threat of democratic revolution? In this article, I argue that state failure and civil war in Tajikistan have imposed limitations on the country's emergent path of authoritarian development. Scarce resources and limited rent-seeking opportunities in postwar Tajikistan weakened the informal bases of presidential power and fragmented the country's state security institutions. As a consequence of its weakened presidential power and fragmented coercive capacity, Tajikistan's leadership has taken a moderated response to the threat of democratic revolution and pursued a slow, graduated strengthening of authoritarian rule. While electoral reforms were reversed, restrictions imposed on the media and on non-governmental organizations were selective and temporary and the use of force has been relatively circumscribed.

On 27 February 2005, parliamentary elections were held in Tajikistan and Kyrgyzstan. Although both elections were plagued by large-scale irregularities, only in the latter did street protests develop and ultimately topple the regime. In Tajikistan, no significant demonstrations materialized despite opposition parties' bitter charges of electoral fraud and misconduct. While opposition leaders threatened to boycott the upcoming parliamentary session and lodged appeals in court, they made no open call for mass demonstrations to protest electoral results. In sharp contrast to the 'Tulip Revolution' in Kyrgyzstan, Tajikistan's spring of 2005 was relatively tranquil, and the regime's authoritarianism continued unabated.

At the same time, authoritarian rule in Tajikistan has differed significantly from the hard line authoritarian regimes of its other neighbours, Turkmenistan and Uzbekistan.[1] Although the government of Tajikistan has reversed electoral reforms and dealt harshly with outspoken political opponents since 2005, restrictions imposed on the media and on non-governmental organizations (NGOs) have been selective and temporary, and repression has been relatively circumscribed.[2] Tajikistan has exemplified a form of 'soft authoritarianism', in which rulers can 'define the political agenda while relying on relatively little outright coercion' but through an alternative set of instruments.[3] As I demonstrate below, the government relies on a core circle of supporters (drawn primarily from President Emomali Rahmon's home region), it extends its influence to other elites by distributing rents and threatening blackmail (when necessary), it applies coercion in a targeted fashion, and it makes use of information control and discursive narratives to shore up its support. While other countries have responded to the threat of anti-regime protests with hard line authoritarian measures, Tajikistan has taken a more moderated position.

What, then, explains Tajikistan's particular trajectory of authoritarianism? What are the distinct sources of its soft authoritarianism? And how has Tajikistan's particular form of soft authoritarian rule led to a moderated response to the threat of democratic revolution in terms of the regime's strategies of isolation, marginalization, distribution, repression and persuasion? In this article, I argue that Tajikistan's emergent path of authoritarian development is a product of the limitations imposed on the regime by state failure and civil war. After several months of mass demonstrations in the capital over the distribution of political positions and economic resources, state failure began in May 1992, when elites in several regions formed 'self-defense' forces from volunteers and local police units. Local law enforcement and security bodies joined independent militias mobilizing across Tajikistan, paralyzing the central government and leading to a five-year civil war in which 50,000 people died and 800,000 people were displaced.[4] The civil war left the regime extremely weak, unable to fully control large parts of the country and faced with a variety of internal security threats. In this postwar context, scarce resources and limited rent-seeking opportunities in Tajikistan weakened the informal bases of presidential power and fragmented the country's state security institutions. As a consequence of its weakened presidential power and fragmented coercive capacity, Tajikistan's leadership has taken a moderated response to the threat of democratic revolution and pursued a slow, graduated strengthening of authoritarian rule.

A number of scholars have examined the politics of semi-authoritarian rule, but few have tied these regime change trajectories explicitly to questions of stateness that emerge in post-conflict environments.[5] By contrast, specialists on Tajikistan have linked the country's semi-authoritarianism to some feature of its post-conflict environment. Several scholars have described how Tajikistan's post-conflict government has put 'power-building' strategies ahead of genuine state building and has promoted a programme of stability before democratization.[6] Others have argued that international aid to postwar Tajikistan has inadvertently helped consolidate the regime's monopoly on power.[7] All of this is possible because Tajikistan's leadership has legitimated its authoritarianism under international liberal intervention through discursive performances of democratic peace-building that overlay deeper processes of re-establishing authoritarian rule after civil war.[8]

Building on this secondary literature, I draw on print sources and ethnographic fieldwork – primarily newspaper articles and semi-structured expert interviews that I conducted in 2007 with lawyers, journalists, government officials and

NGO staff – to examine how resources and rents have limited Tajikistan's postwar presidential power and coercive capacity, and have given form to its particular soft authoritarian rule. The remainder of the article consists of three sections. The first section examines Tajikistan's post-conflict setting, describing how a small resource base and limited rent-seeking opportunities served to weaken informal bases of presidential power and undercut the state's coercive capacity. The politics of rents and resources in the wake of civil war have constrained the reach of the Rahmon regime's use of spoils to extend its informal power and has introduced concrete limitations on how far the state's coercive functions can be carried out on the ground. The second section examines why Tajikistan did not experience mass demonstrations challenging the regime. Alongside structural conditions that make social mobilization difficult to effect in Tajikistan, the memory of demonstrations that preceded the disorder and civil war of the 1990s has left many ordinary people sceptical, even suspicious, of mass protest as an instrument of political change. This has helped buffer the regime from mass protest. The third section demonstrates how these factors have promoted soft authoritarian rule in Tajikistan, resulting in a moderated response to the threat of anti-regime protests. In the wake of Kyrgyzstan's Tulip Revolution, democratic reforms were retrenched, but other levers of hard authoritarianism – a heavy crackdown on NGOs and a broad use of repression for instance – were far more circumscribed. Moreover, Tajikistan's response to possible protests included new initiatives designed to manipulate discursive strands of Islam and nationalism as a means of cooptation of public support. Finally, the article concludes with a brief discussion of these constraints on the feasibility of authoritarian reaction in post-conflict states.

The post-conflict setting

Tajikistan's particular brand of soft authoritarianism, and its relatively moderate response to the threat of mass protest, is intimately linked to the country's post-conflict setting. State failure and a five-year civil war in Tajikistan (1992–1997) had a profound impact on the country's social, political and institutional foundations of state power.

Postwar limits on 'patronal presidentialism'

Emomali Rahmon, put forward by the winning side in the civil war, rose from state farm director in a backwater district to become head of state in just a matter of weeks at the end of 1992. As Rahmon sought to establish his position, competition for access to state rents in the nascent postwar regime turned both competitive and violent. So-called 'bidding wars' broke out among urban and rural militias in the mid-1990s, often between groups from the same side during the war who had turned inward.[9] In many cases, the 'limited nature of rents and resources available-...inexorably led to turf wars' as each side sought 'to cull weaker elements in their own camp'.[10] At the same time, the regime feared that prominent elites were able to 'retain substantial private armies and use administrative resources to build extensive patronage networks' and that they commanded 'solid grassroots support in their patrimonies, which can be transformed from zones of ostensible peace and tranquility into strongholds of anti-governmental resistance overnight'.[11] Throughout the 1990s, Rahmon confronted threats of a coup d'état, insurrection, and opposition forces from the civil war who kidnapped international aid workers and assassinated state officials.[12]

As elsewhere in Eurasia, the political power of the regime rested on the president's informal authority. Henry Hale describes these informal institutions as 'patronal presidential' systems, in which 'power involves not only formal but immense informal authority based on pervasive patron-client relationships and machine politics'.[13] Tajikistan's patronal presidentialism, however, has been weak compared to other Eurasian countries which can be explained by three reasons.

First, the 1997 Moscow peace accord that ended the civil war allocated 30% of national government posts to the opposition, forcing the president into a power-sharing arrangement with senior political elites who were difficult to control.[14] Over time, Rahmon has systematically excluded many of the opposition from national politics, and he has relied more heavily on political elites from Khatlon Province (especially those from his home district of Dangara) to whom he has given favoured access to key political and economic posts in the national government.[15] Yet he has still had to provide some access to state rents for former opposition leaders and field commanders, especially as they gravitated toward a growing drug trafficking economy. At the same time, the selected Khatlon elites and former pro-government field commanders who were tapped to fill senior political posts still aggressively demanded a steady flow of patronage and rents from the presidency.[16] Establishing control over access to state rents, therefore, only occurred incrementally.

With the conclusion of the civil war, the foundations of Tajikistan's economy have provided a clean slate of opportunities for local actors to acquire control over and to create new political arrangements. It furthermore created decentralized controls over its key industries: cotton, energy and aluminum. Laws defining export quotas were altered 40 times in 1994 alone, and from 1994–1996 71 export contracts were granted exemption from state controls due to pressure from senior government officials.[17] Tajikistan's sole smelter was in warlord hands for several years in the 1990s and, in the first half of 2000, over 600 tons of illegally traded aluminum were seized by the national police, the Ministry of Interior (MVD).[18] In contrast to the concentrated rent-seeking that characterized these industries during the Soviet era, Tajikistan's postwar regime has been confronted with diffuse political control over many areas of its economy.

A second reason for Tajikistan's weak patronal presidentialism is the fact that available resources have been scarce and have remained spread across a swathe of actors, constraining the re-establishment of control over elites through patron–client ties. A primary goal of the regime has been to centralize its hold on rents and resources in the republic since postwar ruler-elite bargains have rested increasingly on the regime granting unimpeded access to rents in the cotton sector and from new resources, especially foreign aid and drug trafficking from Afghanistan into Russia. Whereas income from the cotton sector was insufficient, rents derived from the latter two, which are highly mobile forms of capital, have been difficult for the regime to monopolize.

Since 1997, much of Tajikistan's cotton industry, for instance, has been revitalized through World Bank refinancing and commercial loans, which were channelled through Tajikistan's Agro Invest Bank to Tajik companies directing (alongside provincial and district governments) local cotton growing operations. While these bank loans provided start-up capital investment (tens of millions of dollars annually) for global cotton traders such as Switzerland's Paul Reinhardt Corporation and US-based Dunnavant Enterprises to purchase agricultural inputs and finance cotton production,[19] two of the five major Tajik companies in cotton production (that jointly monopolize roughly three-quarters of the industry) – Khima and Sonomi 21st Century – were owned by the head of the National Bank and Rahmon's brother-in-law, respectively.[20] This cotton financing constituted roughly 90% of all agricultural lending in Tajikistan.[21] As in Uzbekistan, as long as cotton rents – commercial loans, foreign aid and revenue from cotton sales on the world market – are funnelled into state banks and companies owned by regime insiders, access to those rents can be controlled and distributed by the central leadership. In contrast to Uzbekistan, however, cotton producing regions only constituted half at best of the republic's localities and cotton rents were insufficient on their own to support the regime's postwar bargains with elites.[22]

Tajikistan's leadership also has sought to control the large amounts of foreign aid (relative to its economy) that has flowed into the country over the last 15 years. Initially focused on humanitarian assistance, this aid is now earmarked for a wide range of projects, including the country's primary industries. As such, this post-conflict development aid has provided Tajikistan's political elite with mobile capital from which it can derive significant rents outside Rahmon's surveillance and control. Attempts by the regime to control this aid have given rise to the Aid Coordination Unit (ACU) inside the Presidential Apparatus, which recorded 89 organizations in 2005 and about US$832 million in agreements.[23] On paper, 'the creation of the AFC gave Rahmon comprehensive control on both state and private finances at all levels'.[24] In practice, the ACU cannot effectively monitor development aid – in part because many loans go through the Ministry of Finance, which is untouched by ACU monitoring.[25] As one report has found, 'Given the high fragmentation of aid, and the lack of unity, supervision and overall direction of the use of foreign aid, "cheap funding" creates too much of a temptation for authorities and actually nurtures corruption.'[26] With the influx of foreign economic assistance, the political elite has found an additional rent to exploit, but one it has struggled to monopolize.

A third area of economic activity from which the regime has sought to generate rents has been a highly lucrative drug trade. In cooperation with the United Nations Office on Drugs and Crime (UNDOC), Tajikistan established the Drug Control Agency (DCA) in 1999 and initially appeared to be a regional leader in drug seizures, taking approximately 90% of all Afghan drugs confiscated in Central Asia in 2003.[27] Since then, as the drug trade has become a source of centralized rents, these efforts have dropped each year, declining from 5600 kilograms in 2003 to 1132 kilograms in 2009.[28] Rather than eliminate drug trafficking, the DCA has become an instrument by which Tajikistan's leadership has sought to establish control over the drug trade, 'forcing out political rivals that had maintained alternate smuggling routes'.[29] These attempts have been stymied, however, by the heavy involvement of political elites – from both sides of the civil war – in the drug trade, by the inherently mobile nature of opium and heroin, and by the multiple political and economic divisions among former field commanders who often function as drug lords.[30]

Together, a divided postwar elite and a limited resource base from which Rahmon can distribute state rents have served to undermine the reach of Tajikistan's regime. The rents that President Rahmon controlled (for example, from the cotton industry) have generated insufficient rents to competing elites, while lucrative rents (especially from foreign aid and drug trafficking) have not been fully under Rahmon's control. As a consequence, Rahmon's government does not rest on a full-fledged 'patronal presidential' system that can 'selectively direct vast sources of material wealth and power outside of formal institutional channels'.[31] Though sufficient to prevent elite defection from his supporters, Rahmon's command over rents remains less centralized than oil-rich Azerbaijan or cotton-producing Uzbekistan, forcing the Tajikistan leadership to pursue a trajectory of soft authoritarian rule.

Fragmented state security institutions

Similarly, the coercive capacity of the state to enforce hard line authoritarianism after the civil war has been weak and internally divided. Tajikistan's leaders were constrained in ways that moderated their ability to carry out pre-emptive and protective policies of authoritarianism. If, as Lucan Way has argued, 'a strong coercive apparatus that has won a major violent conflict' is an important basis of authoritarian organizational power,[32] then Tajikistan clearly lacked such organizational power after a decade of state security fragmentation, state failure and civil war. Much of Tajikistan's security apparatus was split from within and left dependent on the rent-seeking activities of individual field commanders who had become state security or law enforcement officials.[33]

In fact, following mass demonstrations in Georgia, Ukraine and Kyrgyzstan – and the brutal repression used by Uzbekistan's regime against protests in Andijan Province in May 2005 – top government officials in Tajikistan indicated a willingness to use force as a means of eliminating rivals and reasserting control over large areas of the country. Statements by the deputy head of Tajikistan's dominant People's Democratic Party, Abdumajid Davlatov, described protestors in Andijan as 'extremists' seeking to challenge state authority.[34] The head of Tajikistan's National Security Council, Amirkul Azimov, argued that the government of Uzbekistan's actions were 'timely and correct', and that similar repression of mass mobilizations in Dushanbe in 1992 would have 'demonstrated firmness' on the part of the regime which would have averted Tajikistan's five-year civil war.[35] The use of force against domestic mobilization was clearly an acceptable policy position by many hard-line members of Tajikistan's leadership.

The state in Tajikistan, however, lacked the capacity to actually carry out coercive controls evenly across the country. State failure and civil war in Tajikistan had entailed the fragmentation of state security institutions into autonomous agents of organized violence.[36] Since 1997, competition over rents between former civil war combatants who were absorbed into security and rule of law institutions has extended these internal divisions well beyond the conclusion of hostilities. A 2007 survey of 50 legal experts by this author found that they assessed local prokurators' enforcement of crop extraction (especially grain and cotton) and debt collection in some regions much lower than other regions. Using a two-tailed difference of proportions test, it was found that differences in on-the-job performance between these regions are statistically significant at the .05 level.[37] Even within a single province, respondents identified specific resource-rich localities as having powerful district governors and weak, ineffective rule of law institutions 'where investors and other rich people can solve problems with money'.[38] As a result, Tajikistan remains defined by big disparities in its rule of law institutions and in the application of coercive power.

Fragmented state security institutions in Tajikistan have undercut domestic and international state-building efforts by subsuming post-conflict state reconstruction to disparate agendas of competing groups within the country's fractured state apparatus. The emergence of fragmented state security institutions after Tajikistan's civil war is a product of two developments. First, Tajikistan's peace settlement called for militias to be reintegrated into state security organs without being demobilized. Reintegration of paramilitary forces before they were demobilized has imported into the state apparatus informal ties based on locality, region, clientelism and clan.[39] Anecdotal evidence suggests that the parochialism of these ties has been difficult to extinguish within these institutions. For example, the National Guard was created to protect the interests of the presidency, and its real power stems from its proximity to the president. Yet this praetorian guard has nonetheless remained under the authority of former progovernment militia commander Gaffor Mirzoev who commands the personal loyalty of several thousand (many of whom left the Guard when he was transferred to the National Drug Control Agency (AKN) in 2004).[40] Over time, moreover, the government's initial reliance on a formula of amnesty and reintegration has been whittled down to just occasional expressions of amnesty (without genuine reintegration).[41] As a result, law enforcement's limited autonomy has been compounded by high levels of partisan politics within regions of the former opposition.

Second, the regime's reliance on informal bases of support within its security and legal apparatus have undermined its development and use of courts, procurators and police in the maintenance of public order. Lucrative rents continue to play a role in perpetuating divisions within Tajikistan's security apparatus. Both pro-government and former opposition units have been implicated in drug trafficking, providing protection for dealers and traders as well as personally transporting narcotics themselves. Many newly-integrated United Tajik Opposition (UTO) units in the police and Ministry of Emergency Situations were involved in rebel activity (including hostage taking and insurgent attacks) even as they held these official positions.[42] Likewise, government attempts to minimize the role of UTO commanders in these and other government offices have exacerbated internal divisions. As a result of government efforts to gradually dismiss, arrest, or exile former UTO leaders and their fighters from law enforcement agencies, this distrust and suspicion remains embedded in these institutions – occasionally producing militarized conflict within the MVD, belying the country's veneer of stability. In early 2008, a firefight broke out between a Dushanbe-based, pro-government paramilitary group and a Garm-based anti-organized crime unit that left several dead. [43] Likewise, a battle was waged between pro-government security forces and a brother of the former leader of one of the militia forces that brought President Rahmon to power. Suhrob Langariev allegedly enjoyed protection from former commanders and used this to engage in transnational drug trafficking.[44] The regime's slow elimination of those like Langariev, who enjoy protection from those in government, remains a significant challenge in Dushanbe's ability to control even those regions that are supposedly its base of support. As a result, attempts by the government to carry out a hard line set of policies beyond the capital continue to remain in doubt, often depending on the allegiances of the security forces.

This has forced the regime to rely heavily on renewing top-down patronage ties to local elites to the detriment of rule of law and state security institutions. As a lawyer explained, appointment to political office ensures protection to engage in corruption, embezzlement and other illegal activities: 'while any leader has power, no prokurator and no part of the Prokuratura can move against him'.[45] However, the regime's use of rents as a means of pressuring local elites to bind themselves to the regime has yielded mixed results. In localities where the regime has succeeded, local law enforcement bodies 'have become a weapon in the hands of government for the elimination of those commanders, businessmen, and politicians that do not ingratiate themselves'.[46] In localities where rent-seeking has not bound local elites to the regime, law enforcement agencies 'openly serve the interests of commanders [chinovnikov]', and not those of the central government.[47] In short, Tajikistan's coercive capacity and its rule of law institutions remain deeply divided internally, its cohesion dependent on the regime's provision of rent-seeking opportunities. In a postwar environment of scarce resources, mobile capital and limited rent-seeking opportunities,

Tajikistan's regime commands weak 'patronal presidential' power and a fragmented state security apparatus. As a result, a trajectory of soft authoritarian rule has emerged, which has been only slightly focused by the threat of democratic revolution.

Barriers to mass protest in postwar Tajikistan

Few observers believe that Tajikistan confronts a significant threat of democratic revolution, or any other transfer of power inspired by mass mobilization.[48] Several structural factors that led to democratic revolution in Serbia, Ukraine and Georgia – such as mobilized urbanites, civil society groups and student activists – were not prominent in any of the Central Asian countries.[49] This is particularly true of Tajikistan. It is the poorest, most rural republic of the former Soviet Union, with an urban elite spread across two cities (Khojand and Dushanbe) and clan divisions in society.[50] Although Tajikistan's civil society sector is relatively well developed for such a small country, its NGOs are largely donor-driven, dependent on the state, or some combination of the two.

Tajikistan, moreover, is unlikely to host a democratic revolution even by Central Asian standards. Most of the conditions that were crucial in bringing about the 'Tulip Revolution' in Kyrgyzstan, such as an autonomous business elite or a partial political opening caused by a succession crisis, are absent in Tajikistan.[51] So far no significant business or financial elite has emerged outside the state in Tajikistan. Members of the economic elite remain intimately connected to (and reinforce the power of) the country's political leadership.[52] Since signing a power sharing pact to end the civil war in 1997, the space for political debate and public dissent has steadily narrowed as the current leadership has forced opposition elites out of key posts and has monitored mass media outlets. Similarly President Rahmon has given no indication that he plans to leave office; on the contrary, he has changed the constitution so his rule could be extended until 2020.[53]

In addition, Tajikistan possesses a strong aversion to mass mobilization, which many in the country believe had led to Tajikistan's five-year civil war. Because mass demonstrations helped lead to the outbreak of the conflict, political mobilization today remains discredited among many people. Most attempts by dissidents to foster a similar revolution received virtually no mass-based support within the country. A prominent effort to replicate mass mobilization against the Rahmon regime, for instance, was attempted by exiled journalist Dodojon Atovulloev, who founded the Vatandor (Patriot) party.[54] Yet his efforts to mobilize Tajikistan's sizeable labour migrant population in Russia to back his drive for a 'violet revolution' have failed. As one migrant labourer explained, 'We don't need rallies, reforms, or new parties. It's hard for us to find work in our country with the current regime, but if there's a new one, what's the guarantee that life will get any better?'[55] As a 2008 Freedom House report concluded, 'chances of a liberal so-called colour revolution remain rather slim, as the population is generally depoliticized: some enjoying their economic gains and others worrying about daily subsistence'.[56] Given the regime's ability to marginalize political opponents, stabilize the country and bring about economic growth, there has been little likelihood of democratic revolution.

President Rahmon has deftly capitalized on this postwar political culture, using it to justify his stasis over change to the political programme by invoking memories of the political turbulence that preceded the country's civil war. Rahmon has repeatedly advanced a standard refrain of autocratic rulers – that, if he is removed, chaos and war will follow. Democratic revolution would not happen, he has suggested, because 'the people of Tajikistan already understand what civil war and instability are'.[57] In the decade following the civil war, most popular protests appear to be localized expressions of discontent arising from the lack of basic state services, such as electricity, gas and water.

In Tajikistan, therefore, the absence of significant threats of mass mobilization against the regime has provided the leadership with more room to manoeuver than its Central Asian counterparts and has not pushed it toward hard authoritarian rule. Of course, developments in Serbia, Ukraine and Georgia, and especially the forced abdication of President Askar Akaev of Kyrgyzstan, had a significant effect on the Rahmon leadership, surprising many in the government that 'democratic revolution' had reached Central Asia. And it is clear that since 2005 policies targeting opposition groups, NGOs and media outlets in Tajikistan were influenced by the positive example of crackdowns and restrictions imposed in neighbouring states.[58] But in Tajikistan many of these developments were far more selective and limited. On the surface, Tajikistan's strategies look much like those of its Eurasian neighbours: undercutting and dividing the political opposition, driving out international NGOs and tightly controlling local ones, harassing human rights organizations, marginalizing independent media and strengthening Rahmon's political party's majority in the legislature.[59] Yet, the absence of mobilization within society and effective exclusion of any open political opposition has given the regime some space to pursue its particular form of soft authoritarianism. Far more important to explain the absence of mass mobilization have been the constraints on the regime's political foundations and coercive capacity in a context of diffuse rent-seeking opportunities and debilitated state structures after civil war.

Authoritarian reaction moderated

Tajikistan's response to the possibility of regime change has highlighted the limits of traditional levers of state power and the importance of political and ideological mechanisms available to the regime. The Rahmon leadership has reversed electoral reforms, but it implemented a selective and temporary crackdown on media and NGOs, and applied its use of force in a circumscribed fashion. At the same time, the regime has sought to engender public views of moderate Islam and initiate the cultivation of myths of ethno-genesis as central to Tajik national identity. While present in other countries, these mechanisms in Tajikistan are due to the constraints placed on the country's leadership, giving rise to a moderated form of authoritarian reaction.

Reversed electoral reforms

In the wake of 'democratic revolutions' during national elections in Serbia, Georgia, Ukraine and Kyrgyzstan, the regime in Tajikistan rapidly reversed or side-lined electoral reforms. In particular, large-scale irregularities during Tajikistan's 2005 parliamentary election and 2006 presidential election undermined several promising procedural and legal changes enacted in 2004. Amendments to the Constitutional Law on Elections in 2004 incorporated provisions for political party observers, improved candidate access to mass media outlets and immediate posting of election results at each polling station. The revamped legislative framework could have provided a basis for democratic elections had it been fully implemented. Instead, intimidation and arrest of leading opposition figures, glaring errors in tabulating ballots and extensive interference by local authorities ensured that neither election was open and competitive.[60]

In particular, the regime utilized Tajikistan's electoral administration to direct the outcome of the parliamentary and presidential elections. Tajikistan has a three-tiered system of election commissions: a national-level Central Commission on Elections and Referenda (CCER), district election commissions (DECs), and polling state commissions (PSCs). Members of the CCER are proposed by the president and elected by parliament's lower house, the Lower Majlis, although the dominance of the president's party, the People's Democratic Party of Tajikistan (PDPT), in the legislature ensured PDPT control over the body. As a result, the promise of open meetings of the CCER was neglected and the decision-making and functioning of the CCER remained non-transparent. At the local level, the staffing of DECs was so compromised by local government interference that it was at times difficult to distinguish between the two.[61]

The 27 February 2005 legislative elections consolidated PDPT control over the legislative branch. The Lower Majlis has 63 seats, to which 22 members are elected from party lists and 41 from single-member constituencies. Of the six parties that entered candidates, the PDPT took 52 seats, whereas the pro-government Communist Party won three seats, the Islamic Renaissance Party won two seats, and independent candidates took the remaining six seats. OSCE/ODIHR election observers noted widespread multiple voting and unmonitored tabulation processes in district commissions, where many protocols were illegally altered. Moreover, restrictive registration requirements (including a newly imposed US$500 deposit, higher education, and 500 signatures of eligible voters from the constituency) resulted in the exclusion of approximately 100 prospective candidates by DECs.

In addition, just months before the election criminal charges were brought against prominent candidates, including Mahmadruzi Iskandarov (head of the Democratic Party) and Sulton Kuvatov (head of the unregistered Taraqqiyot Party), disqualifying them from electoral competition. Both the timing of the criminal charges and the disqualification of opposition candidates raised serious concerns about the openness of the election. Immediately following the election three opposition parties (IRP, DP, and the Social Democratic Party) declared that they would not recognize the election results. In addition, complaints filed with the CCER and in several district courts were either overruled or ignored.[62]

Changes to Tajikistan's constitution in 2003 gave President Rahmon the legal basis to run for two more seven-year terms in office, possibly extending his tenure until 2020. The 6 November 2006 presidential election returned Rahmon to office with 79.3% of the vote, followed by Olimjon Boboev (6.3%), Amir Karakulov and Ismoil Talbakov (each with 5.2%), and Abduhalim Ghafarov (2.8%). None of the major opposition parties ran in the election, leaving Rahmon facing a field of unknown candidates.[63] In the months leading up to the 2006 presidential election, various members of the political opposition were arrested and detained in a clear pattern on the part of government authorities of using the state's law enforcement and judicial organs as a means of reining in the opposition. In December 2004, Mahmudi Iskandarov, leader of the Democratic Party and likely presidential candidate, was arrested in Moscow by Russian authorities at Tajikistan's request. Immediately after his release by Russian authorities in April 2005, he disappeared (allegedly abducted), and ultimately resurfaced in Tajikistan government custody. On 5 October 2005, he was sentenced to 23 years in prison and fined 1.5 million Tajik somoni (US$470,000) for terrorism and unlawful possession of weapons. Taraqqiyot Party Deputy Chair Rustam Faziev and Chair Sulton Kuvatov were both arrested and sent to prison on charges of insulting the president after publishing an open letter critical of President Rahmon. In mid-2005, Social Democratic Party parliamentary candidates Nizomiddin Begmatov and Nasimjon Shukurov were arrested and sentenced to a year and 18 months, respectively, for hooliganism (allegedly for using foul language during a court hearing).[64] In early 2006, Islamic Renaissance Party member Tojiddin Abdurahmonov – convicted of involvement in organized criminal activity, possession of weapons and possession of forged documents – was sentenced to 16 years imprisonment.[65]

The weakness and rudderlessness of the opposition was partially due to the arrests of Iskandarov and Kuvatov and the death of IRP leader Said Abdullo Nuri in August 2006.[66] But it was also a result of limitations imposed on candidates' access to media outlets, basic security concerns when travelling, and the heavy involvement of local authorities in organizing local PDPT political machines.[67] While Rahmon did not officially campaign, his four challengers held no independent rallies and campaigned in joint gatherings organized by local government or the CCER.[68] This reversal and sidelining of electoral reforms reflects the most effective dimension of Tajikistan's anti-democratic measures.

Selective crackdown on media and NGOs

Since the civil war, Tajikistan has seen a significant rise in NGOs, many of which focus on post-conflict peace-building, socio-economic development and humanitarian projects.[69] While these groups were unable to significantly testify against or influence government policy or legislation, recent moves by the government have significantly increased its pressure on NGOs. In the spring of 2005, the government ordered financial audits of several international organizations in Tajikistan and later that year, authorities refused registration to several NGOs, including Freedom House and the National Democratic Institute for International Affairs.[70] In March 2006, the government extended its restrictions by passing the Law on Public Associations, which requires NGOs to register annually.[71] Through these and other mechanisms, government authorities continue to pressure civic organizations, local and international. According to data provided by Minister of Justice Davlat Suleimonov, only 1040 organizations were re-registered in 2007 out of more than 3500 organizations that were registered in 2006.[72]

Yet restrictions on NGOs have been far less severe than in other Eurasian states, especially on those organizations engaged in economic development and institution building. As a result, the crackdown on foreign NGOs has been selective. Political watchdog organizations, such as Freedom House and the National Democratic Institute for International Affairs, have been denied the right to operate in the country or face considerable government pressure. Yet many foreign NGOs that are involved in social and economic development, promoting rule of law institutions, and providing humanitarian assistance have been encouraged to operate relatively unhindered. This is because these organizations bring in significant financial assistance and they provide services that the government does not have to fulfill itself. One list of foreign NGOs engaged in health sector development alone identified over 95 grants underway in 2006 and 2007, many of which are several million dollars.[73] Estimates for foreign aid in food security and health are predicted to be roughly $10 billion from 2005–2015.[74] Tajikistan's crackdown on NGOs does not extend to those that provide financing, which the regime can – directly or indirectly – access.

Similarly, government authorities have used various methods to restrict the activity of independent media organizations. A new requirement that non-state media outlets obtain licences from the Ministry of Culture was only one of 40 amendments to Tajikistan's media laws in 2005.[75] In August 2004, the government closed Tajikistan's sole independent publishing house, making it impossible for opposition papers to turn out editions. The government has continued, since 2004, to force independent print newspapers out of circulation; *Nerui Sokhan*, *Ruzi Nav*, and *Odamu Olan* were denied accreditation for failure to pay taxes or technical violations.[76] At the time, Tajikistan Prokurator General Bobojon Bobokhonov accused international organizations of funding these 'slanderous papers' and undermining the country's progression toward post-conflict recovery.[77] The government has arrested and/or intimidated editors and reporters, including correspondents for the British Broadcasting Corporation (BBC) and *Sardoi Mardum* (Tajikistan's parliamentary paper), and *Nerui Sokhan*.[78] The editor of the latter was convicted of theft (for siphoning electricity from street lights) and sentenced to two years imprisonment and the confiscation of 20% of his earnings during this time.[79] As Shahram Akbarzadeh describes, government authorities saw these independent and opposition publications as supported politically and economically by the United States.[80]

In early August 2006, the BBC's application for a broadcasting licence was refused by Tajikistan's licensing commission for failing to meet the 2005 law 'On Licensing Certain Types of Activities'.[81] Since the shutdown of Tajikistan's last independent television station, Somonien, in 2005, broadcast media have been dominated by three state television stations, which have received a 25% increase in government funding.[82] In October 2006 (one month before the election), the Ministry of Communications blocked domestic access to five news websites published abroad: *Centrasia*, *Ferghana*, *Arianastorm*, *Charogiruz* and *Tajikistantimes*.[83] However, government restrictions on the media have relaxed since the presidential election in 2006, and the country was ranked higher in press openness than Russia, Kazakhstan, Turkmenistan and Uzbekistan in 2007.[84]

In short, the state has intensified its use of onerous laws on registration requirements, tax liabilities and libel to impose excessive fines or imprisonment on print and broadcast media outlets as part of its authoritarian reaction. Alongside these tactics, state authorities have stifled critical press and media through the use of extra-legal intimidation, arbitrary arrest and detention. Overall, however, Tajikistan has moderated its crackdown on the media, as well as on NGOs, which have been more temporary and more selective than similar state actions in other Eurasian states.

Redefining the debate on Islam and the nation

In the wake of civil war, Tajikistan's small resource base, limited rent-seeking opportunities, and fragmented coercive capacity have weakened the regime's ability to punish subversive elites by denying them access to rents or through repressive measures. As a result, the government has supplemented these strategies with instruments of persuasion, focused on promoting public definitions of nationalism and Islam, as a means of advancing the cooptation of elite and public support. Since 2005, government authorities have attempted to curtail certain fundamental religious freedoms. In March 2006, the government prepared a single law on religion that would codify existing practices and add new restrictions on religious freedoms, including a 200 signature requirement to register religious associations, state control over religious education, a limit on the number of mosques in Tajikistan, and the imposition of state control over pilgrimages to Mecca. To date this law has not been passed due to opposition from religious communities.[85]

Instead, the state has pursued a two-pronged strategy toward Islam: on the one hand, it has continued to target groups it defines as extremist and on the other it seeks to shape popular beliefs by focusing on redefining elements of cultural and religious practice. State monitoring of Islamist movements, however, has steadily increased since the Islamic Movement of Uzbekistan (IMU) used Tajikistan to launch armed incursions into Uzbekistan. Under Article 187 (which bans the arousal of religious and ethnic dissension) and Article 307 (which bans calls to overthrow the government) in Tajikistan's criminal code, government authorities have arrested about 500 alleged members of Hizb ut-Tahrir between 2000 and 2005. Although only 189 cases were brought to court, there are an estimated 150–200 Hizb ut-Tahrir members currently imprisoned.[86] The government's monitoring and pressure on Islamist groups such as Hizb ut-Tahrir may carry ethnic overtones as many of the group's activities are reportedly among Uzbek minority populations (who constitute 16% of the population) in Tajikistan.[87] As a result, crackdowns on Hizb ut-Tahrir have fallen disproportionately on the Uzbek minority. More recently, the Salafiya movement has been banned by the Supreme Court in January 2009 and the Prokurator General arrested 40 of its members, including the movement's leader Mullo Sirojiddin, in Dushanbe for fomenting religious animosity and posing a security threat to the state in June 2009.[88]

Yet at the same time, the regime has sought to create new ideological messages of Islam and the nation. In March 2007, headscarves were banned in educational institutions (though women are allowed to wear a hijab when photographed for official documents).[89] Beginning in 2009, Islam has become a mandatory subject within Tajikistan's public school system.[90] While Tajikistan appears to be separating 'bad' Islam from 'good' Islam, what is different since 2005 is a concerted attempt to craft a message of Islam that will compete ideologically with Hizb-ut Tahrir and other groups.

In addition, Tajikistan has also embarked on an attempt since 2005 to promote a 'secularized national ideology', both to provide a competing discourse to Islam and to promote a unifying message that claims Aryan origins of the Tajik people. 2006 was declared the 'year of the Aryan civilization' and school textbooks with rewritten Tajik history have been produced.[91] This marks a shift from public policies relating to the nation in post-Soviet Tajikistan. While Tajik cultural identity has been reinforced in school texts, through national monuments in public spaces, and in language policies, Tajikistan has not overtly advanced national identity to the same degree as Uzbekistan or Turkmenistan.[92] Yet Tajikistan's central government now appears to be pursuing just such a strategy of nation-building as an alternative lever of authoritarian reaction.

Conclusion

In contrast to other Central Asian countries responding to pressures of democratization, Tajikistan is a weak, post-conflict state, which carries implications for the nature of its authoritarian reaction. Political mobilization in Tajikistan – already unlikely given its structural conditions – remains discredited since protests are believed to have led to civil war in the 1990s. Post-conflict regime survival in Tajikistan, moreover, required strategies of openly consolidating power that were highly similar to those implemented in the course of authoritarian reaction.

Concentrating presidential power through institutional controls, eliminating rivals, and commanding enormous rents from Tajikistan's limited pie of wealth were central features of Rahmon's government prior to rising concerns over democratic change from below. Yet the regime has struggled to monopolize access to rents. Since 2005, efforts to control and disburse rents have remained varied, in some cases strengthening Rahmon's leverage over elites through political patronage and in others attenuating his influence.

Finally, state failure led to the fragmentation of state security apparatuses in Tajikistan, which has severely constrained the implementation of authoritarian reaction. As the case of Tajikistan demonstrates, authoritarian reaction is not necessarily a reflection of the incentives of political elites. It must also be carried out on the ground, raising the question of what constraints and opportunities confront the regime. In post-conflict states, constraints – such as vested interests and fragmented coercive capacities – may emerge as far more significant than in other countries seeking similar paths of authoritarian reaction. As a result, the use of coercion has focused on politically active NGOs and civil society groups rather than 'real' opponents to the regime based within Tajikistan's security apparatus and in its regional governments.

The weak demand for authoritarian reaction, the minimal shift in strategies of rule that it required of Tajikistan's leadership, and the weak capacity of the state all conspire to produce a moderate case of authoritarian reaction. As the Tajikistan example demonstrates, moderate authoritarian reaction consists of several components. First, it involves the reversal of electoral reforms, which exact little cost to even the weakest regimes. Along this dimension of authoritarian reaction, there is no distinction between severe and moderate cases. Second, actions taken to crack down on the media and NGOs, however, are far more temporary and selective than authoritarian reaction in more severe cases. In addition, efforts by the regime to enforce a rule of law in cases of moderate authoritarian reaction result in a far more circumscribed application of the use of force against mobilized populations. Finally, it entails efforts by the regime to compensate for its political and institutional weaknesses by promoting alternative mechanisms of persuasion – in this case, it advanced new definitions of the nation and of Islam to Tajikistan's population – as an extension of its evolving soft authoritarianism.

This article highlights the specific features of authoritarian reaction within a post-conflict state. In Tajikistan, scarce resources and limited rent-seeking opportunities can be critical sources of soft authoritarianism by weakening the bases of autocrats' informal authority and perpetuating internal divisions within state security structures. Like Tajikistan, many leaders of post-conflict countries who struggle to monopolize state rents will find strategies of soft authoritarian rule the only viable ways of staying in power. Even when mass protests bring down neighbouring regimes, authoritarian reaction that is pursued by leaders in a post-conflict setting confronts constraints of weak statehood that mitigate rather than exacerbate authoritarian policies.

Notes

1. Schatz, 'Access by Accident'.
2. Foroughi, 'Tajikistan (2011)'.
3. Schatz, 'The Soft Authoritarian "Tool Kit"'.
4. Rubin, 'Russian Hegemony and State Breakdown in the Periphery'.
5. See for instance, Ottaway, *Democracy Challenged*; and Levitsky and Way, *Competitive Authoritarianism*.
6. Buisson, 'State-Building, Power-Building and Political Legitimacy'; Matveeva, 'Tajikistan: Stability First'.
7. Nakaya, 'Aid and Transition from a War Economy to an Oligarchy in Post-war Tajikistan'.
8. Heathershaw, *Post-conflict Tajikistan*.
9. Driscoll, 'Commitment Problems or Bidding Wars?'.
10. Nourzhanov, 'Saviours of the Nation or Robber Barons?', 125.
11. Ibid., 124.
12. Heathershaw, *Post-conflict Tajikistan*.
13. Hale, 'Democracy or Autocracy on the March?', 307.
14. Driscoll, 'Commitment Problems or Bidding Wars?'.
15. Nourzhanov, 'Saviours of the Nation or Robber Barons?'.
16. Ibid.
17. Nourzhanov, 'Alternative Social Institutions and the Politics of Neo-Patrimonialism in Tajikistan'.
18. Atkiner, *Tajikistan: Disintegration or Reconciliation?*, 74.
19. Meyer et al., 'Rural Finance in Tajikistan', 47–8.
20. Nakaya, 'Aid and Transition from a War Economy to an Oligarchy in Post-war Tajikistan', 266.
21. Meyer et al., 'Rural Finance in Tajikistan', 33.
22. Markowitz, 'Unlootable Resources and State Security Institutions in Tajikistan and Uzbekistan'.
23. Nakaya, 'Aid and Transition from a War Economy to an Oligarchy in Post-war Tajikistan'.
24. Ibid., 265.
25. Dzalaeva, 'Foreign Aid Management and the State Budget Cycle in Tajikistan'.
26. Aminjanov, Kholmatov, and Kataev, 'Case Study on Aid Effectiveness in Tajikistan', 45.
27. United Nations Office on Drugs and Crime and Ministry of Counter-Narcotics of Afghanistan, *Afghanistan Opium Survey 2010, Summary Findings*.
28. The drop in Tajikistan's heroin seizures cannot be explained by a drop in opium production. Opium cultivation in Afghanistan has risen from 80,000 ha in 2003 to a peak of 193,000 ha in 2007 before levelling off at 123,000 ha in 2009 and 2010. Ibid.
29. Lewis, 'High Times on the Silk Road: The Central Asian Paradox', 40.
30. Engvall, 'The State Under Siege: The Drug Trade and Organised Crime in Tajikistan', 845.
31. Hale, 'Regime Cycles, Democracy, Autocracy, and Revolution in Post-Soviet Eurasia', 138.
32. Way, 'The Real Causes of the Color Revolutions', 60.
33. Nourzhanov, 'Saviours of the Nation or Robber Barons?'.
34. Jonson, *Tajikistan in the New Central Asia*, 147.
35. Ibid.
36. Markowitz, 'Unlootable Resources and State Security Institutions in Tajikistan and Uzbekistan'.
37. For more on procurators' performances in specific regions, see ibid.

38. Interviews #9, #11, #32, #49, and #59 with lawyers, Dushanbe, Tajikistan, August–September 2007.
39. Torjesen and McFarlane, 'R before D: The Case of Post Conflict Reintegration in Tajikistan'; Collins, *Clan Politics and Regime Change in Central Asia*.
40. Institute for War and Peace Reporting, 'Tajikistan: Fall of Praetorian Guardsman'.
41. 'Tajik President Declares Amnesty For Former Militants'.
42. Engvall, 'The State Under Siege: The Drug Trade and Organised Crime in Tajikistan'; Heathershaw, *Post-conflict Tajikistan*, 122–4.
43. International War and Peace Reporting, 'Murder Invokes Ghosts of Tajikistan's Past'.
44. International War and Peace Reporting, 'Cops and Robbers in Tajikistan'.
45. Interview #52 with lawyer, Dushanbe, Tajikistan, August–September 2007.
46. Interview #11 with legal expert, Dushanbe, Tajikistan, August–September 2007.
47. Interview #2 with legal expert, Dushanbe, Tajikistan, August–September 2007.
48. Matveeva, 'Tajikistan: Stability First'.
49. Radnitz, 'What Really Happened in Kyrgyzstan?'.
50. Collins, *Clan Politics and Regime Change in Central Asia*.
51. Radnitz, *Weapons of the Wealthy*; Hale, 'Regime Cycles, Democracy, Autocracy, and Revolution in Post-Soviet Eurasia,'.
52. Heathershaw, *Post-conflict Tajikistan*.
53. Foroughi, 'Tajikistan (2011)'.
54. 'Tajikistan: Dushanbe Wants Russia to Extradite Opposition Activist'.
55. Pisaredzheva, 'New Tajik Party Seeks Émigré Vote'.
56. Muhutdinova, 'Tajikistan (2008)', 5.
57. Hale, 'Democracy or Autocracy on the March?', 320.
58. For more on how elites drew upon the successful examples of others in limiting democratization, see Beissinger, 'Structure and Example in Modular Political Phenomena: The Diffusion of Bulldozer/Rose/Orange/Tulip Revolutions'.
59. Foroughi, 'Tajikistan (2011)'.
60. *OSCE/ODIHR Election Observation Mission Final Report, Republic of Tajikistan, Parliamentary Elections 27 February and 13 March 2005.*
61. Ibid., 6; *OSCE/ODIHR Election Observation Mission Report, Republic of Tajikistan, Presidential Elections 6 November 2006.*
62. *OSCE/ODIHR Election Observation Mission Final Report, Republic of Tajikistan, Parliamentary Elections 27 February and 13 March 2005.*
63. Azimov, 'Islamists Shun Tajik Election with Eye to Future'.
64. 'Tajikistan: Country Summary', *World Report 2006*.
65. 'Tajikistan: Country Summary', *World Report 2007*.
66. 'Tajikistan: Opposition Disorganized as Presidential Election Nears'.
67. *OSCE/ODIHR Election Observation Mission Report, Republic of Tajikistan, Presidential Elections 6 November 2006.*
68. Pannier, 'Tajikistan: Presidential Candidates Take to Campaign Trail – Together'.
69. One source estimated that over 1200 NGOs registered in 2002 alone. See Freizer, 'Neo-liberal and Communal Civil Society in Tajikistan: Merging or Dividing in the Post War Period?', 227.
70. Muhutdinova, 'Tajikistan (2008)'.
71. Freizer, 'Neo-liberal and Communal Civil Society in Tajikistan: Merging or Dividing in the Post War Period?'.
72. 'Novosti: Ministerstvo yustitsii Respubliki Tadzhikistan priostanovit deiatel'nost' vsekh organizatsii, ne proshedshikh pereregistratsiyu.'
73. Aminjanov, Kholmatov, and Kataev, 'Case Study on Aid Effectiveness in Tajikistan', 54–63.
74. Ibid., 71.

75. See the chapter on Tajikistan in IREX, *Media Sustainability Index 2005*.
76. CPJ, 'Government Controls on News Compromise Vote in Tajikistan'.
77. 'Tajik Prosecutor Slams International Organizations for Supporting Opposition'.
78. RSF, 'Tajikistan – 2006 Annual Report'.
79. Organization for Security and Co-operation in Europe, 'Human Rights in the OSCE Region'.
80. Akbarzadeh, 'Geo-politics versus Democracy in Tajikistan'.
81. 'Tajik Government "Tightening the Screws" on Independent Media'.
82. Committee to Protect Journalists, 'Attacks on the Press in 2006: Tajikistan'.
83. CPJ, 'Government Controls on News Compromise Vote in Tajikistan'.
84. Muhutdinova, 'Tajikistan (2008)', 10.
85. 'Tajikistan: Country Summary', *World Report 2007*.
86. Karagiannis, 'The Challenge of Radical Islam in Tajikistan: Hizb ut-Tahrir al-Islami', 2.
87. Saidazimova, 'Central Asia: Radical Islamists Challenge Government Efforts at Control (Part 3)'.
88. Gufronov, 'Salafiya' ob'yavlena v Tadzhikistane vne zakona'; Majidov, 'Tajikistan Cracks Down on Radical Religious Movements'.
89. Najibullah, 'Tajikistan: Authorities Exclude Miniskirt, Hejab on Campuses'.
90. Najibullah, 'Islam Becomes Mandatory Study in Secular Tajik Schools'.
91. Laruelle, 'The Return of the Aryan Myth: Tajikistan in Search of a Secularized National Ideology'.
92. March, 'From Leninism to Karimovism: Hegemony, Ideology, and Authoritarian Legitimation'.

Notes on contributor

Lawrence P. Markowitz is Assistant Professor of Political Science at Rowan University. His research has appeared in *Comparative Political Studies*, *Ethnic and Racial Studies*, *Central Asian Survey*, and several edited volumes.

Bibliography

Akbarzadeh, Shahram. 'Geo-politics versus Democracy in Tajikistan'. *Demokratizatsiya* 14 (2006): 563–78.

Aminjanov, Rustam, Martin Kholmatov, and Firuz Kataev. 'Case Study on Aid Effectiveness in Tajikistan'. *Working Paper 13*. Washington, DC: Wolfensohn Center for Development, Brookings Institution, 2009.

Atkiner, Shirin. *Tajikistan: Disintegration or Reconciliation?* London: The Royal institute of International Affairs, 2001.

Azimov, Dadojan. 'Islamists Shun Tajik Election with Eye to Future'. *RCA No. 467*, October 5, 2006. http://www.iwpr.net/?p=rca&s=f&o=324364&apc_state=henirca2006 (accessed February 16, 2007).

Beissinger, Mark R. 'Structure and Example in Modular Political Phenomena: The Diffusion of Bulldozer/Rose/Orange/Tulip Revolutions'. *Perspectives on Politics* 5 (2007): 259–76.

Buisson, Antoine. 'State-Building, Power-Building and Political Legitimacy: The Case of Post-Conflict Tajikistan'. *The China and Eurasia Forum Quarterly* 5 (2007): 115–46.

Collins, Kathleen. *Clan Politics and Regime Transition in Central Asia*. Cambridge: Cambridge University Press, 2006.

Committee to Protect Journalists. 'Attacks on the Press in 2006: Tajikistan'. 2006. http://www.cpj.org/attacks06/europe06/taj06.html (accessed February 16, 2007).

CPJ. 'Government Controls on News Compromise Vote in Tajikistan'. New York: Committee to Protect Journalists (CPJ), 2006. http://www.cpj.org/news/2006/europe/tajik03nov06na.html (accessed February 16, 2007).

Driscoll, Jesse. 'Commitment Problems or Bidding Wars? Rebel Fragmentation as Peace-Building'. *Journal of Conflict Resolution*, in press.

Dzalaeva, Sabina-Margarita. 'Foreign Aid Management and the State Budget Cycle in Tajikistan'. *NISPAcee News 2007* 14 (2007): 1–6.

Engvall, Johann. 'The State Under Siege: The Drug Trade and Organised Crime in Tajikistan'. *Europe-Asia Studies* 58 (2006): 827–54.

Foroughi, Payam. 'Tajikistan (2011)'. In *Nations in Transit.* (pp. 501–518) Washington, DC: Freedom House, 2011.

Freizer, Sabine. 'Neo-liberal and Communal Civil Society in Tajikistan: Merging or Dividing in the Post War Period?' *Central Asian Survey* 24 (2005): 205–29.

Gufronov, Daler. 'Salafiya' ob'yavlena v Tadzhikistane vne zakona'. *Asia-Plus*, January 8, 2009. http://asiaplus.tj/news/47/44944.html (accessed December 13, 2009).

Hale, Henry. 'Democracy or Autocracy on the March? The Colored Revolutions as Normal Dynamics of Patronal Presidentialism'. *Communist and Post-Communist Studies* 39 (2006): 205–329.

Hale, Henry. 'Regime Cycles, Democracy, Autocracy, and Revolution in Post-Soviet Eurasia'. *World Politics* 58 (2005): 133–65.

Heathershaw, John. *Post-conflict Tajikistan: The Politics of Peacebuilding and the Emergence of Legitimate Order.* London, New York: Routledge, 2009.

Human Rights Watch. 'Tajikistan: Country Summary'. *World Report 2006.* New York: Human Rights Watch, 2006.

Human Rights Watch. 'Tajikistan: Country Summary'. *World Report 2007.* New York: Human Rights Watch, 2007.

Institute for War and Peace Reporting. 'Tajikistan: Fall of Praetorian Guardsman'. *RCA No 306*, August 10, 2004.

International War and Peace Reporting. 'Cops and Robbers in Tajikistan'. *RCA No 624*, June 6, 2008.

International War and Peace Reporting. 'Murder Invokes Ghosts of Tajikistan's Past'. *RCA No 533*, February 20, 2007.

IREX. *Media Sustainability Index 2005.* Washington, DC: International Research and Exchanges Board (IREX), 2005. http://www.irex.org/programs/MSI_EUR/2005/MSI05-Tajikistan.pdf.

Jonson, Lena. *Tajikistan in the New Central Asia: Geopolitics, Great Power Rivalry and Radical Islam.* London, New York: IB Tauris, 2006.

Karagiannis, Emmanuel. 'The Challenge of Radical Islam in Tajikistan: Hizb ut-Tahrir al-Islami'. *Nationalities Papers* 34 (2006): 1–20.

Laruelle, Marlene. 'The Return of the Aryan Myth: Tajikistan in Search of a Secularized National Ideology'. *Nationalities Papers* 35 (2007): 51–70.

Levitsky, Steven, and Lucan A. Way. *Competitive Authoritarianism: Hybrid Regimes after the Cold War.* New York: Cambridge University Press, 2010.

Lewis, David. 'High Times on the Silk Road: The Central Asian Paradox'. *World Policy Journal* 27 (2010): 19–49.

Majidov, Surhob. 'Tajikistan Cracks Down on Radical Religious Movements'. *CACI Analyst*, July 1, 2009.

March, Andrew. 'From Leninism to Karimovism: Hegemony, Ideology, and Authoritarian Legitimation'. *Post-Soviet Affairs* 19 (2003): 307–36.

Markowitz, Lawrence P. 'Unlootable Resources and State Security Institutions in Tajikistan and Uzbekistan'. *Comparative Political Studies* 44 (2011): 156–83.
Matveeva, Anna. 'Tajikistan: Stability First'. *Taiwan Journal of Democracy* 5 (2009): 163–86.
Meyer, Richard L., Dennis R. Sheets, Bakhtier Abduvohidov, and Rasuljon Khudoidodov. *Rural Finance in Tajikistan. Rural Finance in Central Asia (TA No. 6078-Reg)*. Dushanbe: Asian Development Bank, 2004.
Muhutdinova, Raissa. 'Tajikistan (2008)'. In *Nations in Transit*, 515–531. Washington, DC: Freedom House, 2008.
Najibullah, Farangis. 'Islam Becomes Mandatory Study in Secular Tajik Schools'. *RFE/RL Report*, August 31, 2009. http://www.rferl.org/content/Islam_Becomes_Mandatory_Study_in_Secular_Tajik_Schools/1811693.html (accessed December 13, 2009).
Najibullah, Farangis. 'Tajikistan: Authorities Exclude Miniskirt, Hejab on Campuses'. *Eurasianet.org*, April 25, 2007. http://www.eurasianet.org/departments/insight/articles/pp041507.shtml (accessed December 13, 2009).
Nakaya, Sumie. 'Aid and Transition from a War Economy to an Oligarchy in Post-War Tajikistan'. *Central Asia Survey* 28 (2009): 259–73.
Nourzhanov, Kirill. 'Alternative Social Institutions and the Politics of Neo-Patrimonialism in Tajikistan'. *Russian and Euro-Asian Bulletin* (1996).
Nourzhanov, Kirill. 'Saviours of the Nation or Robber Barons? Warlord Politics in Tajikistan'. *Central Asian Survey* 24 (2005): 109–30.
'Novosti: Ministerstvo yustitsii Respubliki Tadzhikistan priostanovit deiatel'nost' vsekh organizatsii, ne proshedshikh pereregistratsiyu'. *Tribun.TJ*. http://www.tribun.tj/news.php?n=4038&a=2 (accessed December 13, 2009).
Organization for Security and Co-operation in Europe. 'Human Rights in the OSCE Region'. *IHF Report 2006*. http://www.ihf-hr.org/viewbinary/viewdocument.php?download=1&doc_id=6865 (accessed February 16, 2007).
OSCE/ODIHR Election Observation Mission Final Report, Republic of Tajikistan, Parliamentary Elections 27 February and 13 March 2005. Warsaw: Organization for Security and Co-operation in Europe, Office of Democratic Institutions and Human Rights, 2005. http://www.osce.org/documents/odihr/2005/05/14852_en.pdf (accessed February 16, 2007).
OSCE/ODIHR Election Observation Mission Report, Republic of Tajikistan, Presidential Elections 6 November 2006. Warsaw: Organization for Security and Co-operation in Europe, Office of Democratic Institutions and Human Rights, 2007. http://www.osce.org/documents/odihr/2007/04/24067_en.pdf (accessed February 16, 2007).
Ottaway, Marina. *Democracy Challenged: The Rise of Semi-Authoritarianism*. Washington, DC: Carnegie Endowment for International Peace, 2003.
Pannier, Bruce. 'Tajikistan: Presidential Candidates Take to Campaign Trail – Together'. *Eurasianet.org*, October 28, 2006. http://www.eurasianet.org/departments/insight/articles/pp102806.shtml (accessed February 16, 2007).
Pisaredzheva, Nafisa. 'New Tajik Party Seeks Émigré Vote'. *RCA No. 484*, February 27, 2007. http://www.iwpr.net/?p=rca&s=f&o=333632&apc_state=henirca2007 (accessed November 3, 2009).
Radnitz, Scott. *Weapons of the Wealthy: Predatory Regimes and Elite-Led Protests in Central Asia*. Ithaca, NY: Cornell University Press, 2010.
Radnitz, Scott. 'What Really Happened in Kyrgyzstan?'. *Journal of Democracy* 17 (2006): 132–46.
RSF. 'Tajikistan – 2006 Annual Report'. Paris: Reporters Without Borders (RSF), 2006. http://www.rsf.org/article.php3?id_article=17480 (accessed February 16, 2007).
Rubin, Barnett R. 'Russian Hegemony and State Breakdown in the Periphery: Causes and Consequences of the Civil War in Tajikistan'. In *Post-Soviet Political Order: Conflict*

and State-Building, ed. Barnett R. Rubin and Jack Snyder, 128–61. London: Routledge, 1998.

Saidazimova, Gulnoza. 'Central Asia: Radical Islamists Challenge Government Efforts at Control (Part 3)'. *RFE/RL*, August 8, 2005. http://www.rferl.org/specials/religion/archive/central-asia3.asp (accessed November 3, 2009).

Schatz, Edward. 'Access by Accident: Legitimacy Claims and Democracy Promotion in Authoritarian Central Asia'. *International Political Science Review* 27 (2006): 263–84.

Schatz, Edward. 'The Soft Authoritarian "Tool Kit": Agenda-Setting Power in Kazakhstan and Kyrgyzstan'. *Comparative Politics* 41 (2009): 203–22.

'Tajik Government "Tightening the Screws" on Independent Media'. *Eurasianet.org*, August 25, 2006. http://www.eurasianet.org/departments/insight/articles/eav082506a.shtml.

'Tajik President Declares Amnesty For Former Militants'. *The Associated Press*, June 20, 2007.

'Tajik Prosecutor Slams International Organizations for Supporting Opposition'. *Asia-Plus*, December 14, 2004.

'Tajikistan: Dushanbe Wants Russia to Extradite Opposition Activist'. *Eurasianet.org*, September 28, 2008. http://www.eurasianet.org/departments/insight/articles/eav09290 8a.shtml (accessed November 3, 2009).

'Tajikistan: Opposition Disorganized as Presidential Election Nears'. *RFE/RL*, August 24, 2006. http://www.rferl.org/featuresarticle/2006/8/CE926B40-A58F-4215-8171-025B D977EBCE.html (accessed February 16, 2007).

Torjesen, Stina, and S. Neil McFarlane. 'R before D: The Case of Post Conflict Reintegration in Tajikistan'. *Conflict, Security and Development* 7 (2007): 311–32.

United Nations Office on Drugs and Crime and Ministry of Counter-Narcotics of Afghanistan, *Afghanistan Opium Survey 2010, Summary Findings*. 2010. http://www.unodc.org/documents/crop-monitoring/Afghanistan/Afg_opium_survey_2010_exsum_web.pdf (accessed July 24, 2011).

Way, Lucan. 'The Real Causes of the Color Revolutions'. *Journal of Democracy* 19 (2008): 55–69.

Democracy promotion, authoritarian resiliency, and political unrest in Iran

Güneş Murat Tezcür

Department of Political Science, Loyola University, Chicago, USA

This article argues that recent de-democratization in Iran can be best understood by analysing the interplay of domestic Iranian politics and two external developments. These were the colour revolutions in several post-communist states and the hostile US policies toward Iran after the invasion of Iraq in 2003. Together they generated a political climate in Iran conducive to hardliner attempts to discredit and neutralize the reformist opposition. The regime tried to delegitimize the opposition by portraying it as being in the service of foreign elements and claiming it was seeking to foment a popular uprising. The consequences were twofold. On the one hand, the regime's identification of civic and political activism as threats to national security greatly reduced the manoeuvrability of the reformist opposition and contributed to their marginalization. These developments point to the limits and unintended consequences of democracy promotion in Iran. On the other hand, the post-electoral protests of 2009 exposed the limits of conspiracy discourse in silencing mass discontent. This article argues that the regime's attempt to portray the unrest as a foreign conspiracy failed to convince a large segment of the population.

On 27 April 2006, Iranian security officers arrested Ramin Jamenbegloo, an Iranian-Canadian scholar, at Tehran airport. He was released on bail after spending four months in Evin prison, Tehran. In exchange for his freedom, he was required to give a televised interview and declare that his studies, especially his comparative study of civil society in Eastern Europe and Iran, could have been used by foreign agents in their efforts to topple the Islamic Republic of Iran (IRI). In May 2007, Haleh Esfandiari, the director of the Middle East Program at the Woodrow Wilson International Center for Scholars in Washington DC, Kian Tajbakhsh, a scholar of urban planning and politics and a consultant to the Open Society Institute, Ali Shakeri, a businessman and political activist, and Parnaz Azima, a correspondent for the US government-funded Radio Farda, experienced a similar ordeal. These individuals, all dual citizens of the United States and Iran, were arrested and held in Evin Prison, without any formal charges for about four months. A programme broadcast on Iranian state television (IRIB), aired the 'confessions' of Jamenbegloo, Esfandiari and Tajbakhsh, who declared that their activities served to undermine the Iranian regime. Tajbakhsh admitted that the Soros Foundation he worked for aimed gradually to create a rift between the society and the regime through elections and other soft methods, as happened in Georgia.[1]

That the Iranian regime did not field any formal charges against these individuals, did not take them to the court and released all four on bail was perplexing, given the scope and scale of the accusations published by the Iranian press. For example, Esfandiari was publicly accused of acting against the national security of Iran, a crime punishable by death. While legal persecution of political dissidents has a long history in modern Iran, the timing and nature of these arrests were signs of a new era of authoritarianism in the IRI after 2004. The Islamic Republic witnessed the growth of one of the most influential Muslim reformist movements and vibrant civil societies in the Middle East in the late 1990s. This dual growth led to a partial opening of Iran's political system. The Polity IV Project improved Iran's score to 3 in 1998 from −6 (10 being most democratic and −10 being least democratic). Yet Iran's score sharply dropped to −6 in 2005 and remained at this level at the end of 2010.[2] This was the most dramatic reversal of democratization in the Middle East in a decade. The scope of political freedoms and civil liberties available for Iranian citizens contracted considerably, especially with the advent of Mahmoud Ahmedinejad's presidency.

It is the central contention of this article that US policies in the Middle East and popular uprisings in post-communist regimes had unanticipated consequences for the rising authoritarianism in the IRI. 'Colour revolutions' that overthrew ruling regimes in several post-communist countries between 2000 and 2005 and the increasing hostility between the US and Iran appeared to have rather unexpected implications for domestic politics in Iran. The US invasion of Iraq in 2003 and colour revolutions were conducive to the formation of a political climate in which the regime cracked down on civil society activism and rolled back the democratic achievements of the Mohammad Khatami presidency (1997–2005). There can be two mechanisms through which these international events affected political struggles in Iran. First, it can be argued that the ruling elite in Iran became increasingly suspicious of civil society activists, especially rights advocates, intellectuals, labour organizers, ethnic leaders and journalists, fearing that the US pursued a strategy similar to recent post-communist 'colour revolutions' to destabilize the Islamic Republic.[3] In this sense, the regime developed an acute threat perception of civil society activism. The spectre of a disenchanted public withdrawing its loyalty from the regime has been a recurrent concern for the IRI leadership. The problem is that it is empirically difficult, if not impossible, to demonstrate if threat perception of the ruling elite was genuinely aggravated. The elite can use a discourse of external threats and their domestic agents as a purely manipulative strategy to discredit political opposition and mobilize public support. Alternatively and consistent with the theory of securitization, one may argue that the ruling elite tried to associate a wide range of civil society and political actors with foreign-led conspiracies in order to delegitimize them and perpetuate its monopoly over power especially in the aftermath of the controversial 2009 presidential elections.[4] After all, the IRI neither was vulnerable to external democratizing pressure nor had extensive linkage with Western countries (dense commercial, cultural, political and organizational ties).[5] Regardless of the scope of the threat to their rule, international developments became an excuse for the elite to significantly reduce already limited political pluralism in Iran by excluding the reformist opposition from the political system and restricting civil society activism.

Yet the regime's attempt to capitalize on the Iranian tradition of conspiracy theories failed to end popular support for the opposition in 2009. As discussed below, the ruling elite's attempt to portray post-election protests as a regime change strategy pursued by foreign powers and fringe domestic groups failed to delegitimize the opposition and to eliminate political unrest. While the IRI exhibited remarkable resiliency, increasing monopolization of power came at the expense of extensive political unrest. In summary, a comprehensive understanding of changes in regime behaviour requires an analysis of how the ruling elite exploited international developments for its own purposes. Such an analysis supplements studies that primarily focus on domestic factors in understanding changes in the Iranian landscape such as the growing military involvement in politics and rise of a new generation of hardliners.[6]

Resiliency in fragmentation: power dynamics in the Islamic republic

A growing literature analyses the sources and dynamics of authoritarian rule in the Middle East. In particular, this scholarship discusses how power is institutionally distributed to minimize and neutralize elite defections and disagreements, political participation is structured to preempt popular uprisings, and economic liberalization is pursued without political liberalization.[7] A central insight of this literature is that authoritarian resiliency cannot be just explained by a regime's repressive capacity.[8] Several institutional, economic and historical factors are relevant for understanding authoritarian resiliency in Iran. Interestingly, single-party rule, a factor that is typically thought to be central to authoritarian persistency, is not present in Iran. Single-party and hegemonic-party authoritarian regimes are perceived to be more lasting and stable than military and personal dictatorships and weakly institutionalized oligarchies.[9] Single-party regimes offer greater avenues for political participation, prevent elite defections, are capable of co-opting their opponents, and weather economic crises.[10] Yet the IRI, which has lacked a ruling party since 1987, proved to be both durable and resilient 'under conditions that are believed to be debilitating, namely persistent and deep-rooted elite conflicts'.[11] It can be argued that the absence of a hegemonic party does not translate into weak institutionalization of political power in the IRI. Politics in the IRI has

been characterized by the existence of multiple centres of power and factional bick-
ering that introduce a degree of political pluralism absent in one-party regimes in
the Arab Middle East and Central Asia.[12] The leader of the revolution (*rahbar* or
faqih) Ali Khamenei, who has practically tenure for life, is constitutionally empow-
ered to dismiss the president, appoint the head of the judiciary and control the composition of the Guardians Council (*Shura-ya Negahban*), which can veto
parliamentary legislation and presidential bills and disqualify candidates from
running in the elections.[13] Additionally, he appoints most members of the Expe-
diency Council (*Majma-ye Tashkhis-e Maslehat-e Nezam-e Eslami*), a body that
is entrusted with resolving conflicts between the Guardians Council and the parliament, and decides on the composition of the Supreme National Security Council
(*Shura-ya Ali ye Amniyet-e Melli*), a body of high-ranking officials setting
broadly defined security policies. Furthermore, he appoints the powerful Friday
Prayer leaders in each city, has representatives (Islamist commissars) in every
major state institution and oversees the governance of powerful parastatal enterprises called *bonyads*. The Special Court for the Clergy, which imposes ideological
conformity among the clerical ranks and punishes dissidents, is also under the
direct control of the *faqih*. Finally, all armed forces including the powerful
Iranian Revolutionary Guards Corps (*Pasdaran*) and the directors of the state
TV and radio report to the *faqih*.

Given this picture, it may be tempting to characterize the Islamic Republic as a
(neo)sultanist regime where a single individual monopolizes all decision-making
and has unlimited discretionary power.[14] Yet such a classification of the IRI
would not only underestimate its durability and downplay its legitimacy but also
overlook pluralism and competitiveness inherent in the regime.[15] Khamenei has
no claims to rule based on his superior knowledge, charismatic authority, or dynas-
tical lineage. Equally important, Khamenei has to contend with the presence of
elected positions that may elude his direct control and is not in a position to
appoint his successor. Electoral competition has been an integral aspect of the
regime and provides an institutionalized avenue to factions to vie for power and
develop platforms with popular appeal.[16] The effects of elections on authoritarian
resiliency tend to be ambivalent. On the one hand, the electoral system contributes
to political stability by limiting the scope of elite defections and channelling anti-
system oppositional activity into formal channels, even in the absence of a hegemonic party. As a result, 'legalized opposition becomes domesticated opposition'
and does not represent a serious threat to the stability of the regime.[17] On the other
hand, elections generate a dynamic of competition that is absent in many other
authoritarian regimes. Depending on a variety of situations, this dynamic contributes to the expansion or shrinking of human and political rights. Elections serve to
regulate and shape the contours of factional conflict that has characterized Iranian
politics since the foundation of the Islamic Republic. This conflict has its roots in
different interpretations of the founder of the regime, Ruhollah Khomeini, whose
political thought and practices gave rise to competing political visions that claim to
represent the authentic and true legacy of the revolution.[18] In fact, Iran can be

classified as the only 'competitive authoritarian' regime in the Middle East where opposition perceives formal democratic institutions, which are regularly manipulated by incumbents, as primary means to power.[19] A strong indicator of this has been relatively high turnout rates in presidential and parliamentary elections in Iran in the last 15 years that are comparable to post-communist competitive authoritarian regimes.[20]

The elaborate institutional structure of the IRI is funded by revenues coming from oil and natural gas exports. According to a 2008 International Monetary Fund (IMF) report, oil revenues provide more than 40% of Iran's total budget revenues and an estimated 21% of the country's gross domestic product (GDP).[21] The effects of these revenues on authoritarian resiliency in Iran are several.[22] First, the oil wealth has sustained a vast subsidy system that keeps the prices of essential consumer items artificially low at the cost of a greatly inefficient and corrupt allocation of economic resources and lack of political accountability, at least until the reforms of 2010.[23] While Iran's economic growth is severely affected by fluctuations in oil prices, its GDP per capita (power purchasing capacity) increases regardless of the trajectory of the oil market.[24] Next, the regime pursues strategies funded by oil and natural gas exports in order to restrict the ability of social actors to collectively organize protest action. For instance, the Tehran Bazaar, which was the centre of commercial activity in the country and an autonomous entity capable of effective political action vis-à-vis the state under the Pahlavis, witnesses its political mobilization capacity seriously weakened under the Islamic Republic.[25] The regime has also reduced the capacity of the clerical class (*ulema*) to act collectively against the interests of the state through a combination of pecuniary incentives and coercion. The content of Friday sermons is centrally decided, clerics are directly put onto the state payroll and dissident clerics marginalized or put on trial at the Special Court for Clerics.[26] The ironic outcome of the Islamic Revolution has been the declining ability of the religious establishment to act autonomously vis-à-vis the state.[27] Finally, the regime commands a vast patronage network that incorporates multiple constituencies including families of the martyrs and veterans of the Iran–Iraq War (1980–1988), urban poor and segments of the security forces.[28] These constituencies are readily mobilized for political purposes such as setting up pro-regime demonstrations or physically intimidating dissident activities.[29]

Another set of factors that affects the resiliency of the IRI concerns the ideological nature of the regime which was founded by popular revolutionary struggle and survived a very destructive war with Saddam Hussein's Iraq. Although the utopia of an Islamic state as the enforcer of a morally upright and pious society has never had an appeal similar in its scope and intensity to the communist ideal, it has inspired revolutionary passions and loyalty to the Islamic Republic among many Iranians.[30] While it is usually true that the weakness of an authoritarian regime is exposed only when the regime starts to collapse, it would be too facile to dismiss the Islamic Republic as a regime completely out of touch with society and lacking any semblance of popular legitimacy.[31] The regime commands considerable capacity to articulate an ideology that informs popular political attitudes and guides political action.[32] Available survey evidence indicates that Iranian citizens who are critical of the regime's performance do not necessarily oppose the Islamic nature of the state and state enforcement of Islamic norms.[33] Finally, the war with Iraq in which millions rallied to the front in defence of the motherland and the nascent revolutionary state was a critical development in cementing the linkages between the populace and the new regime. The Iraqi invasion rallied Iranian people behind the regime that used the war to silence the remaining political opposition in the early 1980s. A new generation of hardliner Islamists, including many former members of the *Pasdaran*, who have risen to top positions in the IRI in the recent years, spent their formative years battling the Iraqi army.[34] This generation is highly critical of the earlier presidencies of Rafsanjani and Khatami whom they accused of secularism, consumerism and rapprochement with the West, and disregard for the combative spirit of the revolution.[35]

In this authoritarian setting that allows for limited pluralism and competition, the hardliners, who oppose any change to institutional distribution of power and dominate unelected positions, confronted the reformists who demand institutional changes entailing increased popular accountability of the rulers. The next section discusses how the hardliners used the hostile US policies and popular uprisings in several post-communist countries in order to marginalize the reformist opponents and to restrict civil society activism in the wake of the US invasion of Iraq.

Iranian reactions to colour revolutions and the US policies

The US invasions of Afghanistan in the autumn of 2001 and Iraq in spring 2003 had ambivalent implications for the IRI. On the one hand, the invasions destroyed the Taliban and Saddam Hussein regimes, two arch-enemies of Iran.[36] The US invasion of Iraq resulted in political mobilization along sectarian lines and the rapid rise of powerful Shiite parties. The formation of a Shiite-dominated friendly government in Iraq has been a major positive development for Iran's geopolitical situation.[37] On the other hand, the appearance of hundreds of thousands of American soldiers on both sides of Iran unnerved the IRI rulers. Available evidence indicates that a frightened Iranian regime approached the US with a grand bargaining proposal in May 2003 immediately after the fall of Saddam Hussein's regime.[38] The US administration swiftly rejected the offer because it hoped for or even anticipated regime change in Iran.[39] Influential figures close to the US administration hoped that the invasion would establish a strong beachhead in the authoritarian core of the Middle East and contribute to the rise of pro-American movements demanding democracy.[40] While the US government never consistently followed a policy of regime change that would also threaten its steadfast allies in the region (for example, Egypt and Saudi Arabia), the vision of democratizing waves emanating from a liberal-democratic Iraq was clearly one of the justifications for the invasion and generated unfounded optimism.[41] In a speech delivered on 6 November 2003, President Bush declared, 'Iraqi democracy will succeed, and that success will send forth the news, from Damascus to Tehran, that freedom can be the future of every nation'.[42] The theme of promoting democracy was also central to his second inaugural speech delivered on 20 January 2005: 'The survival of liberty in our land increasingly depends on the success of liberty in other lands ... So it is the policy of the United States to seek and support the growth of democratic movements and institutions in very nation and culture, with the ultimate goal of ending tyranny in our world.'[43]

The US government soon matched its democracy rhetoric with actual plans – especially after the emergence of a robust insurgency in Iraq made a military invasion of Iran simply unfeasible. In 2005, Congress approved $3.5 million to promote human rights in Iran and made Iranian nationals eligible for the money for the first time. The then Undersecretary for Political Affairs, Nicholas Burns, maintained that the fund would contribute to the US efforts to reach out to ordinary Iranians.[44] A year later, then Secretary of State, Condoleezza Rice, asked Congress during a Senate Foreign Relations Committee hearing to increase spending on 'democracy programmes' for Iran to $85 million. While the State Department officials did not explicitly call for regime change, they claimed the fund would enable society-driven political changes in Iran and explicitly cited the Solidarity Movement in Communist Poland as a successful example. The more recent models they had in mind were colour revolutions of Ukraine and Georgia.[45] A fund of $75 million was subsequently established to support democracy in Iran.[46] In early spring 2006, the State Department created a special office primarily to 'promote a democratic transition in the IRI'.[47] These developments were described as a major shift in US policy toward Iran that would seek regime change and not just contain Tehran's nuclear ambitions.[48] The critics warned that the strategy would backfire and strengthen the hardliners at the expense of the reformists and civil society activists.[49] Meanwhile, the US tried to play the ethnic card against Iran. According to journalist Seymour M. Hersh, the US established linkages with the Azeri, Baluchi and Kurdish nationalist groups in Iran with the goal of instigating ethnic tensions.[50] These clandestine networks would be free from congressional oversight. While anti-regime popular demonstrations took place in Azeri and Kurdish regions in summer 2006, it is unlikely the US or US-funded groups were primarily responsible for ethnic unrest. In addition to the State Department fund to promote democracy, the Bush administration sought funds to sponsor covert operations in Iran. Congress agreed to that request in late 2007. The operations would involve the Arab and Baluchi armed groups and attacks against Iranian security forces.[51] In fact, political violence intensified in the Khuzestan and Sistan and Baluchistan regions of Iran by 2008.[52] The US also continued to fund projects that 'promote democracy, human rights, and the rule of law' in Iran. The United States Agency for International Development (USAID) announced that it allocated up to $20 million to fund institutions for this purpose in June 2008.[53]

Given this strong emphasis on democracy promotion, it is not surprising that the Iranian regime became increasingly uneasy with US policies.[54] On the one hand, the Iranian leadership realized that the chance of a US military attack was very low given the growing unpopularity of the Iraq War among American people and the tremendous problems facing the US forces in Iraq.[55] Tehran also seemed to calculate that its linkages with Hezbollah, Hamas and powerful Shiite groups in Iraq provided the regime with considerable leverage vis-à-vis the US. In a speech addressing the commanders and personnel of the Air Force on 8 February 2007, Khamenei dismissed the possibility of a US attack against Iran: 'The enemies are well aware that any sort of aggression would be followed by a full blown reaction of the Iranian nation against the aggressors and their interest anywhere in the world'.[56] On 3 January 2008, Khamenei declared that 'the likelihood of an attack [American attack against Iran] is lower today'. On the other hand, the ruling elite interpreted colour revolutions as events instigated by the US in order to establish pro-Western regimes in post-communist countries. In the same speech, Khamenei announced his opposition to the re-establishment of formal relations with the US 'Any relations [with the US] would provide the possibility to the Americans to infiltrate Iran and would pave the way for their intelligence and spy agents'.[57] It seemed that Khamenei's major concern was the possibility that 'the Islamic Republic either decay and dissolve like the Soviet Union or go the way of the "velvet revolutions" of Eastern Europe, i.e., abrupt change spurred by "pro-Western" intellectuals'.[58] He allegedly spent time analysing the causes of the collapse of the East European regimes and the US tactics of regime change.[59]

The threat of non-violent popular uprisings (that is, 'velvet revolution') and US-supported 'subversive' civil society became central to the discourse of the ruling elite in the IRI by 2006. In July, several months after the substantial increase in US funding for democracy promotion in Iran, Prosecutor General Ghorbanali Dorri-Najafabadi announced that the US was trying to launch a 'velvet revolution' in Iran similar to those in the former Soviet Union.[60] The hardliner antipathy towards civil society actors allegedly funded by the US intensified in 2007. According to Minister of Culture and Islamic Guidance, Mohammed Hossein Saffar Harandi, the US attempts to encourage colour revolutions had backfired and no more of these revolutions would take place.[61] In August 2007, a spokesman for the parliament's National Security and Foreign Relations Commission, Kazem Jalali, warned Arab countries against the US plans for encouraging colour revolutions.[62] According to an article in the *Kayhan* newspaper published on 19 March 2007, the US-based Human Rights Documentation Centre for Iran, which received substantial support from the US democracy promotion fund, organized a human rights training workshop in Dubai. The article accused Ramin Jahanbegloo and human rights and women's rights activist Mehrangiz Kar,[63] who had been arrested in April 2000 and now lived in exile in the US, of being affiliated with the centre. The article claimed the goals of these workshops were to teach 'the theories of velvet revolution', to form 'a political movement which supports velvet revolution in Iran', and to extend 'activity among the Iranian students residing in Dubai'. Another newspaper *Jomhuri-ye Eslami* published an editorial on 11 June 2007 focusing on the activities of George Soros. The editorial characterized Soros as a

'Zionist American capitalist' and 'sponsor of colour revolutions' in post-communist countries. It argued that the recent arrests of Esfandiari, Tajbakhsh, Shakeri and Azima were likely to be related to Soros' organized plots in Iran. Less than a month later, Hassan Haddad, deputy for security at Tehran's Revolutionary Court, announced that Esfandiari and Tajbakhsh were charged with espionage.[64] The state TV broadcasted the 'confessions' of Jahanbegloo, Esfandiari and Tajbakhsh on 18 and 19 July.[65] Most importantly, the hardliners deliberately attempted to delegitimize all civil society activism by portraying them as projects sponsored by the US. For instance, Tehran's deputy Friday Prayer leader Ayatollah Ahmad Khatami, who was also a member of the Assembly of Experts, accused the US of seeking a 'velvet revolution' in Iran in his sermon on 20 July:

> America has been pursuing the project of soft coup d'état or the velvet revolution not only in Iran but also in other independent countries. . .First that the basis of a soft coup d'état or a velvet revolution is to promote the western model of governance in the context of the so-called civil society. Second, the primary task ... is ... recruiting and organizing certain individuals and starting psychological propaganda warfare in society. Third, the operations headquarter of this soft coup d'état was a collection of the press, intellectual circles, infiltrating student groups and feminist and pseudo-feminist currents.[66]

Similarly, the hardliners tried to associate the reformists with the US plans and to discredit them in the eyes of the Iranian public. *Kayhan* accused the reformists of criticizing the arrests of Esfendiari and others and questioning the authenticity of the accusations.[67] The same newspaper published a commentary by Pedram Malek Bahar on 21 November. The author labelled the 10-year period from 1997 to 2007 as the 'decade of velvet war' and accused Jahanbegloo of being the US agent responsible for fomenting a 'velvet coup' in Iran, and Esfandiari for being a 'Zionist spy'. He mentioned how these two organized CIA-backed conferences imitated the Polish Solidarity Movement and decided to recruit intellectuals and students in Iran in order to prepare the ground for a 'velvet revolution'. Moreover, he suggested that Columbia University president Lee Bollinger insulted Ahmedinejad in a visit to the university in September 2007 because the Iranian president had already exposed 'Columbia University's role in orchestrating a velvet coup in Iran'.[68]

In July 2007, the Press Supervisory Board banned the popular *Sharq* newspaper for publishing an interview with a woman accused of being a 'counter-revolutionary' homosexual.[69] Government spokesman Gholamhossein Elham denounced political groups that 'want to prepare the ground for enemy's infiltration and pave the way for a velvet revolution'.[70] Several days later, Minister of Interior Mostafa Pour-Mohammadi declared that the Iranian nation would not be deceived by the proponents of velvet revolutions.[71] In response, the reformist press and politicians criticized the hardliners' strategy of associating all opposition with the US plans. They argued that the regime released four individuals charged with espionage, a crime that carried a possible death penalty, only after keeping them for several months in detention because charges against them were not serious and served political purposes.[72]

This political atmosphere in which any kind of civic activism and political opposition was likely to be identified as being 'subversive' contributed to the deterioration of the human rights situation in Iran.[73] Pressures on women's movements, human rights associations, independent unions and civil society activists intensified in 2007 and 2008.[74] In a particularly notorious case, the security forces arrested two doctors, who were brothers and worked on AIDS-related issues and operated AIDS treatment clinics in Iran, in June 2008. The doctor brothers participated in a US-funded people-to-people exchange programme and visited medical centres in the US with other Iranian doctors in 2006.[75] It appears that they were later secretly tried and formally accused of fomenting a 'velvet revolution' in Iran.[76]

Iranian government officials continued to express their unease with a US-sponsored velvet revolution even after Barack Obama became president.[77] Mohammad Javad Zarif, a former Iranian ambassador to the United Nations, argued that a US interest section in Tehran would be in line with Washington's regime change project. 'The concept of a velvet revolution in Iran should not be considered as groundless fear' [sic], he asserted.[78] Several days later, the deputy chairman of Iran's Joint Chiefs of Staff, Gholamali Rashid, declared that US threats against Iran would continue even with Obama as president. He alleged that the US planned a 'velvet revolution in Iran after the September 11 attacks'.[79] In summary, the hardliners put the reformists on the defensive by associating civil society activism with the US regime change policies. It became increasingly difficult for the reformists and civil society actors to pursue sociopolitical activism for the expansion of rights when the hardliners used the US policies as an excuse to further blur the distinction between acts of dissent and 'subversion'.

The June 2009 uprising and its aftermath

By the end of 2008, the reformists were politically marginalized, disorganized and lacked a long-term strategy. Yet the presidential elections in June 2009 provided them with a golden opportunity to capitalize on widespread discontent with Ahmedinejad who was generally expected to win a second term. Mir Hossein Mousavi, a former prime minister, announced his candidacy in March 2009 and mobilized most of the reformists including former presidents Khatami and Hashemi Rafsanjani under his banner. He quickly became a credible alternative to Ahmedinejad. His campaign, named the Green movement (*Jonbashe-Sabz*), energized vast segments of the population and attracted the support of a variety of social classes, especially the urban middle-classes, who were politically marginalized under Ahmedinejad's presidency.

Public participation in the elections turned out to be very high, reflecting public enthusiasm and the competitiveness of the race. When Iranian authorities declared

Ahmedinejad victor by a huge margin and the results were quickly certified by the Guardians Council, Mousavi and the other two candidates immediately challenged the legitimacy of the results and claimed widespread fraud.[80] Public protests spontaneously took place in various cities on 13 June and culminated in a massive rally attended by Mousavi in Tehran on 15 June. Despite the fact that security forces opened fire on demonstrators and killed scores of them, the protests continued throughout the week.[81] In a key speech delivered during Friday sermon on 19 June, Khameini demanded an immediate end to the protests. While he tried to secure the loyalty of Mousavi, Rafsanjani and other reformist leaders by endorsing their 'insider' status, he categorically rejected the allegations of fraud, urged all parties to accept the legitimacy of the electoral results, and implicitly threatened leaders of the opposition with persecution if they insisted on street protests. He also accused foreign powers of taking advantage of the situation in Iran. He argued that Iran is not Georgia where a 'Zionist-American capitalist' spent 10 million dollars to incite a 'velvet revolution' a few years ago.[82] Following his sermon, the security forces violently dispersed the demonstrators.[83] The regime tried to curb the momentum of protests by coercive strategies that involved extrajudicial killings, torture, mass arrests, purges, defamation campaigns against opposition figures and harsh censorship practices. Yet the demonstrators periodically continued throughout the rest of 2009.[84] Moreover, the demands of the protestors gradually escalated from a repeat of the presidential elections to a major restructuring of the IRI.[85] Ironically, the Islamic regime's worst fears were realized when presidential elections became a catalyst of mass protests and resulted in political instability unprecedented since the consolidation of the Islamic regime in 1982.[86]

From the beginning, the ruling actors, especially the commanders of the *Pasdaran*, which increased its political and economic power during Ahmedinejad's presidency, aimed to delegitimize the protestors by characterizing them as being pawns in the hands of foreign powers intent on overthrowing the Islamic regime.[87] Even before the elections, a senior *Pasdaran* officer accused supporters of Mousavi of fomenting a 'velvet revolution'. He argued that the 'green' campaign was a continuation of a long strategy of destabilizing the regime that started with the election of Khatami in 1997 and continued with the 1999 student demonstrations, and the 2004 parliamentary sit-in.[88] The goal of associating opposition with foreign-led plots continued with post-election trials of hundreds of activists, including prominent reformist leaders. Reminiscent of the 1980s when the ruling elite made opposition figures publicly 'confess' their crimes in order to completely destroy their political credibility, these trials included self-accusing statements by the defendants. The indictments were primarily based on the poorly documented claim that demonstrations were part of a foreign-inspired, long-planned and centrally coordinated project that involved many different activities. The first indictment, read on 1 August 2009, was mostly based on the 'confessions' of an unidentified former 'spy'.[89] According to the prosecutors, many Western institutions such as the Open Society Institution, the Ford

Foundation and German Marshall Fund were preparing the ground for regime change in Iran.[90] This alleged regime change project involved many Iranian actors including the women's movement, human rights associations and students, and aimed to repeat the examples of post-election demonstrations in Serbia, Georgia, Ukraine and Kyrgyzstan. Ironically, the prosecutors, as well as IRI rulers, kept confusing regime changes in communist states such as Czechoslovakia and Poland, and more recent electoral revolutions that took place in post-communist states. From their perspective, there was no difference between 'velvet' and 'colour' revolutions as both would undermine the monopolization of power in the hands of the hardliner elite.

A second indictment read on 8 August 2009 also aimed to discredit post-election demonstrators by portraying them as agents of hostile Western powers and anti-IRI opposition. It characterized diverse activities such as demanding international supervision of elections, travelling to Western countries for training and educational purposes as evidence of a regime change project instigated by various Western governments and organizations.[91] Interestingly, the main culprit was said to be the British (not US) government that had been central to conspiracy theories in Iran since the late nineteenth century. Main Iranian actors who were accused of carrying out this project were the Freedom Movement of Iran (*Nehzat-e Azadi-ye Iran*), People's Mojahedin (*Mojahedin-e Khalq-e Iran*), the ethnic separatist groups and the royalists. A fourth session held on 25 August included leading figures of the reform movement such as Saeed Hajjarian, Mohsen Mirdamadi and Mostafa Tajzadeh, who were also accused of being part of a foreign-controlled regime change project. In his 'confession', Hajjarian accepted that Western theories, including Max Weber's conceptualizations of political regimes, were not applicable to Iran, and he was at fault for teaching these theories at university.[92] Yet these televised sessions and 'confessions' did not have the effect desired by the ruling elite. The protests periodically continued on special dates such as Jerusalem Day on 18 September 2009, the anniversary of the storming of the US Embassy on 4 November 2009, the Students' Day on 7 December 2009, and the anniversary of the martyrdom of Imam Hossein on 29 December 2009, before the opposition lost its viability as a street force on the anniversary of the revolution on 12 February 2010.[93]

Conspiracy theories, repression and protest in the Islamic republic

The recent authoritarian backlash in Iran can be best understood as the result of the interplay between external and domestic factors. This article focused on the international dimension of the process through which the hardliners increasingly restricted the scope of civil society activism and political opposition in Iran. Colour revolutions and US policies toward Iran induced the hardliners to intensify their repression of civil society and political actors, arguing that their activities threaten national security. The ambivalent signals emanating from the US administration and funds for 'democratic promotion' in Iran gave credibility to the hardliner discourse of US designs on Iran. Regardless of whether the IRI leadership believed that the US discourse and policies of regime change in Iran presented a serious threat to their rule, they had no qualms justifying their authoritarian practices on the grounds that they fight against subversive plots sponsored by foreign entities. The hardliners saw an opportunity to marginalize further the reformists in the absence of any serious evidence of collision of interests between the reformists and foreign powers. The government officials and their allies in the press constantly warned the population to be on alert against hostile US plans implemented by Iranian citizens. The 'usual suspects' were the secular-oriented middle class Iranians with links to the West, who challenged the ideological conformism imposed by the regime.[94] Their activities on human rights and women's issues were particularly 'subversive' in the eyes of the ruling class. The hardliners threw the net as wide as possible so that all groups critical of the government's political and human rights record, regardless of their political goals, could be linked to subversive plots sponsored by the US. In this political atmosphere, the reformists, with fewer means to propagate their views, bitterly complained that the US intervention in Iranian politics (that is, when the US administration called for an electoral boycott in 2008) made them vulnerable to the hardliner accusations of serving US interests.[95] In summary, recent developments in Iran largely confirm the argument that democracy promotion is likely to backfire in authoritarian contexts that have only limited cultural, political, economic and diplomatic ties with Western countries.[96]

As became evident in the aftermath of the 2009 elections, the regime's discourse of domestic agents employed by foreigners did not convince a substantial segment of society, including the educated, urban middle class and most resourceful citizens. The regime had a difficult time seeking to restore its credibility, shaken by images of unarmed citizens being beaten and killed by the security forces during post-election demonstrations. Thousands of people continued to demonstrate despite the regime's attempts to link domestic unrest with foreign powers intent on destabilizing Iran for the rest of 2009. It can be reasonably argued that the protests gradually died out not because the public now believed in the regime discourse but primarily because it lost faith in the viability of the Green movement that failed to establish a large and robust coalition involving different segments of the society. These findings are consistent with the recent arguments that claim that effective securitization is 'audience-centred' in the sense that it becomes successful to the extent that it persuades its target audience.[97] It fails when the securiziting agent and the target audience fail to share a common threat perception. A regime discourse accusing foreign conspiracies fell on deaf ears among a large segment of the society who harboured widespread economic and political grievances.

Along similar lines, this article also argued that the persistence of a discourse centred on foreign-led conspiracies primarily depends on the instrumental utility of this discourse in marginalizing political opponents. Some may argue that the ruling elite's paranoia with 'subversive' activities directed by foreign forces reflects uniqueness of Iranian political history. The notion that foreign powers employ local agents to set plots to the great detriment of the Iranian people has been a common theme in Iranian politics since the late nineteenth century when foreign involvement in Iran was increasing and the power of the Qajar dynasty was disintegrating. 'Although the paranoid style can be found in many parts of the world, it is much more prevalent in modern Iran than in most Western societies...In Iran, however, the paranoid style permeates society, the mainstream as much as the fringe, and cuts through all sectors of the political spectrum.'[98] Ahmad Ashraf observes that the widespread appeal of conspiracy theories in Iran is caused by the experience of semi-colonialism, persistence of cultural beliefs about satanic forces, and the effectiveness of such theories in combatting feelings of defeat and helplessness in the face of foreigners with superior resources.[99] The feeling of lack of control over and comprehension of events affecting one's life gives rise to illusionary perceptions characterized by superstitions and conspiracies.[100] The overthrow of Mohammad Mosaddeq in 1953 by a US and British-supported coup greatly contributed to the fear of conspiracies among Iranian political actors.[101]

Yet the events of 2009 demonstrate that conspiracy theories are circulated by elites as long as they have instrumental value and serve certain political goals. After all, many authoritarian rulers fabricate 'internal enemies' subservient to foreign powers, but these fabrications are not taken seriously by a disenchanted public. In reaction to mass protests following the 2009 elections, the ruling elite identified hostile foreign powers and armed groups, such as *Mojahedin-e Khalq*, as the main culprits of political unrest. Reformist leaders, students and ordinary citizens supporting or participating in the protests were accused of being guilty by association to these two actors. While this strategy aimed to restore the legitimacy of the regime and discredit opposition in the eyes of public, it failed to achieve this goal given the continuation of political polarization and tensions. In this sense, the persistence of conspiracy thinking in Iranian politics is not reflective of the uniqueness of Iranian history and culture, but its utility to the ruling elite. Conspiracy theories have specific instrumental purposes and lose their effectiveness when they cease to hold sway over large segments of the population.

Notes

1. Tajbakhsh was also one of the defendants on post-election trials following the political unrest in summer 2009.
2. http://www.systemicpeace.org/polity/irn2.htm.
3. Khosrokhavar, 'The Islamic Revolution in Iran'; Sedghi, *Women and Politics in Iran*, 246–61.
4. For securitization, see Wæver, 'Securitization and Desecuritization'.
5. Levitsky and Way, 'Linkage versus Leverage' argues that extensive linkage significantly contributed to democratization in Central Europe and Latin America.
6. For instance, see Arjomand, *After Khomeini*; Ehteshami and Zweiri, *Iran and the Rise of its Neoconservatives*.

7. For instance, see Pripstein Posusney and Penner Angrist, *Authoritarianism in the Middle East*; Lust-Okar and Zerhouni, *Political Participation in the Middle East*; Schlumberger, *Debating Arab Authoritarianism*. The Arab uprisings of 2011 may lead to reconsideration of some of the claims of this literature.

8. Parsa, *States, Ideologies, and Social Revolutions*, 291.

9. Geddes, 'What Do We Know about Democratization', 131–3; Huntington, *The Third Wave*, 117–21; Magaloni, 'Credible Power-Sharing'; Smith, 'Life of the Party'.

10. Brownlee, *Authoritarianism in an Age of Democracy*, 42.

11. Keshavarzian, 'Contestation without Democracy', 65.

12. Moslem, *Factional Politics in Post-Khomeini Iran*; Kamrava and Hassan-Yari, 'Suspended Equilibrium in Iran's Political System'.

13. Buchta, *Who Rules Iran?*, 6–10, 46–57; Arjomand, *After Khomeini*, 172–91.

14. For example, Ganji, 'The Latter-Day Sultan', 49–50; Arjomand, *After Khomeini*, 188–91.

15. Sultanist regimes are vulnerable to violent overthrows and succession crises because of the concentration of power in the hands of a single individual. Chehabi and Linz, 'A Theory of Sultanism 1: A Type of Nondemocratic Rule'. Moreover, Khamenei, is not indispensable for the stability of the regime as in the regimes of Ceausescu of Romania, Pahlavi of prerevolutionary Iran, or Marcos of Philippines. Brownlee, *Authoritarianism in an Age of Democracy*, 204.

16. Tezcür, 'Intra-Elite Struggles in Iranian Elections'.

17. Gandhi and Przeworski. 'Authoritarian Institutions and the Survival of Autocrats', 1283.

18. Brumberg, *Reinventing Khomeini*.

19. Diamond, 'Elections without Democracy'; Levitsky and Way, 'Elections without Democracy', 52.

20. For turnout rates in these regimes, see Bunce and Wolchik, 'Defeating Dictators'.

21. http://www.imf.org/external/pubs/cat/longres.cfm?sk=22282.

22. There is an extensive literature discussing the pernicious effects of oil for democracy. For instance, see Ross, 'Does Oil Hinder Democracy'.

23. Esfahani and Taheripour, 'Hidden Public Expenditures'.

24. Tezcür, *Muslim Reformers in Iran and Turkey*, 95–7.

25. Keshavarzian, *Bazaar and State in Iran*, 255–67.

26. Arjomand, 'Civil Society and the Rule of Law'; Khalaji, *The Last Marja*; Kamrava, *Iran's Intellectual Revolution*, 120–72.

27. Philpott, 'Explaining the Political Ambivalence of Religion', 507–8.

28. Alamdari, 'The Power Structure'.

29. Wehey et al., *The Rise of the Pasdaran*, 25–9, 32–3.

30. For the declining appeal of communism, see Furet, *The Passing of an Illusion*, 446–51. The attraction of the Islamic state among Muslims elsewhere was mostly limited to Shiite Muslims, see Roy, *The Failure of Political Islam*, 189–93.

31. Kuran, 'Now out of Never', 7–48.

32. cf. Linz, *Totalitarian and Authoritarian Regimes*, 167–8.

33. Tezcür and Azadarmaki, 'Religiosity and Islamic Rule in Iran'.

34. Naji, *Ahmedinejad*.

35. This observation is based on the author's interviews with Ahmedinejad supporters in Tehran in June 2005 and March 2008.

36. Rashid, *Taliban: Militant Islam*, 203–6.

37. This does not mean the formation of a transnational Shiite alliance confronting the power of Sunni regimes of the Arab Middle East as Nasr argues. Nasr, *The Shia Revival*.

38. Parsi, *Treacherous Alliance*, 341–2.
39. Glenn Kessler, 'In 2003, U.S. Spurned Iran's Offer of Dialogue', *Washington Post*, June 18, 2006.
40. Gordon and Trainor, *Cobra II*, 497.
41. Packer, *The Assassins' Gate*, 8–99.
42. Woodward, *State of Denial*, 268–9.
43. The full text of the speech is available at http://www.washingtonpost.com/wp-dyn/articles/A23747-2005Jan20.html.
44. Barbara Slavin, 'US Doesn't Have Needed Support in UN to Punish Iran, Official Says'. *USA Today*, May 19, 2005.
45. Howard LaFranchi, 'The Bush Team Unveils a Plan to Push for Iranian-led Reform', *The Christian Science Monitor*, February 17, 2006; Farah Stockman, 'Rice Wants Funds for Democracy Initiative in Iran', *Boston Globe*, February 16, 2006.
46. Many Iranian dissidents argued against Bush administration policies of bringing 'democracy' to Iran on the grounds that his policies undermine the credibility of the indigenous democratic movement in the country. For instance, see Shirin Ebadi and Muhammad Sahimi, 'The Follies of Bush's Iran Policy', *The New York Times*, May 30, 2007.
47. Elise Labott, 'US to Sharpen Focus on Iran', *CNN*, March 2, 2006.
48. Seymour M. Hersh, 'The Iran Plans', *The New Yorker*, April 17, 2006; Laura Rozen, 'The Revolution Next Time', *Los Angeles Times*, October 10, 2004.
49. For instance, Charles A. Kupchan and Ray Takeyh, 'The Wrong Way to Fix Iran', *Los Angeles Times*, February 26, 2006.
50. Hersh, 'The Iran Plans'. These linkages would be free from congressional oversight.
51. Seymour M. Hersh, 'Preparing the Battlefield', *The New Yorker*, July 7, 2008.
52. For instance, a series of bomb attacks killed several dozens of people in Ahvaz, the capital of Khuzestan between 2005 and 2006. A Baluchi armed group, *Jundallah*, kidnapped 16 police officers in June 2008. The group later executed 15 of these officers.
53. http://www.usatoday.com/news/pdf/usaid.pdf.
54. Sadjadpour, *Reading Khamenei*, 16.
55. For instance, see the comments of Pasdaran Admiral Morteza Saffari reported by *Press TV*, September 9, 2009.
56. Khamamei speeches are compiled from an electronic newsletter periodically sent by his official website http://www.leader.ir.
57. Sadjadpour, *Reading Khamenei*, 17.
58. Ibid., 17–8.
59. Ibid., 18.
60. Reported by ISNA, July 9, 2006.
61. Quoted by *Iran Daily*, March 1, 2007. A few months later he was quoted as saying that the print media was carrying out a 'velvet revolution'. Reported by *Iran Daily*, July 19, 2007.
62. *Press TV*, August 22, 2007.
63. Kar's husband, Siamak Pourzand, was abducted in April 2001 and sentenced to 11 years in prison. After his sentencing, he was made to 'confess' his crimes on TV. He admitted belonging to a network aspiring to 'culturally overthrow the Islamic Republic'. The hardliners used these confessions to question the patriotism and loyalty of the reformists.
64. *Iran Daily*, July 7, 2007.
65. Forced confessions have had a long and tragic history in the Islamic Republic. Abrahamian, *Tortured Confessions*.
66. *Press TV*, July 20, 2007; *Iran Daily*, July 21, 2007.

67. *Kayhan*, August 2, 2007.
68. *Kayhan*, November 21, 2007. Also see *Iran Daily* article on a documentary on Ahmedinejad's visit to the USA, November 1, 2007.
69. AFP, August 6, 2007.
70. *Iranian Daily*, November 20, 2007.
71. *Press TV*, November 25, 2007.
72. For instance, a reformist commentator responded to Hossein Shariatmadari, the chief editor of *Kayhan*, who accused the student protestors of being supported by foreign governments. The commentator asked Shariatmadari to provide credible evidence to back his accusations. Reported by ISNA, October 31, 2007.
73. Iran's Physical Integrity Right Index (constructed by David L. Cingranelli and David L. Richards) declined from 2 in 2003 to 1 in 2007. This index ranges from 0 (widespread torture, extrajudicial killings, political imprisonment, disappearance by government) to 8 (full government respect for these four rights). For more information see http://www.humanrightsdata.org.
74. For instance, see Human Rights Watch, *Iran: Country Summary*. There was also a significant increase in the number of executions. In 2005, there were 86 executions. In 2006, 177 individuals were executed, and in 2007, more than 300. Reported by Amnesty International, *Iran-Amnesty International Report 2007*, http://www.amnesty.org/en/region/iran/report-2007; Human Rights, *Iran: Rights Crisis Escalates*, http://www.hrw.org/reports/2008/09/18/iran-rights-crisis-escalates-0.
75. Farah Stockman, 'Iran's Arrest of Doctors Jeopardizes US Program', *Boston Globe*, September 9, 2008.
76. Paul Grondahl, 'AIDS Doctors Tried in Secret in Iran', *Times Union*, January 3, 2009.
77. Obama subsequently cut funding for the Iranian opposition. Reported by the BBC, October 20, 2009.
78. *Press TV*, November 18, 2008.
79. *Press TV*, November 22, 2008.
80. Mousavi and Mehdi Karroubi, the other reformist candidate, pointed to a very large number of electoral irregularities including ballot stuffing, voter intimidation, duplicate voting and attacks against their campaign managers and workers.
81. For instance, see Nazila Fathi, 'Protestors Defy Iranian Efforts to Cloak Unrest', *New York Times*, June 17, 2009.
82. Full English translation of his sermon is available at http://www.presstv.com/classic/detail.aspx?id=98610&sectionid=3510302.
83. It seems that the IRI rulers were convinced that electoral revolutions in post-communist countries were successful because the authorities refrained from using lethal force against protesters. For a discussion of how electoral protests facilitated mass mobilization, see Tucker, 'Enough! Electoral Fraud'.
84. Mass mobilization capacity was a necessary but not a sufficient condition for successful democratization in East Europe. See Bunce, 'Rethinking Recent Democratization', 171–4.
85. Slogans shouted in the demonstrations were a good indicator of this radicalization. Khamenei replaced Ahmedinejad as the main target of protestors by December 2009.
86. These events defy the observation that authoritarian regimes in oil exporting countries are less likely to experience political protest than similar regimes in resource poor countries. Smith, 'Oil Wealth and Regime Survival', 232–46.
87. For a detailed discussion of the rising power of the Pasdaran and the second generation of hardliners under Ahmedinejad, see Arjomand, *After Khomeini*, 149–91.
88. http://www.bbc.co.uk/persian/iran/2009/06/090610_si_ir88_sepah_velvetrevolution.shtml.

89. A transcript of the indictment is available at http://www.farsnews.com/newstext. php?nn=8805100074. An English translation by Evan Siegel is available at http:// www.qlineorientalist.com/IranRises/the-indictment.
90. In early January 2010, the Ministry of Intelligence prohibited Iranian citizens from having contacts with 60 Western institutions, including Yale University, for their alleged role in fomenting unrest. See http://www.farsnews.com/newstext.php?nn= 8810141571.
91. A transcript of the indictment is available at http://www.farsnews.com/newstext. php?nn=8805170594. An English translation by Evan Siegel is available at http:// www.qlineorientalist.com/IranRises/the-complete-text-of-the-indictment-of-the-second-group-of-accused-in-the-project-for-a-velvet-coup.
92. A summary of the session is available at http://www.bbc.co.uk/persian/iran/2009/08/ 090825_he_ir88_mass_trial4.shtml.
93. There are many examples of the role of street protests in effecting political change in modern Iran. In this sense the reformists did not just imitate electoral revolutions in post-communist regimes. For instance, see Abrahamian, 'The Crowd in the Iranian Politics'.
94. Gheissari and Nasr, *Democracy in Iran*, 126.
95. This observation is based on the author's interviews with reformist politicians in Tehran in March 2008.
96. Stewart, 'Democracy Promotion'.
97. Williams, 'Words, Images, Enemies'; Balzacq, 'The Three Faces of Securitization'.
98. Abrahamian, *Tortured Confessions*, 112.
99. Ashraf, 'Conspiracy Theories'.
100. Whitson and Galinsky, 'Lacking Control'.
101. Gasiorowski, 'The 1953 Coup D'Etat in Iran'.

Notes on contributor

Güneş Murat Tezcür (PhD, University of Michigan, 2005) is an Associate Professor of Political Science at Loyola University Chicago. His research interests include political violence, democratization, judicial activism, Muslim public opinion and electoral politics. He is the author of *Muslim Reformers in Iran and Turkey: The Paradox of Moderation* (University of Texas Press, 2010).

Bibliography

Abrahamian, Ervand. 'The Crowd in the Iranian Politics, 1905–1953'. *Past & Present* 41, no. 1 (1968): 184–210.
Abrahamian, Ervand. *Tortured Confessions: Prisons and Public Recantations in Modern Iran*. Berkeley; Los Angeles: University of California Press, 1999.
Alamdari, Kazem. 'The Power Structure of the Islamic Republic of Iran'. *Third World Quarterly* 26, no. 8 (2005): 1285–301.
Arjomand, Saïd Amir. *After Khomeini: Iran under His Successors*. New York: Oxford University Press, 2009.
Arjomand, Saïd Amir. 'Civil Society and the Rule of Law in the Constitutional Politics of Iran under Khatami'. *Social Research* 67, no. 2 (2000): 283–301.
Ashraf, Ahmad. 'Conspiracy Theories'. *Encyclopedia Iranica* 6, no. 2 (1993): 138–47.
Balzacq, Thierry. 'The Three Faces of Securitization'. *European Journal of International Relations* 11, no. 2 (2005): 171–201.

Brownlee, Jason. *Authoritarianism in an Age of Democracy.* Cambridge: Cambridge University Press, 2007.

Brumberg, Daniel. *Reinventing Khomeini: The Struggle for Reform in Iran.* Chicago, IL: University of Chicago Press, 2001.

Buchta, Wilfried. *Who Rules Iran? The Structure of Power in the Islamic Republic.* Washington, DC: Washington Institute for Near East Policy, 2000.

Bunce, Valerie. 'Rethinking Recent Democratization: Lessons from the Postcommunist Experience'. *World Politics* 55, no. 2 (2003): 167–92.

Bunce, Valerie J., and Sharon L. Wolchik. 'Defeating Dictators: Electoral Change and Stability in Competitive Authoritarian Regimes'. *World Politics* 62, no. 1 (2010): 43–86.

Chehabi, H.E., and Juan J. Linz, 'A Theory of Sultanism 1: A Type of Nondemocratic Rule'. In *Sultanistic Regimes,* ed. Chehabi and Linz, 3–25. Baltimore, MD: John Hopkins University Press, 1998.

Diamond, Larry. 'Elections without Democracy: Thinking about Hybrid Regimes'. *Journal of Democracy* 13, no. 2 (2002): 21–35.

Ehteshami, Anoush, and Mahjoob Zweiri, *Iran and the Rise of its Neoconservatives: The Politics of Tehran's Silent Revolution.* London: I.B. Tauris: 2007.

Esfahani, Hadi Salehi, and Farzad Taheripour, 'Hidden Public Expenditures and the Economy in Iran'. *International Journal of Middle Eastern Studies* 34, no. 4 (2002): 691–718.

Furet, François. *The Passing of an Illusion: The Idea of Communism in the Twentieth Century.* Chicago, IL: University of Chicago Press, 1999.

Gandhi, Jennifer, and Adam Przeworski. 'Authoritarian Institutions and the Survival of Autocrats'. *Comparative Political Studies* 40, no. 11 (2007): 1279–301.

Ganji, Akbar. 'The Latter-Day Sultan'. *Foreign Affairs* 87, no. 6 (2008): 45–66.

Gasiorowski, Mark J. 'The 1953 Coup D'Etat in Iran'. *International Middle East Studies* 19, no. 3 (1987): 261–86.

Geddes, Barbara. 'What Do We Know about Democratization after Twenty Years?' *Annual Review of Political Science* 2 (2000): 115–44.

Gheissari, Ali, and Vali Nasr. *Democracy in Iran.* New York: Oxford University Press, 2006.

Gordon, Michael R., and Bernard E. Trainor. *Cobra II: The Inside Story of the Invasion and Occupation of Iraq.* New York: Pantheon Books, 2006.

Human Rights Watch. *Iran: Country Summary.* New York: Human Rights Watch, 2008.

Huntington, Samuel. *The Third Wave: Democratization in the Late Twentieth Century.* Norman: Oklahoma University Press, 1991.

Kamrava, Mehran. *Iran's Intellectual Revolution.* New York: Cambridge University Press, 2008.

Kamrava, Mehran, and Houchang Hassan-Yari. 'Suspended Equilibrium in Iran's Political System'. *The Muslim World* 94, no. 4 (2004): 495–524.

Keshavarzian, Arang. *Bazaar and State in Iran: Politics of the Tehran Marketplace.* Cambridge: Cambridge University Press, 2007.

Keshavarzian, Arang. 'Contestation without Democracy: Elite Fragmentation in Iran'. In *Authoritarianism in the Middle East: Regimes and Resistance,* ed. Martha Pripstein Posusney and Michelle Penner Angrist, 63–88. Boulder, CO: Lynne Rienner, 2005.

Khalaji, Mehdi. *The Last Marja: Sistani and the End of Traditional Religious Authority in Shiism.* Washington, DC: Washington Institute for Near East Policy, 2006.

Khosrokhavar, Farhad. 'The Islamic Revolution in Iran: Retrospect after a Quarter of Century'. *Thesis Eleven* 76, no. 1 (2004): 70–84.

Kuran, Timur. 'Now out of Never: The Element of Surprise in the East European Revolution of 1989'. *World Politics* 44, no. 1 (1991): 7–48.

Levitsky, Steven, and Lucan A. Way. 'Elections without Democracy: The Rise of Competitive Authoritarianism'. *Journal of Democracy* 13, no. 2 (2002): 51–65.

Levitsky, Steven, and Lucan A. Way. 'Linkage versus Leverage: Rethinking the International Dimension of Regime Change'. *Comparative Politics* 38, no. 4 (2006): 379–400.

Linz, Juan. *Totalitarian and Authoritarian Regimes*. Boulder, CO: Lynne Rienner, 2000.

Lust-Okar, Ellen, and Saloua Zerhouni, eds. *Political Participation in the Middle East*. Boulder, CO: Lynne Rienner, 2008.

Magaloni, Beatriz. 'Credible Power-Sharing and the Longevity of Authoritarian Rule'. *Comparative Political Studies* 41, nos. 4–5 (2008): 715–41.

Moslem, Mehdi. *Factional Politics in Post-Khomeini Iran*. Syracuse, NY: Syracuse University Press, 2002.

Naji, Kasra. *Ahmedinejad: The Secret History of Iran's Radical Leader*. London: I.B. Tauris, 2008.

Nasr, Vali. *The Shia Revival: How Conflicts within Islam Will Shape the Future*. New York: W.W. Norton, 2007.

Packer, George, *The Assassins' Gate: America in Iraq*. New York: Farrar, Straus and Giroux, 2005.

Parsa, Misagh, *States, Ideologies, and Social Revolutions: A Comparative Analysis of Iran, Nicaragua, and the Philippines*. New York: Cambridge University Press, 2000.

Parsi, Trita, *Treacherous Alliance: The Secret Dealings of Israel, Iran, and the United States* New Haven, CT: Yale University Press, 2007.

Philpott, Daniel. 'Explaining the Political Ambivalence of Religion'. *American Political Science Review* 101, no. 3 (2007): 505–25.

Pripstein Posusney, Marsha, and Michele Penner Angrist, eds. *Authoritarianism in the Middle East: Regimes and Resistance*. Boulder, CO: Lynne Rienner, 2005.

Rashid, Ahmed. *Taliban: Militant Islam, Oil and Fundamentalism in Central Asia*. New Haven, CT: Yale Nota Bene, 2001.

Ross, Michael L. 'Does Oil Hinder Democracy?'. *World Politics* 53, no. 3 (2001): 325–61.

Roy, Olivier. *The Failure of Political Islam*. Cambridge, MA: Harvard University Press, 1994.

Sadjadpour, Karim. *Reading Khamenei: The World View of Iran's Most Powerful Leader*. Washington, DC: Carnegie Endowment for International Peace, 2008.

Schlumberger, Oliver, ed. *Debating Arab Authoritarianism: Dynamics and Durability in Nondemocratic Regimes*. Palo Alto, CA: Stanford University Press, 2007.

Sedghi, Hamideh. *Women and Politics in Iran: Veiling, Unveiling, and Reveiling*. New York: Cambridge University Press, 2007.

Smith, Benjamin. 'Life of the Party: The Origins of Regime Breakdown and Persistence under Single-Party Rule'. *World Politics* 57, no. 3 (2005): 421–51.

Smith, Benjamin. 'Oil Wealth and Regime Survival in the Developing World, 1960–1999'. *American Journal of Political Science* 48, no. 2 (2004): 232–46.

Stewart, Susan. 'Democracy Promotion Before and After the "Colour Revolutions"'. *Democratization* 16, no. 4 (2009): 645–60.

Tezcür, Güneş Murat. 'Intra-Elite Struggles in Iranian Elections'. In *Political Participation in the Middle East and North Africa*, ed. Ellen Lust-Okar and Saloua Zerhouni, 51–74. Boulder, CO: Lynne Rienner, 2008.

Tezcür, Güneş Murat. *Muslim Reformers in Iran and Turkey: The Paradox of Moderation*. Austin: University of Texas Press, 2010.

Tezcür, Güneş Murat, and Taghi Azadarmaki. 'Religiosity and Islamic Rule in Iran'. *Journal for the Scientific Study of Religion* 47, no. 2 (2008): 211–24.

Tucker, Joshua A. 'Enough! Electoral Fraud, Collective Action Problems, and Post-Communist Colored Revolutions'. *Perspectives on Politics* 5, no. 3 (2007): 535–51.

Wæver, Ole. 'Securitization and Desecuritization'. In *On Security*, ed. Ronnie Lipschutz, 46–86. New York: Columbia University Press, 1995.

Wehey, Frederic, Jerrold D. Green, Brian Nichiporuk, Nader Alireza, Hansell Lydia, Nafisi Rasool, and S.R. Bohandy, *The Rise of the Pasdaran*. Santa Monica, CA: RAND, 2009.

Whitson, J.A., and A.D. Galinsky. 'Lacking Control Increases Illusory Pattern Perception'. *Science* 322, no. 5898 (2008): 115–7.

Williams, Michael C. 'Words, Images, Enemies: Securitization and International Politics'. *International Studies Quarterly* 47, no. 4 (2003): 511–31.

Woodward, Bob. *State of Denial*. New York: Simon & Schuster, 2006.

Afterword

The Special Issue of *Democratization*, on which the current book is based, was submitted for publication in October 2011. Since then, Russia has experienced arguably the most substantial wave of anti-regime, pro-democracy mass protests since the end of the colored revolutions in Eurasia. Following wide-scale rigging of the parliamentary election in December 2011 by the ruling United Russia party, tens if not hundreds of thousands of Russian citizens took to the streets of Moscow in December 2011 and January 2012. Initially, the intensity and the magnitude of the protest caught the regime by surprise, unprecedented in post-Soviet Russia since 1993. Both the regime and the protesters, most of whom represented Russia's budding middle class, believed the demonstrations were a colored revolution in the making.

Yet, despite further mass demonstrations in May, June and September 2012, the events in Russia did not result in a colored revolution. The authoritarian regime survived the democratizers' challenge, while Putin's twelve-year effective rule was extended by another six years, potentially, through his victory in the March 2012 presidential election. An analysis of the Russian government's reaction to the feared "color threat" indicates that the strategies developed earlier in the decade were effectively redeployed during the 2011-12 crisis. The mixture of isolation, marginalization, distribution, repression and persuasion, strategies described in the introductory chapter, were used by the Russian government in its efforts to suppress a Russian "color threat."

The regime was highly aggressive in its determination to isolate and marginalize opposition leaders, the NGOs active in monitoring electoral fraud, and cyberspace media outlets covering their activities. Golos, the NGO which monitored election fraud, had its site repeatedly attacked and disabled. The NTV television channel (owned by Gazprom, the state-owned natural gas company) aired a prime time exposé of Golos that presented the NGO as a puppet of the West. NTV also portrayed the protesters themselves as paid agents of the US by staging a scene in which protesters were shown receiving bribes to attend an opposition rally. Presenting television programs which "exposed" the opposition as a hostile "other" were frequent throughout 2012.

While government media was aggressive in its negative portrayal of the opposition, the regime intimidated media outlets perceived as sympathetic to the opposition. Thus, state prosecutors launched an investigation into the activities of the internet television channel Dozhd', while Gazprom replaced the Board of Directors of Ekho Moskvy radio station after Putin personally accused its chief editor, Aleksei Venediktov, of slandering him by saying "you [Ekho Moskvy] pour shit over me day and night."

Efforts were made to further isolate and marginalize the opposition from the West and its sources of funding. In the summer of 2012, the Russian parliament adopted a law which forced every NGO with substantial foreign funding, and whose sphere of activities deemed political by the state, to register itself as "foreign agent" with the Ministry of Justice, publicize its foreign agent status in its publications and other activities, and adhere to a frequent and probably crippling reporting requirement. Finally, in September 2012, the Russian parliament expedited the process of amending the law on espionage to greatly expand the definition of treason and espionage to include the passing of information to international NGOs. According to the law, a vaguely defined charge of "harming Russia's security" could result in a twenty-year prison term.[1] The law clearly aims to intimidate foreign NGOs from being active in Russia as well as intimidate Russians from collaborating with or participating in the NGO-supported activities of which the state does not approve.

Hand-in-hand with oppressive new legislation went an effort to minimize Western ability to aid the opposition. In September 2012, the Russian government ordered USAID to cease its activities in Russia effective the following month. Since USAID funded many opposition NGOs, including above-mentioned Golos, its expulsion from Russia was meant to profoundly restrict their activities.2 The expulsion of USAID was also an integral part of a campaign to present the United States as the primary power behind opposition activities. Already in December 2011, Putin had publically accused Secretary of State, Hillary Clinton, of ordering the Russian opposition to stage anti-government rallies. In 2011-12, the Russian regime portrayed the US State Department and its agencies as the institutional embodiment of Western intervention into Russian internal affairs. In addition to the expulsion of USAID, US Ambassador Michael McFaul, known for his contacts with and sympathy for the Russian pro-democratic movement, was constantly vilified in the state media and harassed by the NTV television crews.

In addition to persuasion and isolation, repression strategies were used largely for intimidation purposes. Thus, after rioting took place during the May 6 opposition rally, the apartments and offices of prominent opposition members Aleksei Navalny and Kseniya Sobchak were raided. A large amount of money was found in Ms. Sobchak's apartment (about $1.2 million) and was confiscated under the pretext of investigating its origins and purpose. Dozens of participants in the May 6, 2012 demonstration were arrested and put on trial as well. Moreover, in the summer of 2012, a newly-adopted law drastically increased fines for organizing and participating in "illegal" rallies.

The suppression was extended even to active opposition members who were elected parliamentarians and therefore could not be subject to arrests or searches by virtue of their parliamentary immunity. In September 2012, prominent opposition leader Gennady Gudkov was expelled from the Duma on the grounds that he violated a rule which barred serving parliamentarians from engaging in business activities, a rule which was never enforced in the past. In late July 2012, the most popular opposition leader, the blogger and anti-corruption campaigner, Aleksei Navalny, was accused by Russian prosecutors of embezzlement, a charge that had been dismissed previously as groundless. The case was reopened on explicit orders of Alexander Bastrykin, the head the Investigative Committee, the government's main criminal investigation arm which reports directly to Putin. If prosecuted and convicted, Navalny could spend ten years in jail.

The case of the feminist punk rock band, Pussy Riot, illustrates admirably the combination of intimidation, isolation and persecution strategies. On February 21, 2012, in the midst of the presidential election campaign and as an act of protest against Patriarch Kirill's unambiguous support for Putin, the band staged a five-minute punk prayer in the Church of Christ the Savior in Moscow singing "Mother of God, Chase Putin Out!" The regime transformed a minor act of political performance art, punishable at best by 15 days in a city jail, into a major showdown with the opposition movement. Three of the band members were arrested, put on trial, and sentenced (on August 17, 2012) for two years in jail for alleged hooliganism motivated by religious hatred, despite widespread protest in Russia and abroad. Moreover, in less than a month after the sentencing, Russian state television carried a lengthy exposé of Pussy Riot (Russia Channel, September 11-12, 2012). The band was vilified as cultural agents of the West and lackeys of the exiled tycoon Boris Berezovsky, while its activities were presented as intended to undermine the very foundations of the Russian state and Orthodox Church, its moral pillar.

Finally, the Pussy Riot trial was clearly an unambiguous public demonstration of support for the Orthodox Church's hierarchy for its backing of the regime in its struggle against the opposition. It was an open declaration that the state shared the Church's deeply conservative and anti-Western moral values and its staunch opposition to democracy. As a result of its effort to crash the opposition, the regime elevated the Church to the status of an ideological pillar of the state, helping further to mobilize the millions of believers against the West's immoral "colored threat" which the Pussy Riot band embodied.

Notes

1 The law was first introduced in December 2008, but was quickly shelved because of potential gross human rights violations it could provoke. The 2012 draft is identical

to the law introduced in 2008, see: www.vedomosti.ru/politics/news/4247051/fsb_poluchit_bazu_izmennikov; accessed September 24, 2012.
2 The timing of USAID expulsion was hardly accidental. It meant to hamper efforts of Golos and other NGOs fighting election fraud from effectively monitoring the fall 2012 regional elections which United Russia wanted to win at all cost.

144

Index

Please note: Page numbers in **bold** type refer to figures and in *italic* type to tables

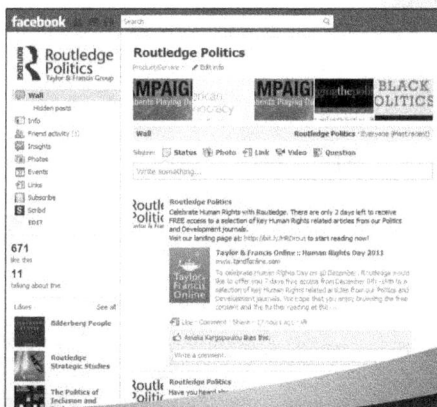

For Product Safety Concerns and Information please contact our EU
representative GPSR@taylorandfrancis.com
Taylor & Francis Verlag GmbH, Kaufingerstraße 24, 80331 München, Germany

www.ingramcontent.com/pod-product-compliance
Lightning Source LLC
Chambersburg PA
CBHW050521280326
41932CB00014B/2400